Love, Inc.

Love, Inc.

*Dating Apps, the Big White Wedding, and
Chasing the Happily Neverafter*

Laurie Essig

UNIVERSITY OF CALIFORNIA PRESS

University of California Press, one of the most
distinguished university presses in the United States,
enriches lives around the world by advancing scholarship
in the humanities, social sciences, and natural sciences. Its
activities are supported by the UC Press Foundation and
by philanthropic contributions from individuals and
institutions. For more information, visit www.ucpress.edu.

University of California Press
Oakland, California

Library of Congress Cataloging-in-Publication Data

Names: Essig, Laurie, author.
Title: Love, Inc. : dating apps, the big white wedding, and
    chasing the happily neverafter / Laurie Essig.
Description: Oakland, California : University of
    California Press, [2019] | Includes bibliographical
    references and index. | Description based on print
    version record and CIP data provided by publisher;
    resource not viewed.
Identifiers: LCCN 2018034895 (print) | LCCN 2018038243
    (ebook) | ISBN 9780520967922 (epub and ePDF) |
    ISBN 9780520295018 (cloth : alk. paper) |
    ISBN 9780520300491 (pbk. : alk. paper)
Subjects: LCSH: Love—Social aspects. | Happiness—
    Social aspects. | Economics—Sociological aspects.
Classification: LCC BF575.L8 (ebook) | LCC BF575.L8 E83
    2019 (print) | DDC 152.4/1—dc23
LC record available at https://lccn.loc.gov/2018034895

Manufactured in the United States of America

26   25   24   23   22   21   20   19
10   9   8   7   6   5   4   3   2   1

For my daughters, Willa and Georgia.
I have always loved you both
without question.

CONTENTS

Conclusion
160

FIGURES

ACKNOWLEDGMENTS

I could never have written this book without the unflagging support of my home institution, Middlebury College. Middlebury gave me financial support, research leave, and so many wonderful research assistants, especially Erin Work and Beatrijs Kuijpers. The Program in Gender, Sexuality, and Feminist Studies at Middlebury lets me teach a course on the sociology of heterosexuality as often as I want. This course, which I have now taught for over two decades, not only undergirds the theoretical scaffolding of this book but also provides me with a lot of smart students who ask really dumb questions—questions that force me to think deeper and harder about romance as an ideology that is both destroying us and keeping us alive.

I also am deeply in awe and rather in love with my many feminist colleagues at Middlebury, especially Sujata Moorti, Carly Thomsen, Kevin Moss, Catharine Wright, and Karin Hanta. At the European University at St. Petersburg, Russia, my colleagues—especially Anna Temkina and Alexander Kondakov—keep me from forgetting how particular love can be.

I am very grateful to the many people who told me about their own journeys through love and romance, friends and strangers alike.

I am thankful for UC Press and my editor there, Naomi Schneider, for bringing this book to fruition. Naomi's utter calm and professionalism made the entire process a fairy-tale come true.

If this is a book about love, it is love that has kept it going. While writing this book I watched as my daughters, Willa and Georgia, and my partner's daughter, Emma, entered the adult world of love and romance. I hope they will always love deeply, but also widely and in ways that do not follow the scripts that have been written for them. All of them have helped me ask questions about dating and other contemporary practices of romance and "anti-romance." Emma tagged along to a wedding expo to find out what all the fuss was about, Georgia went to Disney with me and even taught me how to spot honeymooners, and Willa took photos for the book, her artist's eye always trained on the effects of Love, Inc.

I also had the love and support of my friends, especially my "spouses" Calvin and Gordon White and "our" daughter Addison, Carrie Rigoli, Sue Cronin, Anson Koch-Rein, Patricia Saldarriaga, Glenn Gamblin, Tina Escaja, and Lindsay London, who taught me so many things, like taekwondo and Spanish, and how to cast spells against fascism. And to my canine loves, all of them, but especially Mishka, who loves me no matter what.

Yet there is only one reason this book exists at all and it is because of the love of my life, Suzanna Walters. After initial roadblocks, I was ready to give up on Love, Inc. But Suzanna—who is smarter, more feminist, and a better writer—told me that this book was good and important and deserved to be published. Suzanna insisted that I stop feeling sorry for myself, pull myself together, and get it done. This is exactly what true love looks like: it supports you, it believes in you, and it isn't afraid to tell you to "put on your big girl panties." During our years together, Suzanna has taught me that love is not a fairy-tale, that it cannot promise us a secure future, and that love is not separate from "the world." And that is exactly why love can make us stop and experience joy each and every day of our lives. But I must confess, even after all she has taught me and all I have learned from writing this book, I cannot help myself: I continue to hope, with the full force of romance, that we will spend the rest of our lives together going to political protests, not celebrating Valentine's Day, and watching our girls grow into women. In other words, our very own happily ever after.

Introduction

A Short History of Love

I have a confession: I am a true romantic. I fervently believe in happily ever after and true love always. I am also a cynic. I have a sinking feeling that romance blinds us with fairy dust. I am afraid that romance will, metaphorically speaking, wear off at midnight, leaving us dressed in rags and missing one of our shoes. The romantic in me has spent a lifetime looking for "the one" while the cynic has spent nearly as long teaching and writing about romance from a critical perspective. Environmental collapse and a global transfer of wealth to the billionaire class cannot be solved by seeing someone across the room and feeling our hearts beat faster until we finally lean in for the kiss as fireworks go off in the background. I know that. Most people know that and yet, somehow, the promise of romance as a guarantee of future well-being has become increasingly powerful even as the future itself is increasingly insecure.

That is the argument of this book: that the worse things get, the more we turn to romance to feel hopeful about the future. It is not that capitalism causes romance, but rather that romance is both the most pleasurable and the most future-oriented escape from the grimness of globalized capitalism. Americans turn to a number of belief systems for sustenance: religion, nationalism, football. And some of these, like religion, even promise a better future in the afterlife. Yet romance promises us a better future in *this* life, with the added bonus of an enchantment of the everyday as we hunt for our prince or princess. After all, today could be the day we meet our true love or maybe we are already with our true love and didn't realize it until today. We turn to romance because romance can make our lives better, more bearable, and more sustainable. We turn to romance because unlike having religious faith or even supporting the Jets, only a terrible cynic could begrudge us love.

At the risk of being a terrible cynic, however, I want to point out that romance is a privatized solution to what in fact are structural and global threats. I'm not arguing that married people are less likely to engage in political change, but rather that people who believe that romance will allow them to ride off into the sunset and live happily ever after, many of them single, are looking at the world through rose-colored glasses. True love can no more solve our future than nationalism can. It can only distract us from what we really need: a realistic sense that our future is collective and is seriously endangered at this point in history. Our love affair with romance is like any dysfunctional relationship: the worse things are, the more we believe in the power of romantic love to fix it. When Donald Trump became president of the United States, many Americans insisted that "love trumps hate" and that "love will win." I was too disheartened to respond with that sort of optimism. I looked at this book project, nearly done at the time, and asked myself: Who cares? Why offer a critique of romance as a dangerous ideology when there are far more dangerous ones that now have a place in the White House, ideologies like white nationalism and a worship of wealth and conspicuous consumption? But the worse things got, the more I realized that romance actually is the problem, or if not *the* problem, a problem. Romance lulls us into focusing on our love life rather than politics. Romance teaches us to turn away from the public sphere, to not think about the world, but to focus instead on our relationships and our families. And even when we know the world is bigger than that, even when the world intrudes on us with white nationalists taking over the streets of Charlottesville and global warming producing monster hurricanes on our coasts, we still hold onto the fantasy that true love will save us. I'm not saying that despair causes romance, but rather that romance is a balm for our battered world.

We know, deep in our hearts, that love is not all we need, but love provides a port in the storm. In the winter of 2016–17, nuclear war rhetoric between the US and North Korea was heating up even as global climate change was creating a series of disasters, from raging fires in California to an Arctic vortex throughout much of the country, and Americans responded by turning to the Hallmark Channel. During the 2017 Christmas season, Hallmark aired thirty-three original movies and more than 80 million people watched them.[1] Despite the various "smart" dramas on cable, Americans took pleasure in Hallmark, the only non-news channel with growing viewership in 2017. The company that invented the canned sentiments of greeting cards has now transformed into a network that produces film after film of love saving the day. As Heather Long pointed out in the *Washington Post*, Americans are turning to Hallmark's "feel good" programming to avoid the ugliness of the real world and the even grimmer future it promises.

> Hallmark's ratings have been going up for several years, but it really started in late 2015, right about the time the ... Trump phenomenon took off. During the week of the election last year, the Hallmark Channel was the fourth-most watched channel on TV ... It had more prime-time viewers than MSNBC did and was just behind CNN.[2]

Publicly Americans may pretend to want gritty political dramas like *The Handmaid's Tale*, but privately we're watching Hallmark originals like *A Dash of Love*, a film about love in a restaurant, and *Love Locks*, a romance about college sweethearts reuniting after twenty years.

This war between "good" and "bad" TV mirrors the more existential battle between our inner romantic and inner cynic. The fact that nearly all of us are both romantics *and* cynics can help explain some of the more puzzling contradictions of our time. Our romantic landscape is littered with dating apps and a hook-up culture that encourages young people to not "catch the feels," and yet most Americans want to get married.[3] Although fewer people in the US get married today than ever before, white weddings themselves are ever bigger and more costly.[4] Since 1939, the cost of the average wedding has been rising, from about a fourth of median annual household income to a half.[5] As of 2016, a typical wedding in the US cost a record $32,641. This means that many couples are spending *more* than half their annual income on the big day.[6] People don't read books as much as they used to, yet the romance novel is booming.[7] Romance novels are a billion-dollar industry and account for 13 percent of all adult fiction sold.[8] More to the point, Americans buy even more romances during difficult times. As Motoko Rich explains in the *New York Times,* "Like the Depression-era readers who fueled blockbuster sales of Margaret Mitchell's 'Gone with the Wind,' today's readers are looking for an escape from the grim realities of lay-offs, foreclosures and shrinking 401(k) balances."[9] Movies too provide us with escape from our woes. Just as Esther Williams's films sedated depression-era moviegoers, so today's "chick flicks" offer an equally fantastic escape from the Great Recession and its aftermath. Although unemployment and underemployment are on the rise in chick flicks, they continue to mostly offer up stories of what Diane Negra and Yvonne Tasker describe as

> imperviousness to the recession, largely continuing to trade in hyper-con-sumerist spectacle, situating itself exclusively and unselfconsciously in environments of urban affluence and privilege, and glorifying the elimina-tion of feminism from the "life-scripts" of its female protagonists. This all may seem unsurprising; indeed, it complies perfectly with conventional wisdom that in periods of economic duress, Hollywood renews its charge to gratify audiences through escapism.[10]

Romance has not always been our opiate of choice. Once upon a time, not that long ago, there was no such thing as riding off into the sunset to live happily ever after. Prior to the past few hundred years, humans did fall madly in love, but they did not imagine that love would ever lead to a happy, safe, and secure tomorrow. The idea that true love will keep us safe and happy in the future started with industrialization and modern ideas about sexuality, class, race, and gender. This is not a coincidence. Romance helps people make sense of the modern world and imbues consumption with meaning. Romance not only props up notions of what love is good and what love is bad, but also specifies who deserves good love.

In this way, romance is what Karl Marx called an ideology; as such, it is distinct from the real feelings we have with intimate partners. Romance, like Catholicism or a fervent belief in the power of the free market, is a set of ideas that represents the interests of the ruling class. As an ideology, romance teaches us that certain people (mostly white, mostly straight, mostly well-off, and mostly normatively gendered) deserve happily ever after, as well as full citizenship and extra rights and privileges from the state. As many feminist scholars before me have shown, romance as an ideology tells us stories that keep gender and racial hierarchies in place, with white men as knights in shining armor and white women as damsels in distress; those who would stand in true love's path are often portrayed as middle-aged, power-hungry women, or as queer or not white.

Romance doesn't just sell us ideas about class, race, gender, and sexuality, it also sells us stuff, lots and lots of stuff, from wedding dresses and diamond rings to houses in ideal suburbs and even political candidates. And it imbues that stuff with meaning—marking some items, like diamond rings and wedding dresses, as sacred. Yet even among those Americans who cannot afford the stuff, romance as an ideology still rules. Today nearly everyone wants the promise of a happily ever after. As D'Vera Cohn puts it,

> The romantic ideal of marriage plays out in survey data that show whether they are married or not, Americans are more inclined to choose "love" as a reason for marriage more than any other factor ... over "making a lifelong commitment" ... and "financial stability."[11]

Romance has its own forms of propaganda. Photo by
Willa Cowan-Essig.

Part of the reason nearly all of us are subject to romance's charms is
culture. Hollywood produces film after film telling us that regardless of
the obstacles, we too can find happiness and security if we just tie the
knot. *Knocked Up* showed us that even a night of regretted sex and the
resulting pregnancy can be fixed by falling in love. *My Big Fat Greek Wed-*

ding shows that huge cultural and linguistic divides can be permanently solved by marriage. Even adventure films, like the *Harry Potter* series, end with reproductive, heterosexual, married couples as well as one gay and dead Dumbledore. By the time we see Harry and Ginny and Ron and Hermione send their own offspring to Hogwarts, it is clear to the reader that their love was written in the stars.[12] Hollywood produces a lot of films with a variety of messages, but we all know that a happy ending is one with a wedding and an imagined future where the couple is without conflict and preferably with children. And if a happy ending does not result in the prince and princess riding off into the sunset, it is because such an ending would undermine cultural rules about who deserves love and who does not. In the 2016 Sally Field romantic comedy *Hello, My Name Is Doris,* the humor lies in the romantic fantasies of a quirky sixty-something secretary who mistakenly believes she is in a romantic relationship with a very attractive thirty-something executive. The joke is not about romantic love, per se, but about Field's character, a desexualized older woman who doesn't understand that she is not worthy of this Prince Charming. When the tables are turned, and it is a sixty-something-year-old man with a much younger woman, that's amore. Just look at *Autumn in New York* (Winona Ryder playing twenty-two with a fifty-year-old Robert Redford) or Woody Allen in life or film.

Hollywood is not alone in harnessing the power of romance to seduce us. Advertisers use romantic love as much as they use sex to sell us stuff. There are all the ads for diamond rings and wedding dresses that promise us eternal happiness if we just have the perfect romance with the perfect stuff. But advertisers also use the promise of happily ever after to sell us everything else. Thumb through any fashion or women's magazine and see page after page of beautiful couples staring dreamily into each other's eyes. Buy a minivan or SUV and the promise of a happy family. The right beer can move men from "bromance" to romance. Even cleaning products use the story of romance to convince us to buy the right cleanser. A recent Apple advertisement insists that "medicine, law, engineering—these are noble pursuits and necessary to sustain life. But poetry, romance, love—these are what we stay alive for." Unspoken are the words: buy an iPad.[13]

This turn to the romantic is not just cultural; it is also political. Politicians on the right and the left argue that "romantic love" and "marriage" are the answer to nearly every problem. Poverty? Marriage will fix it. The US government has been running a marriage campaign in poor neighborhoods for over a decade. The campaign, known as the Healthy Marriage Initiative, tells poor, primarily black and Latino Americans that married people earn more money, and therefore the answer to being poor is to get hitched. Despite all evidence that poverty is caused by a lack of money and the lack of any opportunity to earn money, about $300 million is spent annually to do things like place billboards in poor neighborhoods showing the ideal family—mom, dad, two kids—and the words "Marriage makes you richer."[14]

In the 1980s a vibrant national gay and lesbian political movement took a turn toward magical thinking when it decided to put nearly all its resources into the marriage equality movement.[15] On June 26, 2015, the Supreme Court declared that gays and lesbians had a constitutional right to get married. President Obama, along with millions of others, tweeted #lovewins. As Emily Bazelon pointed out a year earlier:

> The win for same-sex marriage overshadowed the loss for voting rights—an abrupt end to a key anti-discrimination provision, which had been hard won by civil rights activists ... Instead of focusing on a court that seemed determined to dilute the power of black and Hispanic voters, the public saw a more neutral court respectfully and retroactively recognizing the same-sex marriage of an 84-year-old widow named Edie Windsor.[16]

Despite the promise of the safe and secure future that "winning" marriage implies, for black and Hispanic citizens both queer and straight, basic constitutional rights like voting were gutted. And regardless of race, there is still no federal employment protection for lesbians, gays, or transgendered Americans.[17] Since love "won," LGBTQ citizens are finding themselves in an increasingly precarious legal landscape. State laws like those in North Carolina and Mississippi allow discrimination against LGBTQ people in everything from whether they can buy a wedding cake to where they can go to the bathroom.[18]

That is the power of romance as an ideology: it can make us feel like our lives are enchanted even when the world around us is collapsing. Those of us who turn to romance to feel hope about the future are not "dupes of ideology." What we are is desperate, and desperate times call for desperate measures. Romance allows us to feel hopeful. It provides optimism about our lives and our futures when we need it most. And so many of us embrace the ideology of romance as a survival strategy even when we know that romance will not actually solve the unprecedented problems we humans now face. We might call ourselves homo romanticus. Like homo economicus, homo romanticus makes choices that might be rational at the micro level of individual survival, but the macro and historical effects of these choices can be devastating. Homo economicus can decide to buy a gas-guzzling car because gas is relatively cheap—as is the gas-fueled car compared to an electric one. Homo romanticus can decide to spend her time going to couples therapy rather than "getting out the vote." The ideology of romance, like the consumption of cheap fossil fuels, allows us to keep going *and* will ultimately make things worse.

CAPITALISM, ROMANCE, AND OTHER FAIRY-TALES

In this way romance is intimately connected to consumer capitalism and its emphasis on individual well-being. It is not that romance and capitalism recently got into bed together. The story of capitalism has always been a love story. Yet most histories of capitalism have left romance out of the picture. Max Weber stressed the importance of what he called the Protestant ethic in the development of capitalism. In *The Protestant Ethic and the Spirit of Capitalism,* Weber argued that certain forms of Protestantism, particularly Calvinism, viewed the accumulation of wealth as a sign of godliness, thereby reshaping the spirit of the culture. Thus, although the structures necessary for capitalism—the currencies, the trade routes, and so on—existed in other places and at other times, it was only in Protestant America, where the accumulation of wealth was seen as godly, that capitalism fully took root. Since wealth signified divine grace, there was an incentive to accumulate more and more wealth by investing in future revenues rather than spending. As capitalism developed, "the strict earning of more and more money ... [became] purely ... an end in itself."[19]

Weber's sense that capitalism relies on a constant investment in the future missed that this future was already always heterosexual, reproductive, and deeply romantic. In other words, at the very core of the capitalist system lay the promise of a more perfect future not just through the predestination of the Calvinist God or even the accumulation of wealth through labor, but also through the narrative of romance leading to the one true love and the happily ever after. In *No Future,* Lee Edelman describes this constant investment in a reproductive sexuality as "futurity."[20] In *The Straight State: Sexuality and Citizenship in Twentieth-Century America,* Margot Canaday argues that an investment in futurity was at the core of American citizenship from the late 1800s onward since "unlike comparable European states, which were well established before sexologists 'discovered' the homosexual in the late twentieth century, the American bureaucracy matured during the same years that scientific and popular awareness of the pervert exploded on the American consciousness."[21] American citizenship has long relied on a heterosexuality that was always already invested in future gains. Like the Protestant ethic, this *romance ethic* promised rewards down the line, even a sense of perfection and completion and yes, heaven, if only we worked hard at it. But like the proverbial bootstraps, the rewards of romance were never available to everyone. Instead, this sexual citizenship demanded heterosexuality, marriage, and even whiteness in order to gain the full rewards of the state. For instance, the federal government rewarded GIs returning from World War II with low-interest loans to buy their suburban homes, but only if they were white, male, and married.[22] Thus whiteness, heterosexuality, and marital status were always central to full citizenship in the US. Even in the twenty-first century, in part because of the expansion of marriage rights to gay and lesbian couples, marriage remains the primary determination not just of federal rights and privileges, but also of adulthood, good parenting, and even American-ness. The idea that the citizen is always already married persists even though for the first time most adult Americans are *not* married.

Since Weber's classic explanation of capitalism was published over a century ago, many theorists have tried to think through how that spirit or "Geist" moves the American economy and culture. In *Self-Help, Inc.*, Micki McGee makes the argument that in the twentieth century, the Protestant ethic morphed into an ethic of continual self-improvement. McGee theorizes that as citizenship and personhood opened up to more than landed white gentlemen, the earlier promise of being a "self-made man" transformed into the far more democratic if just as unlikely promise of being a "fully realized individual." This "hybridization of personal and commercial values [is] eminently evident in the texts of self-improvement culture. [Thus] a calculating rationality was imported into the private sphere."[23] This left Americans with the sense that each one of us is responsible for our own self's happiness, wealth, and health.

Laura Kipnis, in *Against Love*, weaves Weber's Protestant ethic and Karl Marx's alienation of labor with self-help to argue that our romantic relationships are belabored dead-ends, sites of imprisonment and despair. For Kipnis, capitalism, the Protestant ethic, and the culture of constant self-work transform intimate relationships into yet another form of labor. Kipnis asks:

> When monogamy becomes labor, when desire is organized contractually, with accounts kept and fidelity extracted like labor from employees, with marriage as a domestic factory policed by means of rigid shop-floor discipline designed to keep the wives and husbands and domestic partners of the world choke-chained to the status quo machinery—is this really what we mean by a "good relationship"?[24]

For Kipnis, the only way to escape this "domestic gulag" is to put a clog in its machinery and refuse to be productive in our intimate relationships.[25] Yet Kipnis's *Against Love* still leaves us with some sort of pre-capitalist form of emotion, some sort of purer and freer form of intimate expression.

In *Cold Intimacies: The Making of Emotional Capitalism*, Eva Illouz shows how capitalism produces these emotions in the first place. Illouz argues that capitalism is neither cold nor rational, but instead highly emotional. This "emotional capitalism" as Illouz defines it is

> a culture in which emotional and economic discourses and practices mutually shape each other, thus producing ... a broad, sweeping movement in which affect is made an essential aspect of economic behavior and in which emotional life—especially that of the middle classes—follows the logic of economic relations and exchange.[26]

For Illouz, modern love is part of what Max Weber described as our "disenchantment" with our world. "Disenchantment," she writes, "is both a property of belief that becomes organized by knowledge systems and expert cultures ... and a difficulty in believing. This is because both the cognitions and emotions organizing belief become rationalized." Illouz argues that this rationalization of feeling leads to a contradictory relationship between our idea of romantic love and our experience of it, and these contradictions mean that modern love is expressed primarily through irony. According to Illouz, "Modern romantic consciousness has the rhetorical structure of irony because it is saturated with knowledge, but it is a disenchanted knowledge that prevents full belief and commitment. Thus if love is a modern religion ... it is a religion that cannot produce belief, faith or commitment."[27] Illouz is correct. The feelings of romantic love are often infused with disenchantment, yet paradoxically they are also full of hope and possibility and make life bearable.

In this book, I uncover both how capitalism makes romance possible and how romance makes existence possible. I am building off Illouz and

Kipnis to make a different if related set of claims here: romance has always been central to modernity and capitalism, but in ways more contradictory than notions of alienation and disenchantment allow. I am also arguing that capitalism took a particular turn in the 1980s and that turn demanded an ideology that could both disguise the real material effects of global capital while simultaneously allowing people to feel hopeful about the future. In this book, I am tracing the real emotional effects of romance in real people's lives by showing how romance is a story not just about feelings, but about who belongs and who does not and what love matters and what love dare not speak its name. Romance gets so many of us to buy into this story with our hearts as well as with our hard-earned dollars. I argue that in addition to alienation and disenchantment, romance induces a feeling of hopefulness about the future, but that hopefulness is predicated on the lie that love is all we need.

As economic precariousness and global warming started to press down on us, romance rode in on a white horse to whisk us away. Truth be told, all the other heroes, like communism and revolution, had shown themselves to be drunken louts who never really cared about us in the first place. And just then a dashing leading man and a new form of cowboy capitalism rode into our lives to save the day and the future.

ROMANCING REAGAN

On January 20, 1981, Ronald Reagan became president and set in motion a series of neoliberal economic reforms. These reforms, colloquially referred to as Reaganomics or trickle-down economics, promised that as the rich got richer, their wealth would trickle down to the rest of us. It never did. Reagan's policies would help transform American society from one of the most to one of the least equitable countries. Since our love affair with Reagan began, the US has become a country where 10 percent of the population now controls over 75 percent of the wealth. The US is the most unequal of any industrialized country and slightly worse than India, Chile, and South Africa.[28] The 25 percent of the wealth left to be divvied up by the remaining 90 percent of us is hardly randomly distributed. Whites continue to earn about 1.7 and 1.5 times what black and Hispanic Americans earn, respectively, and women get paid about 83 percent of what men earn.[29] These policies of transferring monies to the wealthiest and cutting the social safety net for the poorest have since spread around the world, leaving most people much worse off than they were in 1980. Between 2011 and 2014, 95 percent of the world's population got poorer while the richest 1 percent gained over $27 trillion.[30]

Instead of paying attention to Reagan and his ideological soul mate, Margaret Thatcher, and their fantasy that a "rising tide floats all boats," most of us were too focused on a different sort of fantasy. Seven months after Reagan took office, Charles, Prince of Wales, and Lady Diana Spencer got married in the most fairy-tale of weddings; 750 million people watched it around the world.[31] If only that many had paid attention to Reagan and Thatcher's dreams of giving money to the wealthiest and ending government programs and legal protections for the poorest and most marginalized. Most people, myself included, ignored the deregulation of banking. Many of us, however, knew all the details of the twenty-five-foot train of Princess Di's ivory taffeta wedding dress and her poufy princess sleeves and how dashing Prince Charles looked in his full naval attire complete with white gloves and gold braid. In fact, the two looked so like Prince Charming and Cinderella that even today the keeper of Diana's wedding dress, Nick Grossmark, says the reason it is a priceless gem is because "it is a fairytale fantasy, a typical princess's wedding gown. It's like something out of Walt Disney."[32]

Disney, in fact, was a key player in this global turn to romance over reality. The corporation managed to turn itself around at the end of the 1980s by reinvigorating romance as its genre of choice. After not so great sales of its far less romantic films, like *Honey, I Shrunk the Kids* and *Oliver and Company,* Disney went back to its romantic roots. In 1989, Disney hit the jackpot with *The Little Mermaid* and *Pretty Woman.* According to press reports, earnings from the movies pushed profits up 34.5 percent; videocassette sales increased profits by 56.8.[33] In *Pretty Woman,* a prostitute becomes worthy of the love of a wealthy "john" as their romance transforms them into a prince and princess. In *The Little Mermaid* a fish/princess hybrid is made human through the love of a prince. Both these stories demanded a suspension of reality ("johns" don't fall in love with prostitutes and marry them; mermaids don't exist and if they did, why would they want to be human?).

Disney and trickle-down economics both promised us that things would get better. We now know the economic policies didn't work, and with the advent of Occupy Wall Street and other social movements calling for the redistribution of wealth, the fantasy of trickle-down economics is no longer very popular. There has been, however, no large-scale movement to stop fantasizing about a future saved through romance. To the contrary, in much of the world today people willingly swallow the central tenet of the romantic ethic: work hard at relationships, discipline yourself sexually, invest in the future through marriage, and you will be rewarded. You can be gay or black or even old and have failed at the enterprise of love over and over again, but just keep trying. Heaven in the form of a fairy-tale ending is just around the corner if you follow the rules, show yourself to be a good romantic citizen, and buy the right stuff. No wonder many of us feel disenchantment; but, also, no wonder many of us feel a sense of purpose that is the foundation of the ideology of romance. This is where the marriage of romance and capitalism draws its strength: by promising us a better world at some future point *if* we are willing to sacrifice now. We are being sold hope in increasingly hopeless times, and many of us are buying it like never before, not just in the US but globally, because romance, like capital and the problems it creates, travels.

In the past few decades, romance as an ideology *and* as a material force has been gaining ground worldwide. As Utopian visions of collective well-being or magic markets faded into the dustbin of history and arguments over "capitalism versus communism" began to seem as quaint as landlines and TV networks, romance gained new life as a solution for the future. Nation-states turned away from economic camps and began to align themselves along notions of good and bad romance. We might call this a new romantic cold war. Unlike the Cold War of old, which neatly divided states into East and West, this new romantic cold war is a global one. It does not exist in one place or another, but circulates. No longer confined to Russia or the US, East or West, fights over what it means to be a good sexual citizen and what constitutes good love happen in surprisingly similar ways here, there, and everywhere.

ROMANCE TRAVELS

On Valentine's Day 2010, I stood in the small Tuscan village of Volterra, Italy, and listened as Russian, British, American, and German tourists prattled on about teen vampires and true love. It was then that I understood that romance travels. I have been trying to travel with romance—going to the royal wedding of Kate and William in London and wedding expos across North America, touring with teen vampire fans, and interviewing "naughty" middle-aged women obsessed with a love story that involves spanking, lots and lots of spanking. I have also been following romance's shadow, the dark space left behind where love and happy endings are not allowed. In these dark spaces, circulating between Russia, Uganda, the United States, and France, a story of bad romance threatens not just good love, but nation-states.

That is why the story of how romance travels is a story about ideology, capital, *and* emotion in the twenty-first century. It is a story about romance as an ideological formation that has married a particular form of economic policy known as neoliberalism and how this couple works together to produce real emotional commitments. These emotional commitments range from a nearly religious zeal for marriage to an equally religious zeal for destroying homosexuality. In the United States, a place where citizenship has long been defined as the ability to access marriage and individuals are willing to take on huge amounts of debt to create "perfect" weddings, there is also a huge amount of anxiety about single-mother families and gay marriage. In Russia, homosexuality is imagined as a contagious disease that threatens the body politic, and yet there are also a lot of gay and lesbian citizens. That is because citizenship and sexuality are now fractured, existing as a palimpsest, with previous notions written over contemporary ones and families as they actually are coming into contact with a variety of representations of ideal families from a variety of locations.

In the twenty-first century we all exist in fractured time. I live in multiple spaces, languages, cities, and countries. I travel back and forth and in between. Sometimes I listen to Russian news stories in Burlington, Vermont, while I Skype with my daughter in St. Petersburg or my partner in Boston. I am what the advertisers like to call a "global citizen," but in the twenty-first century, we are all global subjects. Even for those who do not exist in the privileged world that I do, nation-states mean less and less as both capital and the problems it produces transcend national borders. We are all in what political theorists call "post-Westphalian" time, a historical moment when nation-states are less important than global corporations. As Nancy Fraser points out, imagining nation-states as sovereign no longer makes sense when it comes to thinking about how the world works. Global climate change, the accumulation of capital among the few, and the simultaneous economic crisis for the many mean that not just ideologies cross borders, but also the real material results of these ideologies, such as rising oceans and air too polluted to breathe. Instead of thinking about romance and neoliberal capitalism as being nationally located, I am trying to trace what Fraser calls "all affected" persons, since "globalization is driving a widening wedge between affectedness and political membership."[34]

Nation, culture, and economy are all working together to convince us that love matters more than gender and racial equity, economic justice, or even environmental salvation. And yet romance is more than an ideology. It is also a survival strategy. Like meditation or a good glass of red wine, romance convinces us that we can survive another day. It is romance's ability to produce this sense of optimism, no matter how grim the world becomes, that is its real magical power. This book is an attempt to unravel how romance travels alongside global capital but also how romance travels in the hearts and minds of many ordinary Americans.

I have tried to follow my head and my heart to examine how love gets incorporated into culture and economy. My head led me to ask questions: What are the scripts of love that our culture teaches us to follow? And what are the products that consumer capitalism sells us in our quest for happily ever after? How is love "produced"? How is it "incorporated" by a variety of industries and ideologies that teach us what to do when we fall in love? All of these industries and ideologies do not have our best interests at heart, but profit. Yet romance is also a set of emotional commitments. That is why so many of us consume romance even when we know that it cannot save us. Romance keeps us going, keeps us from feeling hopeless and provides us with everyday magic that is too easily dismissed as "childish" or "for women." In this sense, romance is both an ideology *and* a strategy, a trap *and* an escape mechanism.

But my heart led me somewhere else. I can see that romance has real emotional effects. Romance does the affective labor that neoliberal global capitalism cannot. It gives so many of us hope in hopeless times. And yet, romance produces a sort of cruel optimism, an optimism that Lauren Berlant describes as

> ignit[ing] a sense of possibility [yet] actually mak[ing] it impossible to attain the expansive transformation for which a person or a people risks striving; and, doubly cruel ... such that a person or a world finds itself bound to a situation of profound threat that is, at the same time, profoundly confirming.[35]

We certainly live in a time of profound threats. Romance has been mobilized to allow us this cruel optimism when what we really need is "kind realism." Kind realism demands that we no longer privatize our futures by searching for our own personal happily ever after, but collectivize our resources to survive environmental destruction, religious fundamentalism, and the seemingly inevitable concentration of resources in the hands of the few. We don't need fairy-tales; we need global movements where we see "humanity" as far more important than our beloved. If such a future seems overly optimistic, consider the cruelty of the alternative.

It was never written in the stars that capitalism be so cruel nor that romance be married to it. Like most marriages, this one is the result of random chance and utilitarianism. Romance helps us bear the effects of global capital, but capitalism could survive without romance and romance could survive without capitalism. In order to disrupt the marriage of romance and capitalism, I have organized this book like a typical love story. Chapter 1, "Learning to Love," considers how romance is a hegemonic ideological formation that instructs us in a variety of things: from how to love, how to be more productive workers, and how to maintain racial and gender hierarchies, as well as to accept the global accumulation of capital among very few people. From Disney to *Twilight* to *Fifty Shades of Grey*, love stories are primers in the ideology of romance, and the ideology of romance is deeply wedded to capital. The second chapter, "Finding Love," considers contemporary practices of dating, partnering, and the rituals of becoming a couple. I consider how finding our "perfect" mate is now part science, part consumer product, and how Americans buy into it no matter how often they fail at the happy ending. Chapter 3, "Marry Me?," looks at how couples move into the increasingly sacred and *spectacular* space of "engaged to be married." By considering the somewhat new phenomenon of YouTube proposals, I look at how the wedding proposal has moved from a private conversation between a man and a woman to highly watched videos of dancing flash mobs and singing grooms. Chapter 4, "White Weddings," considers how the ideology of romance solidifies into romantic subjects and sexual citizens through marriage and its most fetishistic ritual, the white wedding. By examining the global circulation of perfect weddings, I try to map out the close connection between economic redistribution under neoliberalism and the sexual apartheid created under romance. Chapter 5,

"The Honeymoon," considers romantic travel and consumption as a colonizing process that allows the ideology of romance to reproduce racial, gender, and class hierarchies. I go to Disney World in Florida to find out why the most magical place on earth is also the number one destination in the continental US for honeymooners. The book's conclusion, "Happily Never After," considers how people actually experience the culmination of romance. I travel to the world's most fantastical suburb, Celebration, Florida, a town designed by the Disney corporation to embody the space of ideal families, and consider how Celebration's entanglement in the "real"—the housing crisis, increasing homelessness, and globalization—disrupted it as an imaginary space and led to Disney selling off this dreamscape and its nightmarish problems. As can be seen from the book's organization, the research is based on analysis of various cultural texts, fieldwork at various sites of romance, and interviews with people engaged in various forms of romantic behavior. I conducted fieldwork for three days before and during the royal wedding of Kate Middleton and Prince William, as well as at sites of *Twilight* and *Fifty Shades* tourism (Volterra, Italy; Forks, OR, and Seattle, WA). I interviewed nearly a hundred people planning weddings and vendors at three wedding expos (two in the US and one in Canada), conducted a week's worth of fieldwork at Disney World and Celebration, Florida, and conducted twenty semistructured interviews lasting between one and three hours on modern dating. I also went to a mass lesbian wedding, interviewing sixteen brides and four wedding guests. Spending all this time in the world of Love, Inc., convinced me more than ever that love is not all we need, but it sure feels good.

The contradiction between wanting the magic of romance even as we know there is no such thing as magic is the tension at the heart of so much of contemporary life. Most people I interviewed for this book are both hard-nosed cynics and true romantics. Most of us are Jekyll and Hyde when it comes to love. Our cynical selves scoff at the crass commercialism of big weddings and online dating sites that for a fee will find us our "perfect match." And yet that doesn't stop many of us from crying at weddings or even shows about weddings or writing that profile on Match.com. I am trying to speak with my fellow romantics here to tell a different sort of love story, one where our "happily ever after" is about some sense of collective well-being. If this were a typical fairytale I would be the wicked witch showing up uninvited to ruin the wedding of the prince and princess. But please consider that the time for fairy-tales has passed. We can either start telling ourselves new stories with new, more collective endings, or, like the wicked witch, meet our unfortunate ends.

I realize that *Love, Inc.* is hardly a typical love story. I still hope that it will leave you with a true romantic's belief that the future can be better than the present.

CHAPTER ONE

Learning to Love

Gravitation is not responsible for people falling in love.
 Albert Einstein

FIRST LOVE

If Einstein was right and gravitation is not responsible for people falling in love, then what is? In order to answer that question, it is best to start at the very beginning: the body. Neuroscience tells us that the place in the brain where we experience romantic love, the caudate, is part of our primitive and "reptilian" brain, more an instinct than a conscious decision. In addition to animalistic instinct, romantic love is associated with dopamine production. In other words, romantic love is an addiction as well as a reptilian response.[1] If neuroscience is correct and we have a deep-seated biological drive to fall in love, both the historical and anthropological record show that how those instincts and addictions get shaped into action has everything to do with culture. Otherwise love would not be such a many-splendored thing and would look depressingly the same in ancient Greece and contemporary Beijing. Instinct and addiction are always determined, even overdetermined, by culture and history. When it comes to the neuroscience of love, we are more like a toy poodle offering to do tricks like "shake" or "roll over" for a treat than we are a wolf howling at the moon.

In the US for the past 150 years or so, all infants have been subject to having their innate drives toward love twisted and shaped by the ideology of romance and the reality of consumer capitalism. To paraphrase the more philosophical language of Michel Foucault, romance was a temporary aberration, but with modernity, the romantic was born as a species. Or as Karl Marx and Simone de Beauvoir's offspring might have said, one is not born a romantic, but becomes one in conditions not of one's own making.

This may sound abstract, but let me begin with something far more concrete: two temper tantrums. When one of my daughters was ten months old, she wanted to wear her new summer sandals, white and sparkly. I wanted her to put on sneakers because it was raining and cold outside. She lay down on the ground and screamed until I did what all bad parents do and gave in. We could interpret her tantrum as evidence that females have deep-seated preferences for sparkly white things, like sandals or wedding dresses, but I had already polluted the blank slate of my daughter's brain by oohing and aahing over the sandals and telling her that they were "pretty," a word she had already begun to associate with good things. We are not born willing to lie on the floor and scream for certain fetish items. We learn that. I myself taught it to my daughter. American culture teaches most daughters that the fetish items they should be willing to pitch a fit for are not just pretty and white, but bridal.

On WETV's reality show *Bridezilla*, romance-induced temper tantrums are not just a regular occurrence, but actually drive the entire narrative of the show. Many of these tantrums involve young brides not having the perfect things for a perfect wedding. "Bridezillas" throw tantrums over things like wedding dresses and diamond rings and even shoes. The brides scream and yell and throw things and threaten their families, friends, and, especially, their fiancés. In one episode, a young bride by the name of Joraine says, "If my expectations aren't met I'm going to flip out at my own wedding and body slam somebody." In the same episode, bride Amanda threatens to set people on fire, pouring gas on them and lighting a match, if everything is not perfect on her wedding day.[2]

What separates a ten-month old from a twenty-year-old is not the ability to throw a tantrum, but rather that the older girl's desire is obsessively focused on romance and its culmination in the perfect wedding. These tantrums are part of the emotional work of the white wedding. From the time we are very young, we are all molded into romantic beings, even if we do not become "bridezillas." We learn that people fall in love, that falling in love is the most magical thing two humans can do, full of pumpkins turning into carriages and frogs into princes. And most important of all, we learn that falling in love is how we end up adults, with a family of our own, happy and well adjusted because the kind of person (or evil witch or giant octopus) who does not fall in love is ugly and mean and will die a horrible death (usually at the hands of a prince who will run his sword or some other suitably sharp and phallic object through her middle).

Both the culture of romance and the market of romance are part of the story of how we learn to love—and not just to love, but to love in particular ways that turn infant girls into brides and nearly everyone, men included, into romantics. Although not themselves brides or bridezillas, men are also seduced by the promise of a happily ever after. According to research by the online dating service Match.com, men want to get married just as much as women, and they are much more likely to fall in love "at first sight."[3]

The way we learn to love demands not just conformity, but consumption. We learn what to be and what to want in a variety of ways: family relationships, friendship networks, expert advice, and culture, from pop music to animated films to romance novels and romantic comedies and reality TV shows like *Bridezillas*. This chapter teases out these cultural scripts of romance by tracing the history that led us to where we are now: a romantic landscape populated with rich vampires and BDSM tops who save ordinary girls from lives of economic hardship. In order to fully understand romance we have to trace the road from Victorian Valentine's Day cards and early Disney films to the *Twilight* saga and its illegitimate progeny, *Fifty Shades of Grey*.

ROMANCE, CHILDHOOD, AND THE PERVERSE
VICTORIAN IMAGINATION

At some point during evolution between plankton and Bon
Jovi, apes evolved the ability to become emotionally attached
to one another.

Mark Manson, *A Brief History of Romantic Love*
and Why It Kind of Sucks

It would be easy to say that we have always shaped our infants into romantic subjects. After all, it seems so natural to fill our children's heads with ideas of true love. But childhood has not always been awash in the gauzy dreams of two hearts beating as one. A few hundred years ago, American children were not dreaming of riding off into the sunset. Instead, their cultural texts were the ever-grim Grimm's fairy-tales. In these premodern versions, the central story was never about a sweet and innocent girl being rewarded with a happily ever after. In the brothers Grimm version, a vengeful Cinderella puts her evil stepmother into red-hot iron shoes and makes her dance about till she falls down dead from the pain. In the earlier version of "Snow White," it is a jolt from a horse, not a kiss from the prince, that awakens her. Then there are the previous versions of "Sleeping Beauty," where the prince has sex with her while she is unconscious and she bears children in that compromised state. These tales are not exactly romantic in the modern sense of the word.[4] Even more recent tales for children, like Hans Christian Andersen's 1837 "The Little Mermaid," are not about romantic love as much as about the Christian quest for a human soul and thus eternal life.[5]

But all that changed about 150 years ago, when romance and capitalism got involved with each other in ways that demanded a happy ending in order to get us to buy the story. Let me be clear. I am not suggesting that romance and capitalism were fated to be joined, but rather that they fell into together, the way most modern couples do. Modernity saw large structural changes like the development of capitalism, the rise of the middle classes, and a new form of women's labor called shopping. At the same time, new beliefs and business practices were forming to get children involved in Love, Inc. For one, the Victorians were busy inventing the child. Obviously, people were both young and small before the Victorian era, but these young people were not imagined as cherubic little angels who must be kept out of the paid economy as well as the sexual one. Of course, not all children were angels. The angels were blond, blue-eyed, and middle class. Other children had to work in factories, as slaves, as servants, and more. As Robin Bernstein points out in *Racial Innocence,* the child was invented by the Victorians, but that child was invented as white, sexually pure, and in need of protection. According to Bernstein,

> The cult of domesticity demanded performances of sexual innocence within the home ... Sexual innocence then divided white and black children in much the same way it did white and black women. Unique to the polarization of black and white children, however, was the libel ... that black juveniles did not—could not, even experience pain.[6]

This angelic white child, as Bernstein suggests, was disturbingly similar to another invention of the Victorians: the lady.

Prior to capitalism, one was born into one's status: a lord or a serf, a lady or a chambermaid. But with the onset of capitalism and the huge class revolutions that took place throughout the 1700s and 1800s, the lady was not just a status, something you were because your parents were nobility, but also a performance. It was not enough to be wealthy and white. The modern lady had to *enact* purity and innocence, not engage in physical labor, and exist solely for the purpose of serving her family. As Anne McClintock points out in *Imperial Leather,* "For most women from the still-disorganized middling classes ... idleness was less the absence of work than a conspicuous labor of leisure."[7] It was precisely this labor of performing *ladyhood* that allowed the dictionary definition of lady to shift from primarily meaning "a woman of high social position" to a "woman who behaves in a polite way." The shift from position to behavior did not completely unmoor "lady" from race and class hierarchies, but it did require a different set of behaviors and rituals of *ladyness* in order to maintain those hierarchies.[8]

Like the child, the lady also needed quite a bit of protection from sexual predators since the lady's very absence of desires, her purity, was what made her desirable in the first place. As James Kincaid untangles this Victorian hairball in *Erotic Innocence:*

> I'm not the first to announce that both the child and modern sexuality came into being only about 200 years ago, but it isn't often noted ... they got mixed together. One somehow got implanted in the other, and it shouldn't have happened. Despite the loud official protestations about children's innocence, our Victorian ancestors managed to make their concept of the erotic depend on the child, just as their idea of the child was based on their notions of sexual attraction.[9]

It should come as no surprise, then, that the sort of stories the Victorians came up with for white and middle-class children were different, more "innocent," and also more invested in the idea that children, like ladies, ought to be protected by their knight in shining armor. And so things changed. As a culture, we began to produce stories for certain children and stories about children that taught young people to focus on romantic relationships and to embody true love through certain forms of consumption, like big weddings, as well as certain sorts of embodiment, like the white and pure woman-child that is so central to weddings and other romantic fantasies.

The first material artifacts of the marriage of romance and capitalism appeared in about 1850, when Esther Howland started mass-producing Valentine's Day cards in Worcester, Massachusetts. Howland's brilliance was to take the promise of romance and mass produce it for a profit. Howland's cards were a combination of lacy frothiness and images of sweet white children, in pairs and alone. Although never married herself, Howland helped spawn a national holiday that moves American consumers to spend about $18.9 billion every year on the stuff

Valentine's Day cards, part of the nearly $20 billion spent in the US each year on Valentine's Day. Photo by Willa Cowan-Essig.

of romance, $703 million of which is spent on our pets.[10] Hallmark estimates that about 141 million Valentine's Day cards are exchanged worldwide.[11] The cards also introduced Americans to the idea that love is a tangible product that can be bought and exchanged.

From Howland's cards, consumers quickly moved to romance novels. Young women traded in their more complex Jane Austens for the mass-produced paperback romance, which always had a "happy ending." Romance novels ended when a young woman was tamed by marriage and a rough man was tamed by the love of a young woman and the reader could imagine their future as happy, secure, and always reproductive. These modern romance novels were made possible by modern technological inventions like synthetic glue and a network of grocery and drug stores that more and more women began to frequent.[12] Harlequin and other modern stories of romance helped us believe in things like true love, but also about why certain groups deserved true love and others did not.

ROMANCE AS MODERN IDEOLOGY

> Visionary speculation, especially of an unrealistic or
> idealistic nature.
>> Definition of "ideology," *Oxford Dictionary*

In this sense, the modern era put romance into marriage for the first time. Premodern notions of romance, such as chivalry, placed romantic love firmly outside of marriage. A man wanted a woman and that woman was nearly always attached to another man, either a husband or a father. Lady Guinevere and Sir Lancelot with King Arthur in tow, Romeo and Juliet with the families' refusal to allow their marriage, or even King Henry VIII, who always had a wife in the way of his true love. Romance went from being a set of ideas about love and sex that rarely involved two people married to one another to something that was properly situated within marriage. As Anthony Giddens puts it:

> Romantic love became distinct from *amour passion,* although at the same time had residues of it. *Amour passion* was never a generic social force in the way in which romantic love has been from somewhere in the late eighteenth century up to relatively recent times. Together with other social changes, the spread of notions of romantic love was deeply involved with momentous transitions affecting marriage as well as other contexts of personal life ... Unlike *amour passion,* which uproots erratically, romantic love detaches individuals from wider social circumstances.[13]

This new romantic love was not just a sign of modernity, but provided a way of distracting us from conditions as they really are by promising us a happy ending. If religion was the premodern opiate of the masses, then romance was modernity's far more addictive heroin.

Since Howland started churning out Valentine's Day cards, romance has been weaving its magical spell to make gender, race, and class hierarchies appear natural. As Laura Kipnis argues in *Against Love,* we do not notice that romance is doing this because romantic love, like capitalism, "come[s] to subsume and dominate their creators, who don't see it happening, or what they've lost, or that the thing they themselves invented and bestowed with life has taken them over like a hostile alien force, like it had a life of its own."[14] In this sense, as an alien force that moves us to act, romance is both an affect and an ideology.[15]

Like other ideologies, romance tells us that it is for everyone. Just pull yourself up by your heartstrings and you too can find your happily ever after. Yet true love was never meant to be for everyone. As new power hierarchies formed with industrialization, new groups of people claimed the right to decide who could and who could not be in love. Rather than priests and rabbis, Victorian legislators and reformers as well as a burgeoning mass media began to create new rules for love. Victorians passed laws about commercial sex, homosexual acts, and marriage. As historian Nancy Cott explains in *Public Vows: A History of Marriage and the Nation,* the US government became increasingly involved in regulating intimate relationships. Marriage and sex had been primarily community concerns before the 1800s, but by the time of the Civil War,

> a rhetorical relationship had been set up between the institution of marriage and the success of the national compact so that what undermined one put the other at risk.... The reframing of American political society after the Civil War incorporated a preferred model for American marriage, which renewed emphasis on the spouses' being of the same race, highlighted the state's role in the marriage ... The unified nation had newly expressed stakes in every union's being freely chosen, monogamous, and legal.

This newfound state interest in marriage and citizenship also led to an increased policing of relationships outside of legal marriage, including polygamous marriages as well as homosexuality and prostitution.[16]

Victorian sciences, especially sexology, marked certain sexual acts as "racially degenerate" specifically because they indicated the lack of a clear and hierarchical gender binary. In other words, early sexologists tied gender and racial hierarchies into sexual acts to mark some love as central to modern lives and other love as that which "dare not speak its name."[17] To be clear, it was never just homosexuality that had to be silenced, but any sex that was commercial, public, interracial, polygamous, masturbatory, and/or intergenerational. Sex outside reproductive, private, married, dyadic couples was marked as sick, atavistic, primitive, degenerate, and therefore not fully white.[18] Because modern ideas about romance first developed among the ruling classes to mark some love as worthwhile (that between a man and woman who are married, white, well off, and gender normative) and other loves as perverse (homosexual and interracial relationships, black and working-class sexualities, commercial sex, etc.), romance was always an ideology that privileged the romantic ruling classes over the sexual hoi polloi. As Gayle Rubin put it in her canonical essay "Thinking Sex: Notes Toward a Radical Theory of the Politics of Sexuality,"

> Modern Western societies appraise sex acts according to a hierarchical system of sex. Marital, reproductive heterosexuals are alone at the top erotic pyramid ... All of these hierarchies of sexual value function ... in much the same ways as do ideological systems of racism, ethnocentrism, and religious chauvinism. They rationalize the well-being of the sexually privileged and the adversity of the sexual rabble.[19]

By the end of the 1800s, sex had become a form of class warfare as well as a central project of the nation-state. And most people didn't even notice. Instead Americans bought Valentine's Day cards and paperback romance novels. Soon enough a new form of romance propaganda came along: the cinema. And it got us young. In 1937 Disney released *Snow White and the Seven Dwarfs*, and an entire generation of true romantics was born. *Snow White* and other Disney films taught Americans that love is all you need and that love is blind—but also that only beautiful, young, well-off, white characters get true love. These messages are now so much a part of popular culture that they find expression not just in children's literature, but in literature aimed at teen and adult readers too. Disney teaches us to believe in Love, Inc., but then more grown up stories, like *Twilight* and *Fifty Shades of Grey*, come along to reinforce these lessons throughout our lives.

DISNEY TAUGHT ME TO LOVE

I watched Disney movies almost *Clockwork Orange*-style with
my eyes pried open being completely brainwashed.
  Soman Chainani, NPR interview

Many people have written about how Disney teaches children, but
especially little girls, to believe that "some day her prince will come"
and that all stories should end in a big, white wedding. Most research
shows that the romantic narratives and gendered characteristics of Disney characters have changed over time, with female characters taking
on more traditionally masculine traits such as assertiveness. There is
also ample evidence that Disney films continue to place romance as the
cornerstone of "adulthood" and that children are highly affected by
these cultural scripts.[20] Even those Disney films that are not specifically about romance, including those made by DreamWorks and Pixar,
like *Toy Story* or *Monsters, Inc.,* help educate children about love and
romance, not to mention gender, race, sexuality, and even hard work
and pulling oneself up by one's own bootstraps.[21] More importantly,
Disney and other children's films teach us and our children how to be
romantic subjects while convincing us not to pay much attention since
it is just "mindless entertainment." These films are what Henry Giroux
has called a giant "teaching machine."[22] As Carrie Cokely points out,

> Much of the magic that is produced by Disney is entangled with notions of
> romance, true love, and the white wedding. While promoted as stories of
> adventure, of youthful rebellion, and of coming of age, the majority of Dis-
> ney animated films center on the theme of the marriage plot: finding true
> love and, inevitably, marriage.

We have to pay attention to Disney because that Disney "magic" is
always already paying attention to us and our children.[23]

  Disney is not just a vector of socialization; it is also a highly profitable corporation. Disney is not just selling us an ideology, where the
most appropriately gendered and those with the most racially white
features find true love and happiness and those who are gender nonnor-

mative or nonwhite are punished, but also a lot of stuff. Disney sells vacations and cruises, cheap princess dresses and extremely expensive princess weddings, and, until its recent withdrawal from the project, an entire way of life in the form of Celebration, Florida. Disney's annual revenue is over $55 billion. That includes $3.77 billion for the parks, nearly another $2 billion dollars for various consumer products, and a cool $6.9 billion for Disney Media Networks.[24] Disney might be the chief propagandist for romance, but it also a corporation that exists to produce profit.

TWEEN ROMANCE

Because innocence is sexier than you think.
Love's Baby Soft advertisement, 1975

As important as Disney is in teaching our children to be romantic from a young age, all of this is just the warm-up act for Love, Inc., in the tween years. It is when our children edge toward puberty that the romantic imperative becomes impossible to ignore. Romance is so central to the tween years that entire subgenres of fiction have been invented to sell them romance. Tweens can read books like Leslie Margolis's *Boys Are Dogs*, about a sixth-grade girl who learns she can train the boys in her middle school just like she trained her dog. For the more literary minded, a *Pride and Prejudice*–inspired book by Sarah MacClean, *The Season,* tells the tale of Lady Alexandra, who is less interested in high society than she is in working with the incredibly handsome Gavin to find out who killed his father. There are hundreds of these romance novels that are aimed not at teens or grown women, but at tweens.[25]

Some of these, such as the relatively new and very popular series *The School for Good and Evil,* attempt to move away from the overly simplistic love stories that Disney has offered American children for the past ninety years or so. The author of this series, Soman Chainani, says he grew up on Disney: "My life was Disney. Everything I knew about narrative came from Disney." But he also wanted to show far more complex characters and stories than Disney historically has. In other words, he wanted to break out of romance and tell stories that "ultimately break it all down ... [move] beyond the Disney good and evil matrix."[26] To a large extent, Chainani succeeds because the story centers on the friendship between two girls, one beautiful and evil and the other hideous and good. Although Chainani succeeds in reversing our deeply held cultural belief that beauty is good, he ultimately does not escape from the clutches of romance since Agatha, the ugly but good character, rides off with her prince while Sophie, the princess on the outside/witch on the inside, decides to have a career. It is also true that the love between Agatha and her prince, Tedros, is part of what moves much of the narrative of books 2–4. Romance is a hegemonic ideology. Even when we imagine we are escaping it, it continues to shape how we narrate our books and our lives. Chainani has given young tweens a different sort of story, but ultimately delivered yet another tween romance to them. But who exactly is the tween and how did she come into being?

The Victorians might have invented the child and children's culture, but mid-twentieth-century advertisers invented the "tween." According to Daniel Cook and Susan Keiser, the tween

> in its feminine incarnation, registers social ambiguities regarding maturity, sexuality and gender ... These ambiguities bespeak moral tensions informing the "appropriate" body, as articulated in the idiom of commerce. The tween girl, both as a biographical person and as a commercial persona constructed through market discourses, resides in an unstable cultural space where ambiguities of social identity invite, even tolerate, polysemous and polyvalent renderings of who "she" is.[27]

This figure of the tween, like the Victorian child, is still white and well off, a figure able to buy—and buy into—any trends that advertisers throw her way, but the tween is also already potentially a sexual being. Since the 1960s, the tween has moved from training bras to padded bras, from junior girdles to silk thongs, but she remains the target of not just advertising, but the ideology of romance, which demands that she spend emotional labor and her hard-earned money on Love, Inc.

Just as children enter their tween years, a variety of books, movies, TV shows, and pop songs are sneaking up behind them to kick them into the depths of romance as obsessive-compulsive disorder. Disney gives these tweens a variety of primarily white, good-looking young pop stars who represent both hypersexuality and sexual purity, like the Jonas Brothers and Miley Cyrus of old or today's Calum Worthy and Piper Curda. These Disney tween stars represent a whole series of complicated messages about how sex is bad/good/confusing, but at the center of it all is true love.

Although at this point Cyrus might be best known for her hyper-sexualized performances, like "twerking" on stage at the 2013 MTV Video Music Awards, there was a time when she performed as a sexually innocent tween star on the Disney series *Hannah Montana*.[28] Cyrus's most popular hit as her Disney show alter ego Hannah Montana was "He Could Be the One." "He Could Be the One" is a song that might be about finding her one true love or, alternatively, the boy with whom she has sex for the first time. Either way, it is an anthem to the centrality of romantic love and longing even in a very young girl's life; it was extremely popular, reaching number 2 on the Billboard Hot 100 list.[29] Miley Cyrus/Hannah Montana's popularity as an eroticized virgin is just one indication that tween romance strikes a chord in our culture. Although some scholars of virginity mark the erotic virgin as a young woman, Disney has increasingly sold children and tweens the idea of an erotic virgin as a prepubescent or barely pubescent girl or boy.[30]

In the past couple of decades, tween culture has become big business in the US. The popularity of series like *Harry Potter* or *The Hunger Games* puts tweens at the center of American popular culture. But these adventure stories are not at first glance scripts for how to grow up to be a romantic subject, despite the centrality of love stories and the ultimately "happy" ending of monogamous and reproductive heterosexual love. Another tween series, *Twilight*, made romance the main attraction. In 2010, at the height of the *Twilight* series popularity, I traveled to two

Teaching teens to love romance. Photo by Willa Cowan-Essig.

sites of *Twilight* tourism: Forks, Washington, and Volterra, Italy. In addition to traveling to these sites, I went to the midnight openings of the *Twilight* movies, where I interviewed tweens and their mothers (I never saw any fathers, and rarely saw boys), read all the books, collected stories from some of the series' biggest fans, and generally immersed myself in some of the most powerful cultural scripts we have for "learning to love." What follows is a way to think about how the ideology of romance in *Twilight* reinforces the claims of global capitalism that extreme wealth and whiteness are not merely desirable, but worth dying for.

EDWARD AND BELLA TLA

> Do you believe in destiny? That even the powers of time can be altered for a single purpose? That the luckiest man who walks on this earth is the one that finds true love?
>
> Bram Stoker, *Dracula*, 1897

The story of Edward Cullen and Bella Swan sold 116 million copies and was translated into thirty-seven languages.[31] The five films (based on the four books) made about $3.4 billion worldwide,[32] making it one of the top-grossing movie franchises in the world, slightly behind the *Harry Potter* series, but more popular than the *Star Trek* movies.[33]

The love story between Edward and Bella is fairly formulaic: an ordinary girl meets her prince, the one who will save her from the dreariness of her existence, and it is love at first sight and eternal passion and commitment thereafter. This narrative mirrors many Disney tales, including "Cinderella," "The Little Mermaid," and "Snow White." In the *Twilight* series, Bella is a young and completely ordinary high school girl who is abandoned by her flakey mother and goes to live in Forks, Washington, with her father, who works as a police officer. Forks is dark and gloomy, located in the proverbial forest full of dangerous and magical creatures like a Native Indian tribe whose members are actually werewolves, as well as a clan of "vegetarian" (i.e., they don't consume human blood) vampires, the Cullens. The moment Edward Cullen and Bella Swan encounter one another, we know he will be her prince and transform her ordinary life into something magical. Bella notices Edward (and his vampire "siblings") immediately. And when he finally looks at her, we know they are fated for one another.

> Edward Cullen's back stiffened, and he turned slowly to glare at me—his face was absurdly handsome—with piercing, hate-filled eyes. For an instant, I felt a thrill of genuine fear, raising the hair on my arms. The look only lasted a second, but it chilled me more than the freezing wind.[34]

From that moment to the end of the last book in the series, *Breaking Dawn,* the reader knows that Edward and Bella will eventually be married and living in the modern-day equivalent of a castle with no financial worries, their union completed by the birth of a child.

Much has been written about the *Twilight* series and its messages. The series author, Stephenie Meyer, is a Mormon and many of the themes in the books mirror Mormon teachings, like sexual abstinence until marriage, the ever-present threat of sexual danger, and the immorality of abortion.[35] In the stories, Bella and Edward must wait until they are married (as soon as she finishes high school) to have sex, but sex itself presents a danger since Edward's superhuman strength and animalistic desire to suck Bella's blood make intimate relations even more fraught than they would be among mere mortal teens. When Bella wakes up after their wedding night, she is happy and at peace; she feels that she is where she is meant to be, and is completely unbothered by the fact that she has been bruised and battered by her new vampire husband. As she realizes their conjugal bed has been ripped to shreds by Edward's excess desire, Bella looks down at her body to find that "large, purplish bruises were beginning to blossom across the pale skin of my arm. My eyes followed the trail they made up my shoulder, and then down across my ribs." Although Edward, the batterer/husband, feels sorry that he has hurt his wife, Bella insists that the violent sex makes her feel "perfectly happy. Totally and completely blissed out."[36]

This bridal night sexual union results in a pregnancy—except the half-vampire fetus is literally eating Bella alive. Carrying the child is an exercise in excruciating pain ending in certain death and an object lesson in never getting an abortion no matter what. Edward considers abortion because he is so distraught watching a pregnancy that is "sucking the life from her while I stand there helpless! Watching her sicken and waste away. Seeing it hurt her." But Bella refuses to even discuss terminating the pregnancy that will kill her.[37]

In addition to Mormonism, the *Twilight* series is permeated by Victorian beliefs about sex, gender, race, and class. The series preaches that a real woman should preserve her sexual purity till marriage, that she values motherhood over all else, even her own life, and that sex is dark and dangerous, possibly resulting in bruising and battery—not because the man is a monster, but because he cannot help himself; violent sexuality is in his nature. Indeed, as in many a gothic romance, it is the lady's purity and devotion that can turn the monster into a prince.

Bella = Belle and Edward = The Beast. *Twilight* also has not-so-subtle lessons about race and class, since Bella must choose between two men: the much older, but wealthier and sparkly white Edward, in his ultra-modern mansion and with his ridiculously expensive cars; and the down-and-out werewolf, Jacob Black, who is a poor Quileute Indian living in a shack on a reservation and driving a motorcycle he put together himself from junk parts. There is never any doubt that Bella will save herself for Edward, the white man; a life of extreme wealth and luxury, as well as racial purity, will be her reward.

Mirroring the Book of Mormon's notion of free will, the characters desire sex, but exert their will not to have sex until they are married. As feminist studies scholar Danielle Borgia puts it, "These novels consistently represent lust as enthralling, but proscribe the consummation of love outside of wedlock as weakness."[38] Because the consummation of their love represents Bella's raison d'être, all other aspects of her life are unimportant. Borgia points out that Bella's marriage to Edward and her subsequent cutting of all ties to her past "implies that her relationships with family and friends, as well as her sense of self, before she met her lover were meaningless and unimportant. Her marriage therefore becomes the defining aspect of her identity."[39]

Despite the Victorian and Mormon messages embedded in *Twilight*, most commentators and even the author herself point out that the book has mixed messages, at least when it comes to gender and desire. For instance, although sex is represented as dangerous and even deadly, Bella's desire for Edward is a central part of the narrative. In an interesting twist on the woman as prey and man as predator, *Twilight* and other recent vampire series such as Charlaine Harris's *True Blood* place desire firmly in the female human protagonist. Reversing the monster/victim typology of Bram Stoker's canonical *Dracula*, it is Bella's desire for Edward that cannot be contained. The vampire is not the predator, corrupting innocent women; rather, human women desire the vampires and corrupt them. Perhaps this is no more obvious than in the 1990s classic TV show *Buffy the Vampire Slayer*. When Buffy, a girl destined to destroy vampires, finally sleeps with the vampire Angel, he loses all his human feelings, including any love for her. Buffy destroys Angel not with a stake through the heart, but by making him fall in love with her and thereby lose himself. In this way, young girls obsessed with both romance and the figure of the vampire are learning that women are the sexual aggressors, even if men/vampires are sexually dangerous. Again, to quote Borgia,

> The Twilight series, ... despite its careful censoring of explicit sexuality, portrays its teenage female protagonist as actively seeking to become the vampire's victim based on her sexual desire. Indeed, the disturbing messages of Twilight stem from this switch in its characterization of predator and prey: the deadly vampire is the one who deserves the reader's pity, and the woman he imperils is cast as the one who puts him at risk.[40]

We might imagine this predator/prey reversal as a kind of feminist reclamation of women as sexual beings, and perhaps it is in fact a form of resistance to the sexually chaste Victorian lady. It is also, however, a return to much earlier Judeo-Christian notions of women as more susceptible to sexual desire than men. In this sense, Bella is Eve to Edward's Adam, a fact mirrored in the iconography of the first book, *Twilight,* which is adorned with a bright red apple held in Bella's hands. Clearly the *Twilight* series as well as other contemporary vampire tales are sending mixed messages about sexuality and gender and are read in a variety of ways. Stephenie Meyer argues that her authorial intent was to empower women to make choices in their lives. According to a statement on Meyer's website,

> When I hear or read theories about Bella being an anti-feminist character, those theories are usually predicated on her choices. In the beginning, she chooses romantic love over everything else. Eventually, she chooses to marry at an early age and then chooses to keep an unexpected and dangerous baby ...
>
> The foundation of feminism is this: being able to choose. The core of anti-feminism is, conversely, telling a woman she can't do something solely because she's a woman—taking any choice away from her specifically because of her gender. One of the weird things about modern feminism is

that some feminists seem to be putting their own limits on women's choices. That feels backward to me. It's as if you can't choose a family on your own terms and still be considered a strong woman. How is that empowering? Are there rules about if, when, and how we love or marry and if, when, and how we have kids? Are there jobs we can and can't have in order to be a "real" feminist? To me, those limitations seem anti-feminist in basic principle.[41]

For Meyer, feminism is about choices, any choices, even ones that clearly undermine the liberation of a young woman from the structures of patriarchy. Meyer's words echo some of what Third Wave feminism has said about "choice" and how women's choices are always valid because they come from their lived experiences, which are so varied as to lead to very different choices. But this sort of feminism, laid out by Jennifer Baumgardner and Amy Richards in *Manifesta: Young Women, Feminism and the Future,* insists that those choices must also be done consciously, as feminists, something Meyer's characters do not do even if she, the author, insists on a feminist consciousness.[42] And it is perhaps her notion of Bella Swan as a woman in charge of her own destiny that marks this series as both extremely traditional and even Victorian in its obsession with white female sexual purity and at the same time something that is also more contemporary, even feminist. It is no doubt this very tension between Victorian lady Bella, who marries as a virgin right out of high school, and typical American teenager Bella, who just wants to get into bed with the hottest guy at school, that makes the novels so compelling to so many readers.

SOMEDAY MY PRINCE WILL COME

Once there was a Princess ... And she fell in love ... It was very easy! Anyone could see that the Prince was charming. The only one for me.
Snow White

In order for an ideology to be effective, it has to stay "on point" and in this sense, the *Twilight* series is remarkably able to replicate the lessons of romance that are already contained in Disney, Harlequin romance novels, and romantic comedies. These lessons include the idea that women should be helpless and vulnerable in order to be rescued by men, that these men may be beasts, but true love and beauty can turn them into gentlemen. Most of these rules of the ideology of romance are actually codified by an organization that is the chief propaganda arm of Love, Inc.—the Romance Writers of America (RWA). According to the RWA, a romance has two elements: first, "the main plot centers around individuals falling in love and struggling to make the relationship work" and second, "the lovers who risk and struggle for each other and their relationship are rewarded with emotional justice and unconditional love." Additionally, all romances have an "emotionally satisfying and optimistic ending."[43]

As Anthea Taylor points out, part of the emotional satisfaction of the *Twilight* love story is knowing that Edward will always protect Bella:

> Though presumably attempting to capture teenage angst and anxiety, the narrator's insecurity and lack of self-esteem position her as a pitiful creature ... From the first book, when he initially saves her from a runaway car, Bella comes to rely upon Edward entirely ... The amount of times he rescues her implies her inability to exist in the most mundane way without his (patriarchal) guardianship; in addition to the threat posed by his own "animal" urges, there are always other vampires seeking to kill Bella. Edward thereby becomes her saviour, not only from the dangerous situations (into which he often places her), but from *herself* and her quotidian feminine teenage existence in small town USA.[44]

Think how in *The Little Mermaid*, Ariel watches as Prince Eric defeats Ursula by deflating her, which is actually similar to how Prince Phillip defeats Maleficent in *Sleeping Beauty*. Although not all Disney films end with the prince saving the hapless heroine from evil characters, enough of them do that it is a recognizable trope of romance and one that Meyer plays out again and again in her series.

It is not just Bella's helplessness, but also her ability to perfectly perform the functions of the romantic heroine that make this series so central to modern romance. Bella understands immediately that Edward is "the one," she has an unwavering commitment to being with him even after he abandons her for all of the second book, *New Moon,* and ultimately she possesses the ability to turn her angry and emotionally distant lover, a man who is as cold and hard as marble (not to mention brooding, possessive, and stalker-ish) into a committed and caring father and husband. The ability to transform men from beasts into princes is a standard, not just in Disney films, but in romance novels in general. As Janice Radway argues in her seminal study of romance readers, the emotionally satisfying narrative of female characters who steadfastly work to change their man and the male characters who eventually change is what romance readers want over and over again. And what romance readers want is what sells. Romance novels sell more than any other genre of fiction and account for nearly one in five books, including nonfiction, sold in the US, accounting for over $1 billion worth of book sales a year. In other words, *Twilight* sells because romance sells and *Twilight* is a perfect romance.[45]

Yet there is also an economic fantasy at the center of romance that falling in love can make the future safe and secure primarily in the form of never having to worry about the material world again. In *Twilight,* Bella literally becomes superhuman, a being who no longer ages and who has the strength and speed of a god. She also becomes rich, mind-blowingly rich, escaping the modest financial situation of her family of origin: her father is a police officer and her mother a kindergarten teacher.[46] In her original incarnation, Bella wears jeans and flannel shirts and drives a beat-up 1953 Chevy pickup truck. Her best friend, Jacob, drives a Volkswagen Rabbit that he managed to build himself from spare parts. These forms of transport, like the pumpkin in Cinderella, are transformed after she marries Edward into a Ferrari F430, and her rags become designer frocks.[47] That's because *Twilight* articulates the fantasy of women translating erotic (and racial) capital into financial security. Because the love between Bella and Edward is marked as primal, unavoidable, and fated, we know that Bella will always have the financial support of Edward. He will never leave her for a younger vampire because she will always be perfect. This economic fantasy is a lot better than the economic reality facing most young women in the US, a reality that includes an average student loan debt of $29,000, delayed child birth, delayed marriage, delayed home owner- ship, and a persistent pay gap that will leave them earning significantly less than their male counterparts regardless of educational level.[48]

TWILIGHT GROWS UP

> Woman arrested for masturbating in the cinema while watching *Fifty Shades of Grey.*
> Headline from *Cosmopolitan* magazine, February 24, 2015

It goes without saying that not just American tweens, but adults, par- ticularly adult women, love the promise of romance too. According to the RWA, these romance- reading women are more likely to live in the South, be frequent readers, and live with a spouse or partner. The majority have a household income of somewhere between $50,000 and $100,000 a year.[49] It was these adult women, well schooled in romance, who discovered a bit of *Twilight* fan fiction and turned it into the pub- lishing success of 2012. This book, *Fifty Shades of Grey,* started on an internet site for fan fiction. A later version, in trilogy form, was picked up by an Australian publisher, The Writer's Coffee Shop, and published as an e-book.[50] When Vintage got hold of the series, it went through sixty printings and sold 10 million copies in six weeks. In other words, *Fifty Shades of Grey* accounted for 25 percent of the entire adult fiction market during that time.[51] In order to explore the book more deeply, I read the three books, watched both movies, and took a research trip to Seattle, Washington, where the action of the books takes place. I also read content on fan sites and the Fifty Shades Facebook page for clues about how this literary phenomenon functions as part of Love, Inc.

The *Fifty Shades of Grey* series follows the fated love story of the ter- ribly ordinary and financially struggling Anastasia Steele, a college senior, and the super-rich and powerful yet still young Christian Grey.

Grey, like *Twilight's* Edward, is controlling, possessive, and knows immediately that Anastasia Steele is the one. Steele, like *Twilight's* Bella, is clumsy, awkward, ordinary, powerless, and willing to give herself completely to the far more powerful Grey.

The main difference between the two series is that the narrative in *Fifty Shades* is not driven by the supernatural, but by the erotic. Centering completely on the pleasures of male domination and female submission, *Fifty Shades* moves the narrative along the path of Anastasia's increasing exposure to Christian's sexual kinkiness, which, like Edward's vampirism, both marks him as ontologically different from the woman who loves him and provides the transformation of that woman from ordinary to extraordinary. Christian wants to have sex, just sex, with no romance, no kissing, no eye contact. He wants to be completely in charge. He wants Anastasia to call him "sir." There is a playroom in his home that involves a fair amount of leather and latex. It is the kinkiness of the series—the scenes of bondage and spanking, as well as its popularity with women of a certain age—that earned it the label "mommy porn."

But despite the far more explicit sex scenes of *Fifty Shades*, the sort of sex that happens between the two couples is strikingly similar. The man is all-powerful, dangerous even, and the woman wants it that way. This is Anastasia's reaction when Christian reveals his secret room of BDSM paraphernalia:

> "I'm a Dominant." His eyes are scorching gray, intense.
> "What does that mean?" I whisper.
> "It means I want you to willingly surrender yourself to me in all things ... To please me."
> *Please him! He wants me to please him!* ... And I realize, in that moment, that yes, that's exactly what I want to do.[52]

Like Bella, Anastasia finds that her true desire is to submit to the excess desire of her man even if, or perhaps especially because, it involves physical pain.

Also like *Twilight*, *Fifty Shades* offers the heroine a choice between two men. Christian Grey is white and wealthy, and José Rodriguez is

Hispanic and works a regular job as a photographer. In both *Twilight* and *Fifty Shades,* the nonwhite suitor attempts to force himself on the white heroine, and in both cases the white beloved saves the heroine from the unwanted sexual attentions of brown men. In a scene that echoes the kiss between Jacob and Bella, Anastasia must fight off the attentions of the unsuitable suitor, José. When Anastasia has too much to drink, José attempts to have his way with her.

> "No, José, stop—no." I push him, but he's a wall of hard muscle and I cannot shift him. His hand has slipped into my hair and he's holding my head in place ... He gently trails kisses along my jaw up the side of my mouth. I feel panicky, drunk, and out of control. The feeling is suffocating.
> "José, no," I plead. "I don't want this ..."
> "I think the lady said no," a voice in the dark says quietly ... Christian Grey, he's here ... José releases me.[53]

Katie Roiphe famously argued that *Fifty Shades* is so popular because feminism makes women yearn for such submission. According to Roiphe, it is the fantasy of complete submission and not taking responsibility for any sexual desires that appeals to so many women precisely because women are more educated and more financially secure than they have ever been. As Roiphe put it, "We may then be especially drawn to this particular romanticized, erotically charged, semipornographic idea of female submission at a moment in history when male dominance is shakier than it has ever been."[54] Roiphe's analysis, however, is too focused on the erotic and takes no note of the economic fantasy that is at the heart of both series. It was not feminism but rather the ideology of romance as a way out of economic precariousness that made *Fifty Shades* and *Twilight* so popular. The two series are perfect romances. Both Bella and Anastasia must transform their men from cold and angry lovers to supportive and loving husbands by submitting themselves completely to their lifestyles (BDSM/vampirism). And through their submission they are rewarded with financial and emotional security forever and ever.

Readers, mostly women, were drawn to *Fifty Shades* for the same reason their daughters were drawn to *Twilight* and the same reason younger girls are drawn to *Cinderella* and *Sleeping Beauty* and over a billion dollars of romance novels a year: because we are taught to value these stories of true love at first sight and believe in the transformation of ordinary girls into extraordinary princesses through the desire of a powerful, wealthy man. We grow up on these cultural scripts of romance. We can tell you how love happens by the time we're five or six. And then we just keep telling ourselves these stories over and over again because although they might not happen in real life, they are, like heaven, a promise.

Yet *Twilight* and *Fifty Shades* are also importantly stories about the possibility of escaping economic collapse. As most people worldwide are experiencing economic hardship and a smaller and smaller percentage of people control more and more of the wealth, *Fifty Shades*, like *Twilight* before it, offers us a piece of neoliberal propaganda.[55] Not only does Anastasia "choose" the incredibly rich and powerful Christian over her one other suitor, the Latino and not-rich José, but she manages to translate that choice into a lifetime of economic security. The proverbial castle on the hill and happily ever after comes in the form of an isolated island home off the coast of Seattle. The actual 1932 home where the movie is filmed boasts a golden faucet in the shape of a swan (propaganda slogan: swans mate for life) and, perhaps not coincidentally, a nursery decorated by Disney artists.[56]

In some ways, the magical ending of the *Fifty Shades* series requires even more magical thinking from its readers than the vampire- and werewolf-themed *Twilight* does. Readers are asked to believe that Anastasia, an English major from Washington State University at Vancouver, which ranks 138th nationwide, receives multiple job offers in the publishing industry in Seattle right out of school. Then we are to believe that she manages to move from an entry-level position into ownership of a publishing company by marrying her slightly older and much wealthier boyfriend, Christian. We are also to believe that Christian earned his money through hard work, not the privileges that accrue to a white, straight man whose (adopted) parents are both super-rich. Indeed, when Anastasia suggests that it is "luck" that has brought

Christian his wealth, he responds by quoting an industrialist from the first great redistribution of wealth under capitalism:

> I don't subscribe to luck or chance, Miss Steele. The harder I work, the more luck I seem to have. It really is all about having the right people on your team and directing their energies accordingly. I think it was Harvey Firestone who said, "The growth and development of people is the highest calling of leadership."[57]

Harvey Firestone, of rubber tire fame, got his wealth by producing a product. It is never clear what exactly Christian produces except that it involves "global communication technologies." Yet we are supposed to believe that Grey has acquired so much wealth through his own labor. *Fifty Shades* is littered with images of wealth in those who "work hard"— and therefore deserve their riches. One of the few truly poor people in the book is Grey's mother, the quintessential "bad mother" who was a "crack whore" and whose "bad choices" killed her but also made possible her son's adoption by a wealthy family—as well as dooming him to his lifetime of kink.

Perhaps it should be no surprise that Anastasia, a sexually pure woman who saves herself for the man she eventually marries and subsumes her life to his, is eventually rewarded with all the signs of a good life: a helicopter, expensive cars, a yacht, European vacations. Nor should it come as a surprise that the ending of the *Fifty Shades* series, like *Twilight*, focuses on the couple, now parents of one son and a daughter in utero, safely cocooned in their own community of wealthy relatives.

> I gaze up at the view as the sun sinks behind the Olympic Peninsula ... It's simply stunning: twilight over the Sound. Christian pulls me into his arms.
> "It's quite a view."
> "It is," Christian answers and when I turn to look at him, he's gazing at me. He plants a soft kiss on my lips ...
> "It's home."
> He grins and kisses me again. "I love you, Mrs. Grey."
> "I love you, too, Christian. Always."[58]

Female readers learn that through total submission to a rich and powerful man, a submission based on understanding that such men deserve their wealth because they earned it, they too can find their place of perfect security—their castle in the sky or mansion on the Sound, nestled in the arms of their tamed prince.

CAN'T BUY ME LOVE

Money can actually buy you love, survey finds.
Headline from the *New York Post*, February 11, 2018

Like religious ideologies, romance moves us to act. But most of our romantic actions occur in a strange mix of emotion and consumption—buying objects that we hope and pray will enchant our own lives with romance. *Twilight* lovers can surf on over to Amazon to buy action figures of Bella, Jacob, and Edward (set of three, $39.99) or a 17-inch Edward Cullen doll (for $160), or even a pillow with the (fictional) Cullen family crest on it for $199.99. If you feel safer imagining your possessive and violent vampire lover watching over you at night, you can buy a silhouette of stalker Edward over at Etsy, and if you want to really impress your beloved you can buy her Bella's wedding ring for a mere $149.99 over at Entertainment Jewelry.

The *Fifty Shades of Grey* series not only got women to buy the book, but to buy many of the sex toys they read about, leading to what one erotica business executive described as a "worldwide shortage of pleasure balls." When the movie version of *Fifty Shades* came out, a variety of sex toy producers geared up to produce both sex toys and "softer" accessories, including blindfolds and handcuffs. America's favorite family retailer, Target, carried the official *Fifty Shades* sex toys while other retailers, like Babeland, just tried to capitalize on the growing interest in BDSM accoutrements.[59] On the Lovehoney website, the most romantic among us can buy everything from the *Fifty Shades of Grey* "No Peeking Soft Twin Blindfold Set" ($14.99) to the "Fifty Shades of Grey The

Pinch Adjustable Nipple Clamps" for just $19.99.[60] As if adult toys weren't enough, the Vermont Teddy Bear factory sold a "special edition" *Fifty Shades of Grey* Teddy Bear for Valentine's Day 2015. The teddy bear came with "smoldering gray eyes, a suit and satin tie, mask—even mini handcuffs."[61] It is difficult to know whether the bear represents the total infantilization of adult women or the sexualization of childhood, but it certainly shows how money can be made from the very real emotions of Love, Inc.

As legal scholar Alex Dymock points out in her essay on the commodification of sexuality in the *Fifty Shades* trilogy,

> The revelation that the transgressive "inner experience" of reading Fifty Shades promises is therefore unlikely to be unearthed in the pleasures of breaking sexual taboo or even in the act of speaking female sexual desire, but through the guilty pleasures of shopping … Indeed, even the covers of the novels betray their content … anonymous objects: a tie, a mask and a key.[62]

Dymock is right. *Fifty Shades of Grey* and other romantic texts are both highly produced and completely commodified, yet they are also very real, as a trip to Volterra, Italy, with my young daughter taught me.

THE MOST ROMANTIC VALENTINE'S DAY EVER

> Volterra has … some brilliant New Moon tours to appeal to vampire-fans, "normal people" should not fear. Your neck is not at risk in Volterra. (It's the home of the Vulturi, but you can always wear garlic!)
>
> Volterra tourism guide, visittuscany.com

On Valentine's Day in 2010, I participated in a *Twilight* Vampire Tour in Volterra, Italy, with my then eleven-year-old daughter. Volterra is the site of some of the most exciting scenes in Meyer's vampire saga and, at that age, my daughter was completely mesmerized by the love story of human Bella Swan and vampire Edward Cullen. Both my daughters had read the books and seen the first two movies, and were anxiously awaiting the release of the third *Twilight* movie, *Eclipse,* later that year. When we found out that legions of fans, many of them young tween and teen girls, had turned Volterra into a site of *Twilight* tourism, we just had to go.

Going on a research trip to Volterra was the most romantic, most exciting thing either one of us could imagine doing on Valentine's Day. As the sun set on this postcard-ready medieval village set atop a winding mountain road, we gathered along with twelve other *Twilight* fans, mostly heterosexual couples in their twenties and thirties, at the designated spot. Our tour guide greeted us from underneath the hood of a long black cloak. Her bright eyes and red lips were in stark contrast to the pale makeup on her face. She didn't mention that Volterra is the oldest city in Tuscany, settled about three thousand years ago by the Etruscans. She did not gesture at the ruins of the theater or baths that the Romans had built. Instead our vampire guide showed us where the fountain would have been if the famous fountain scene had been filmed in Volterra.[63] Then she took us along to the Roman sewers, down some steep stairs, and into a dark room where local residents dressed as vampires pretended to attack us. My daughter and I held hands, thrilled and scared and hopelessly in love with Tuscany and *Twilight* and romance. It all ended in a typical Tuscan feast with lots of red wine, smoked meats, and local cheeses, as my daughter and I and the other *Twilight* tourists toasted "the best Valentine's Day ever."

According to Eva Zettelmayer, a spokesperson for the Volterra Chamber of Commerce, this oldest city in all of Tuscany had no idea that it was featured in the *Twilight* books.[64]

> Then in 2007 Stephenie Meyer came to present the book *New Moon* in Italian and we had no idea what it was. But then there were these buses, lots of buses that arrived from all over Italy with posters and apples who came to meet her ... When I came to work here in Volterra I had no idea what these *Twilight* fans were talking about, but starting in November of 2008 we saw a big boom in *Twilight* tourism ... When the news came out that they would shoot *New Moon* in Volterra ... actually they shot in Montepulciano ... but our registrations for hotels have increased over 100 percent ... We are the city in the book, not the movie. Now about a quarter of our tourists come for *New Moon*.

Zettelmayer herself had not read the *Twilight* series before the onslaught of tourists, but once she sat down to read them, she could not stop. Like my daughter and millions of people around the world, Zettelmayer found the love story of an ordinary teenage girl and an extraordinary vampire absolutely addictive. Nonetheless she also, like many residents of Volterra, found the *Twilight* tourism completely baffling. Zettelmayer could not understand trekking up the windy mountain road to this ancient Etruscan city to consume a fictional history and culture rather than the history of the rich and real Volterra. But Volterra relies on tourism, and so the locals had little choice but to start supplying goods to meet the demands of *Twilight* tourists. They started selling alabaster apples to mirror the apple featured on the first book in the series. The innkeepers started having *Twilight* Romance Weekends and someone came up with the idea of vampire tours. As Zettelmayer joked, "Volterra has a high-security prison and the prisoners work all around town, in the restaurants, the public toilets and until the 1970s we had an insane asylum so people are used to prisoners and crazy people running around. The *New Moon* tourists don't really bother them." All joking aside, *Twilight* has boosted their tourism considerably. The Chamber of Commerce there estimates that about one out of four tourists come because of *Twilight*. Residents and shop owners expressed mixed feelings about this make-believe history drawing people to their town. One shopkeeper told me she is trying to connect Volterra's traditions and history to *Twilight* while downplaying the vampire aspect. "We live on tourism," she said, but "we don't want to become the city of vampires."

A FORK IN THE ROAD: ECONOMIC REALITY OR ROMANTIC FANTASY?

Entering Forks
Population 3,175
Vampires 8.5
Souvenir population sign in Forks, Washington

A trip to Forks, Washington, the other site of the *Twilight* saga, revealed a somewhat similar story. Like Volterra, Forks is difficult to reach. It involves a lot of driving on deserted roads with hairpin turns through stunning scenery of ancient forests, mountains, and ocean. However, there is not much to see in Forks other than a couple of stoplights, a slightly bedraggled motel, and two *Twilight*-themed stores. According to a worker at one of the stores, people come from all over the world to see Forks, but especially from Australia, Japan, the UK, and Germany. The worker, a young white man in his early thirties, tells me that the people who come in span all ages, from young teens to grandmothers in their eighties. "They just want to touch the real place, you know? Get a piece of it." He himself doesn't particularly like the *Twilight* books. He couldn't get past the first few pages, but he supposes that "the one true love that lasts forever is what we all want ... I mean there are a lot of times that I can't stand my girlfriend for another minute, but still, we all want the possibility of finding that one true love."

Down the street at the other *Twilight*-themed store, a worker tells me a similar story about who comes and why. She herself loves the books, has read them all at least ten times, and plans to read them again. For her the stories are what love ought to really be about.

> We all want that once-in-a-lifetime love. People are so much more selfish today, but *Twilight* teaches us important lessons. You don't have to be the most beautiful girl or the track star or anything like that. Bella is not the best at anything. For Edward, it's love that really matters. These days it's "I like your face, let's go to bed." These stories take us back to what love is all about.

As in Volterra, *Twilight* tourism has completely changed the town of Forks. According to Marcia Bingham, head of the Forks Chamber of Commerce, seventy thousand visitors stopped by and signed the guest book. Many more actually came to town and supported the local economy, which had been devastated by the slump in timber prices.[65]

Here, at the epicenter of *Twilight* tourism, is a world where anything is possible. This is the promise of romance as an ideology: it can happen to you too if you just have faith and refuse to give up the hope that someday you will find true love. A prince can fall in love with a peasant and an extraordinary vampire can find his soul mate in a very ordinary schoolgirl. Volterra and Forks are indeed real places, but they are also an idea, a manifestation of the ideology of romance in the same way that Lourdes is both a real place and the manifestation of Catholicism's most sacred beliefs. In these small and isolated villages, a romantic phenomenon like the *Twilight* series collides with actual places and transnational tourism to create very real experiences, like a vampire tour on Valentine's Day. The feelings are not fictional: real people experience Forks and Volterra in a bodily state of longing for their own real-life romance and happily ever after. This world, of self-published love stories that become global phenomena that then create tertiary markets and stories that then become actual sites where real bodies collide with fiction and consumption, is a world where anything, even a transcendent and permanent love at first sight, is possible.

Yet once we locate the magical thinking of forever true love in what are in fact places devastated by global capital and neoliberal economic policies, a different sort of vampirism comes to light. In order to fully grasp this, I took a trip to Seattle for some *Fifty Shades* tourism. Seattle, like Forks and Volterra, is very nearly a character in the series. In the books, it represents a land of stunning wealth and opportunity for young Anastasia Steele. But the real Seattle is not exactly the place that romance imagines, or at least not for a gal like Anastasia, with an English degree and lack of dotcom experience. One of the most striking absences in *Fifty Shades* is not so much female desire, but poor people. Yet if you are in the actual physical city of Seattle, the poverty is impossible to not see. For the top quintile of Seattle dwellers in 2014, income had risen to a median of $248,000, but the bottom 20 percent of Seattle earners only averaged $13,000 a year.[66] In 2010, the city's mayor, Ed Murray, reported raising the number of homeless encampments to nine to deal with rising homelessness: there were 30 percent more people without shelter than three years before.[67]

Seattle, like the US and the world more generally, is a land of extremes: homeless encampments and penthouses. Unlike the much more impoverished Volterra and Forks, Seattle was not bustling with *Fifty Shades* tourism. In fact, the few existing *Fifty Shades*–type businesses (a tour through the city, a romantic *Fifty Shades* weekend at the Edgewater Hotel that included a helicopter ride) were fairly difficult to track down. Employees at the Edgewater said the *Fifty Shades*–themed package was not something any of their customers were asking for, and the tour guides recommended a Sex Tour since *Fifty Shades* didn't produce enough tourists to sustain it.[68] Instead of *Fifty Shades* products, Seattle was booming with the sort of consumption outlined in the book itself: $15 artisan cocktails, apartments at Escala, where Christian Grey lived, that sold for $6 million, and shopping for funky frocks on Ballard Avenue. Seattle is a land of unimaginable wealth, a land of people who live in penthouses or mansions on islands, surrounded only by other people like them.[69] It is also, like much of the world, a land of growing income inequality, where most of the population lives with increasing economic hardship. Seattle in *Fifty Shades* is a dreamscape that allows us to get away from our own reality or even the reality of Seattle in order to fantasize about a helicopter ride with a handsome young billionaire who earned his money through his own hard work.

What is interesting from the point of view of Love, Inc., is how both *Twilight* and *Fifty Shades* allow us to dream about a land of (white) plenty. By using romance as a device to lift Bella and Anastasia from economic precariousness into the sort of wealth that none but the top 2 percent can imagine, both series employ romance as an ideology that turns income disparities into matters of "personal choice." Anastasia chooses Christian. Unlike many of the people who go to WSU Vancouver, Anastasia was able to graduate in four years.[70] Anastasia also magically managed to graduate without the $23,000 student loan debt of the average WSU Vancouver student.[71] Even more magically, Anastasia managed to live in her best friend's beautiful downtown apartment in a city that is one of the top ten most expensive for renters.[72] Bella chooses

Edward (not Jacob or the independent pursuit of a career), and that choice leads to a life of bright yellow Ferraris (cost: $239,000) and a beautifully designed home in the woods (cost: $3 million).[73] Outside of the magical thinking of romance, as a high school graduate Bella was destined to earn about $30,000 a year.[74] To live in Forks, Washington, for Edward and Bella—if in fact they were ordinary humans and had a child—would require them both to earn $36,000 a year. A livable wage does not involve nice cars, vacations, or beautiful homes. It just means they would not experience chronic hunger or homelessness.[75]

Reality ruins the magic of romance. When placed against reality, the romance of *Fifty Shades* and *Twilight* is no longer believable and once we don't believe it, it can no longer make the current economic reality in which most of us live bearable. As any romantic knows, reality's a bitch.

CHAPTER TWO

Finding Love

A Modern Tale of Dating, Tindering, OKCupiding,
Ghosting, and Generally Putting Yourself Out There

Every once in a while, in the middle of an ordinary life,
Love gives us a Fairytale.
　　Author unknown—small wall placard
　　in a Home Goods store

Even in fairy-tales, the path to true love always requires some down-right dirty work. In *Sleeping Beauty*, Prince Phillip is locked in a dungeon for a hundred years only to find that he must fight his way through a forest of thorns. Having finally cut a path to the castle in which his true love sleeps, the prince must then face the evil Maleficent. Maleficent, angry that Phillip has pushed through the thorns, transforms herself into a large dragon and screeches, "Now you shall deal with me, oh Prince, and all the powers of HELL!" Planting that first kiss on one's true love is not any easier in the other stories that populate American culture. Prince Eric in *The Little Mermaid* must defeat the evil sea witch Ursula, who has transformed herself into a giant monster. Aladdin must defeat the queer-acting Jafar, who has transformed himself into a giant monster. In non-Disney tales of romance, there are fewer giant monsters to defeat, but the path to true love is no less thorny. In *Twilight*, Bella and Edward must face down an entire army of vampires. Even in

Fifty Shades of Grey, Christian must save Anastasia from a murderous ex-lover made monstrous by her obsession with him as well as mental illness and homelessness.

None of these fictional stories, however, get to what many describe as the true horror of modern mating rituals: dating. In all of the fictional stories of true love, "the one" who is "meant to be" is obvious from the beginning. It is merely a matter of defeating those who would stand in the way. In the real world, "the one" is never so obvious, and a true heart must slog through hundreds, even thousands, of dating profiles, go on a large number of "first dates," and all the while live in a culture where people work more than ever, making leisure time both a highly prized commodity and easily "wasted."[1] In other words, we feel more pressure than ever to find our safe and secure future in the form of "the one," but modern technologies and economies make kissing frogs in hopes of a prince(ss) a far more costly endeavor.

Add to this the fact that many young Americans come to the world of romance through the bleakly unromantic hook-up culture so prevalent at universities; many would rather slay dragons than date. Hook-up culture is a world where sex happens without any sort of emotional attachments or even a date. In the world of hook-ups, it is not unusual to have sex with someone who just happened to be at the same party and then not even say hello to that person the next time you see them. Hook-up culture, according to sociologist Lisa Wade, "is now part of American history, the newest way that young people have come to initiate sexual encounters and form romantic relationships."[2] It is not, as many of our moral gatekeepers would have it, that college students are having more sex than co-eds have been having for at least half a century. They're not.[3] What is different is a pervasive culture on college campuses insisting that sex be completely separated from human emotions. High school and college students often describe emotional attachment, including love, as akin to a contagious disease, as in "catching the feels." The insistence within some youth cultures on having no romantic feelings, no sense of a future, or even necessarily human kindness toward the people you are hooking up with then finds itself at odds with what seems to be a fairly widespread desire on the part of college students to have "real" relationships. According to a recent report by sociologists Arielle Kuperberg and Joseph E. Padgett, based on an analysis of twenty-four thousand college students, hook-up culture does not match up with students' desire for relationship: 67 percent of women and 71 percent of men said they wanted more opportunities for a long-term relationship, that is, for romance.[4] Unfortunately, hook-up culture is not conducive to the "future tense" relationships associated with contemporary romance.[5]

And so, exiting their college years, many educated young Americans, despite a lifetime of Disney, have no idea how to actually pursue the fairy-tale they have been taught to desire. As Rebecca Traister points out in *All the Single Ladies: Unmarried Women and the Rise of an Independent Nation*, American women are not necessarily getting married, and when they are, it is much later than before and long after they have established lives as independent adults with close networks of friends.[6] Yet most of the data shows that Americans, despite declining marriage rates, would still like some sort of marriage-like relationship: two people, in love, monogamous, cohabitating, possibly reproductive, and lasting forever. In that way, as homo romanticus, we have changed very little since we were born as romantic subjects more than a century ago.[7] What has changed is how we find romantic love. Rather than friends or family introducing us, or meeting someone at work or church, Americans now search online and on their phones for their own fairy-tale endings in a digital dating landscape that replicates many of the beliefs of hook-up culture, beliefs that are antithetical to finding "the one." In what follows, I trace the trajectory from suitors visiting potential marriage partners in the front parlor to Tinder and other companies that make money from "matching" potential partners for sex and possibly even romance. I discuss this history of dating in Love, Inc., in relation to the twenty in-depth interviews that I conducted in 2016 with people who were dating online in hopes of finding true love.

DATING, CONSUMERISM, AND THE TWENTIETH CENTURY

> Bundling, or bed courting, as it was known, was introduced to
> the American colonies ... The idea was that if a couple was
> seriously courting, it should spend a night together in the
> girl's bed to ensure compatibility. There were ground rules:
> underclothes must be kept on at all times ... no hanky panky.
> To that end, the bundling board ... might make an appear-
> ance ... a large plank placed between two lovers.
>
> Andrew G. Gardner, "Courtship, Sex, and
> the Single Colonist"

Needless to say, people did not always date. Dating, like many of the other rituals of romance, such as engagements and white weddings, is a fairly recent invention. Prior to companionate marriage and some degree of autonomy in choosing a spouse, there was no need for dating. Parents arranged or at least approved of marriages. Of course, there were some early rituals of "visiting" and "calling upon" and even "bundling" young couples in bed. The historical record shows that early American romantics were having plenty of sex before marriage, but these practices could hardly be described as dating.[8] For dating to occur, several economic and social changes had to take place. First, there had to be the development of consumer culture and a sense of going out in the world to pay for pleasure. Then there had to be enough young people to have enough money to consume in this new world. Then urbanization, mass migration, immigration, and industrialization shaped the spaces and trajectories of consumption for dating. Even so, not everyone could "go out"—clearly couples had to be straight and of the same race. And, of course, couples had to have some disposable income, which meant that going out for poor and working-class young people was not generally in pairs, nor did it involve the sort of consumption that is often associated with dating, such as dinner and a movie.[9] So it is that dating developed primarily as a middle- to upper-class practice and was often most visible on college campuses in the early part of the twentieth century. In the 1950s, dating was primarily seen as a potential route to marriage, a "going steady." By the 1960s and 1970s, dating was no longer a trial run for finding true love, but rather a mix of romance, sexual encounters, and "free love" that by the late twentieth century had morphed into the "hook-up" culture that defines many sexual encounters in the 2010s.

Romantic subjects are, as they were a century ago, moved by the market to pursue romance through consumption. Instead of paying for dinner or a concert, today's lovers pay for dating apps, online dating services, and even old-fashioned matchmakers that they find online. They pay for endless first dates and all the clothing and cosmetics that these dates require. And they pay in the most precious commodity of all: time.

LOVE IN THE ETHER

The research team at eHarmony Labs is dedicated to advancing the scientific understanding of human relationships.
        eHarmony, "Studying the Science of Love"

Apparently as soon as there were computers, humans began to consider how their power might be harnessed to meld individuals into couples. A 1959 Stanford University course used an early IBM computer to pair forty-nine men and forty-nine women. Although most of the couples did not stay together, one couple did in fact get married, and the students received an A on the assignment. In 1995, the first online dating site, Match.com, launched. Match worked like classified ads in that users searched for their perfect mate. Soon there were sites that eliminated the need to search and instead offered to preselect potential partners for users. In 2000 eHarmony launched a site that relied on "scientific romance," creating algorithms that can go through multiple data points from tens of thousands of subscribers to find "the one." More recently, dating sites started to offer genetic and other biometric markers to help users determine whether they are compatible with someone.[10] For instance, GenePartner, whose slogan is "Love is no coincidence," offers the "GenePartner Test" for just $249. Before buying genetic testing, users have to find potential partners through dating sites. This way, the firm can use "science" to establish you and your potential partner's "symmetry of attraction" and even "probability of successful pregnancy."[11]

The popularity of online dating is undeniable. Fifteen percent of Americans have used online dating sites or dating apps, and 27 percent of college-age Americans have. Meeting your mate online is increasingly the new normal.[12] Ten years ago, I had a colleague who was embarrassed to tell people she met her husband online. They would lie and say they met at a party. Now her shame seems rather quaint. According to a 2016 survey, 59 percent of Americans think online dating is a good way to meet people, up from 44 percent in 2005. Five percent of Americans who are married or in a long-term relationship say that they met online.[13]

Online dating sites offer something humans have never faced before: a seemingly endless pool of potential mates. About 30 percent of the Earth's 7 billion inhabitants have access to the internet. In North America, nearly 80 percent of the population can get online. This means that rather than having our pick of tens of eligible partners—or perhaps with classified ads prior to the internet, hundreds of potential partners—many of us now have access to thousands and perhaps even tens of thousands of potential mates.[14] We have landed in a world where meeting online or on your phone is available to most Americans, and we are thoroughly seduced by these new technologies, particularly the ones promising that "science" will help us find our true love.

One of the most popular and oldest online sites is eHarmony. According to media reports, eHarmony has nearly eight hundred thousand active users who are paying customers.[15] eHarmony users can pay up to $700 a year to use the site. According to their website, eHarmony mobilizes the latest science of love so effectively that 438 people get married every day because of their "patented Compatibility Matching System®."[16] And eHarmony marriages are less likely to end in divorce, according to a company survey of twenty thousand of its married couples.[17] It is unclear exactly what the "Compatability Matching System" algorithm is since the formula is proprietary information, the secret sauce of love. eHarmony founder Neil Clark Warren, a clinical psychologist for thirty-five years before starting the company, has been very clear that whatever the algorithm is, it is based primarily on matching for similarities. Warren believes that "opposites attract, but then they attack."[18] According to eHarmony's website, they match people on the basis of twenty-nine different dimensions of compatibility, including core values, intellect, and attitudes toward children.

Warren started the company as part of his deeply held belief as an evangelical Christian that heterosexual marriage is both necessary and good. After Warren was sued for discriminating against same-sex couples, he launched Compatible Partners in 2009. According to Warren, the company is increasingly successful at helping gay and lesbian partners find love. A user today can click on "woman seeking a woman" or "man seeking a man" icons (in pink and blue bathroom–style signage) in the same way a user can click on man seeking woman. Affiliated sites like Compatible Partners are listed at the bottom, not on the main site, alongside Asian, black, Jewish, and Hispanic dating, not to mention senior dating and local dating. On their "Who We Are" page, eHarmony features six couples, all hetero-gendered and white with the exception of one black couple and one Asian woman. The couples all seem to be about the same age as their partners. They also all look fit and have nice smiles with straight white teeth. In the US, both thinness and good smiles signify wealth.[19] A user might read this page as reinforcing the cultural idea of "fulfilling marriages" as for white, straight, and well-off couples.

eHarmony uses not just whiteness and wealth, but claims of science and technology to sell their product. For instance, on the website "tour," they claim that "there's a lot of science that goes into our matchmaking process" and that "we search among millions of singles based on Key Dimensions that are crucial for relationship success ... we understand who you are and who you match best with using the latest technology." Yet eHarmony also uses the key terms of the ideology of romance, like "magic," "fireworks," and "love of their life."

In order to benefit from the magic and the science of eHarmony, a user must first fill out a questionnaire with questions like "How would your friends describe you?" and "What are you passionate about?" The questionnaire takes about twenty minutes. Once you have finished the questionnaire, you can sign up for a plan ranging from $16.95 to $34.95 per month. This allows subscribers to see recommended match photos, browse matches outside their recommended ones, and also to contact others on the site. It also gives the subscriber one phone call for "personalized help from an expert."

Online dating sites that promise to find their customers a happy ending based on the science of love are not really using science as much as they're using hope and optimism to sell us the possibility of a happy ending. Science is verifiable, and none of these sites actually allow external reviewers to see the algorithms they use or their data. As Benjamin Radford, a research fellow at the Committee for Skeptical Inquiry, argues, science is the sales pitch of eHarmony. Radford notes how often the words "science," "scientist," and "scientific" are used. Despite this claim to science, data showing that eHarmony "science" works has not been published in any peer-reviewed journals, and the company has refused to open up its data to external review. The science of love at eHarmony (and other online websites that use science to sell their service) is thus actually pseudoscience.[20] In theory, claims to the efficacy of the product should be regulated under the Federal Trade Commission Act, which prohibits "deceptive advertising" and demands that any claims to performance be substantiated. But eHarmony and other dating sites are not being closely monitored, nor are they meeting the legal requirement to provide information to allow the public, or at least government regulatory agencies, to evaluate the efficacy of their service.[21]

Although this might violate the basic principles of truth in advertising, the fact that eHarmony and other sites marshal the magic of science to convince consumers to use their sites to look for love makes a lot of sense in our culture. Science, like romance, has magical and even metaphysical properties. It claims to lift us up out of our subjective and partial truths and show us something bigger and truer. Science developed alongside romance and capitalism, and thus the three work together. The entanglement of science, romance, and capitalism on sites like eHarmony is a threesome made in heaven. To proffer science as a source of truth and romance as a path to happiness and then sell it for a profit is perhaps the most obvious manifestation of Love, Inc. The fact that the state does not get too involved in regulating love for sale should come as no surprise, since the cost of regulation would be to disappoint so many citizens who need love as a drug. If the state stepped in to say that "there is no scientific way to find love," it would be the same as saying "look at the man behind the curtain."

Love is more like religion in this sense. Although in the US, church and state are supposed to be separate, in practice the state would never announce that there is no God even when religious leaders are exploiting our hope for a life ever after for profit.[22] In the same way, the state cannot announce that romance is dead and that our hope for a better future is being exploited for profit. But many people no longer require the promises of scientific romance to look for love online. In 2008, with the introduction of apps on the iPhone, Love, Inc., jumped into our pockets and our dating lives were forever changed. Dating sites like Zoosk quickly developed.[23] Today there are so many dating apps and so many people on them that journalist Nancy Jo Sales described it as a "dating apocalypse." In Sales's poetic prose:

> As the polar icecaps melt and the earth churns through the Sixth Extinction, another unprecedented phenomenon is taking place, in the realm of sex. Hookup culture ... has collided with dating apps, which have acted like a wayward meteor on the now dinosaur-like rituals of courtship.[24]

In order to see whether dating apps will destroy the world—or at least romance as we know it—I took a look at three popular dating apps,

Tinder, Bumble, and Grindr, to see what sorts of promises they make and whether a happy ending is one of them.

TINDER AND BUMBLE (AND EVEN GRINDR) CAN LEAD TO LOVE

As the saying goes, there are plenty of fish in the sea, and it turned out my sea held 1,946 of them ... And yet, almost comically, I wanted to date only one particular person.

Lauren Petersen, "Wanting Monogamy as 1,946 Men Await My Swipe"

In an episode of the British sci-fi series *Black Mirror,* a future utopia quickly reveals itself as a dystopian world of striving for "likes" throughout every interaction of the day, whether with your local barista, someone at work, or in your most intimate interactions. The heroine, Lacie (Bryce Dallas Howard), has to improve her social media score, based on likes, in order to buy a home. The episode reflects the intense social pressure of constant observation and judgment that social media brings. Lacie cannot be her authentic self, but only a highly curated version of perfection, and this curated self is, in the end, unsustainable.[25] This episode could easily be about dating in the second decade of the twenty-first century. Holding our future in our hand, we now date by swiping right or left, not bothering to even read profiles or take "scientific" compatibility surveys, but merely by glancing at a 2x2 inch images of potential matches. Some young women I interviewed said it increases their self-esteem to see all the people who have swiped right on them; others said the entire process is dehumanizing. In any case, we no longer live in a world where we can avoid knowing how much we are "liked," but we do not yet know what the effects of those "likes" on human connection will be.

Tinder, a primarily but not only heterosexual app, launched in 2014 and today 10 million people around the world go on it each and every day.[26] Tinder is growing so quickly in popularity that twenty thousand people download the app daily.[27] Although the app is free to download, Tinder manages to produce over $800 million in annual revenue, primarily through its membership fees and other features.[28] About a million Tinder users are paying for membership and the company saw a nearly 25 percent rise in total revenue in the first quarter of 2017 alone.[29] By incorporating Facebook information, Tinder allows users to create profiles with six photos and other information such as age and number of Facebook friends in common. Tinder was originally only available as a phone app, but in 2017 Tinder introduced an online version that they describe as "your ... professor's worst nightmare. Mobile phones not allowed in class? Just fire up your laptop and swipe incognito. Cubicle life got you down? Now you can toggle between spreadsheets and Super Likes in a flash."[30] If, as Eva Illouz argues, love is "disenchanted" in modern times, Tinder offers users the chance to imbue their everyday and ho-hum work and school lives with the enchantment of swiping and being swiped.[31]

As others have pointed out, there is a lot of racism and misogyny on Tinder. Sometimes people have been banned for racist and sexist behavior, like when San Francisco Tinder user Nick Vedovi was banned from the site because of messages he sent to a woman who "took too long to respond."[32] Yet most people who engage in bad behavior do not get banned and a lot of bad behavior takes place on Tinder and other dating apps because, as with all social media, people think that no one is watching them. For feminist theorist C. L. Mason, who looks at more subtle forms of racism, whiteness on Tinder is both

> an aspiration and fantasy ... confirmed by the imagery ... This fantasy of whiteness is inextricably embedded within the eroticisms of blackness. Blackness is not a backdrop to white fantasies, desire, and pleasure; rather, the blackness of bodies present ... the erotic possibilities of desiring whiteness.[33]

As for misogyny, it is nearly ubiquitous on Tinder. Feminist users have tried to organize and fight back with campaigns such as feminist_tinder on Twitter or Tindernightmares on Instagram. Bye Felipe is another site of feminist resistance to dating app "bro culture." Bye Felipe collects sexist comments from dating app users and posts them on its Instagram site as an act of both public shaming and feminist critique. Feminist scholar Frances Shaw argues that sites like Bye Felipe are a form of feminist resistance where violent and aggressive threats that are rooted in male entitlement can be contained within the safer space of feminist critique. Shaw also argues that these sites "respond to gaps in the abilities of the services to deal with these problems."[34] In this way, dating apps, like other forms of social media, encourage users to imagine themselves as unobserved, but communities can form to enforce some sense of acceptable behavior even when the corporations that run these sites refuse to do so. Despite the fact that apps have ushered in a radically new form of dating, contemporary dating practices are just as mired in older forms of domination as they were in the 1950s, when sexual coercion and violence were not just commonplace, but largely legal. What new technologies do is make it possible for dominant groups to behave badly with more people and with more of a sense of anonymity. These technologies also allow those bodies acted upon to organize and resist such behavior through public shaming.

In 2014, Whitney Wolfe launched Bumble, a more explicitly feminist dating app. Ironically, Wolfe launched Bumble with money she won in a sexual harassment lawsuit against her former employer, Tinder. This workplace culture of misogyny fits with the larger critiques of the company for allowing male users to flood female users' inboxes with pornographic photos and verbal abuse.[35] Needless to say, at least according to my interviewees, much of dating app interaction between men and women moves quickly from "match" to "dick pic" for reasons that probably have little to do with trying to get a woman to go out on a date and far more to do with displays of male privilege and entitlement.

Bumble attempts to limit this online misogyny by making sure that "ladies always make the first move."[36] It also has a reporting system that allows users to block and un-match with a user. For $9.99 a month (plus more for special features like BusyBee, which allows users to extend the twenty-four-hour window the site allows for matches), users can date in ways that are less likely to feel like a verbal and visual assault to many women. Bumble successfully mobilizes the feminist impulses of early twenty-first-century culture *and* the older, more romantic impulses of homo romanticus. A match made in heaven, for some, and certainly a new form of dating that facilitates both sexual hook-ups and some level of sexual safety all while making a tidy profit.[37]

Grindr, the dating app for men seeking men, launched in 2009 and is, according to their website, the world's largest dating app for men. Grindr has 7 million users in over 190 countries. Grindr replicates the same social hierarchies found in sexual markets like Tinder or eHarmony or even offline. Grindr users' profiles often illustrate the racist, misogynist, ageist, and size-ist nature of the sexual market for gay men. "No spice/No rice" is a common way of saying no to Latino or Asian American users. Also "no femmes/no fats" signifies a distaste for non-normative gender presentations or bodies that are not "fit."[38] This behavior is so ubiquitous that sites like "Douchebags of Grindr" have popped up to document how individuals will engage online in the sort of discrimination considered unacceptable offline.[39]

Yet Grindr is different from other dating sites in its explicitly political messages alongside shots of beautiful and buff men. For instance, on June 13, 2017, Grindr featured a screen about the LA Pride March, which like many Pride marches in the Trump era was refashioned as a "Resist March." Grindr reported on the event: "The streets were lit with equality as a parade became something much more powerful" because it was explicitly political. The app also featured a story about violence against LGBTQ people. The story told users that even without counting the Pulse Nightclub shootings, 2016 saw an all-time high in the number of violent crimes against members of the LGBTQ community. Despite Grindr's reputation as being for men who are only interested in sex with other men—no relationships and NO romance—the site does feature advice on love and relationships. In an article titled "Tough Love: Why You May Never Find the One," Zachery Zane argues that we need not judge relationships by how long they last, but rather how much happiness they bring. In other words, "while you may never find 'the one,' you may find the one for right now, and that may be all you need."[40] In this way, Grindr avoids the claim to a secure future found in romance and explicitly politicizes sex as an identity and an act.

Grindr may be a part of the white supremacist and misogynist culture in which we all live, but it is decidedly not part of Love, Inc. Grindr is not selling its users the promise of romance and a happily ever after, but rather the hope of human connection and community building, which is a very different notion of how to create a better and more secure tomorrow than "meet the one." Grindr is not offering personal solutions to our precarious present. Instead, the app uses progressive politics and a commitment to social justice as a place of hope, offering its users the chance not just to "chat and meet," but also a "welcoming window into a passionate and progressive lifestyle." Not to romanticize a site that makes so many men feel unwelcome, but Grindr may be a model for how a corporation can sell human, bodily connection without imbuing it with the false promises of romance. Instead, Grindr offers its users the very real and very hard work of political action in hopes of a better future.

Still, romance has a way of seeping into even the most unromantic spaces. Some of my interviewees talked about using Grindr in hopes of meeting a partner, arguing that Grindr hook-ups can lead to more lasting connections. One gay man said that if he were just looking for sex, he would use Scruff, another online dating app for men that works similarly to Grindr by using geo-location technologies to match users. This is somewhat inconsistent with research on why men leave Grindr. Interviews with those who no longer use the service consistently mentioned that they were looking for more than just sex and that Grindr was not a good space to create intimate connections.[41] But the fact is the men in this study were looking for "more than sex" on Grindr even if they didn't find the "more" there. Interestingly, none of the queer men I interviewed talked about how Grindr offers pragmatic strategies for creating a better future. Perhaps that is because few open Grindr to think about the midterm elections. Or perhaps it's because romance is just too powerful an ideology to escape.

LOVE IS A BATTLEFIELD: STORIES FROM THE WAR ZONE

> Even in this de-sexualized world, the idea of love and her courtesans—desire, lust, eroticism, the chase, the capture, the devouring—had a stubborn staying power. In the end, for those of us who survived … our last wish didn't turn out to be power or money or property or fame. Everyone's last wish turned out to be love.
>
> Lidia Yuknavitch, *The Book of Joan*

Romance may be a sort of "cruel optimism," but sometimes it is the only optimism we can muster in what increasingly feels like "end times" environmentally, politically, and economically. In Lidia Yuknavitch's novel, *The Book of Joan,* the world as we know it has ended and only the wealthiest few have escaped to a large space ship in the sky. And yet, despite their now sexless and barren bodies, the main characters are moved by a deep and abiding desire for romantic, sexual love.[42] The need for connection, even after the apocalypse, moves the narrator and the narrative forward in what might actually be a better description of our dystopian romantic present than a postapocalyptic future. Contemporary dating practices are, almost by design, the opposite of romance. Although some companies might be promising a romantic ending, both the technologies and the culture of dating complete strangers means that we are less bound by community standards and friend networks than we have ever been. Most social science shows that we behave worse when we do not believe others around us know what we are doing, a phenomenon known as "online disinhibition." We are all just more likely to be jerks when we don't know someone, can't make eye contact with them, and believe there are few if any consequences for our actions.[43] Some research shows that 30 percent of Tinder users are already married and 42 percent already have a partner.[44] In fact the dating site Ashley Madison, which is intended for people already in relationships, was started because such a large number of people looking for dates online are actually already married. Ashley Madison tried to capitalize on this fact with slogans like "Life is Short. Have an Affair!" and scandalous commercials showing hot sexual affairs between people who are "married, just not to each other."[45]

Far scarier than the lying adulterers are the criminals who lurk in the land of online dating, the ones who try to "catfish" romantics, convincing them to send money and more to an online persona who has no relationship to the real-life person who created it. According to data from the Internet Crime Complaint Center, in the US these "online dating romance scams" are among the top five crimes on the internet, with thousands and thousands of complaints per year. By meeting people virtually, criminals can create the perfect object of romantic love, groom the person by offering more and more intimacy, and even though they never meet them in person, asking for or even blackmailing the hopeless romantics for money.[46] Then there are the very real threats of unwanted sexual aggression both online and off that women have always faced when dating.[47]

Yet, like the characters in Yuknavitch's postapocalyptic novel, no matter how grim the landscape of contemporary romance, we still want love. In the summer of 2016, I interviewed twenty people about their dating practices.[48] I found them mostly through a Facebook advertisement that I ran for a month. The advertisement clearly stated that I wanted to speak to people who were dating but hoping to find a long-term relationship. In other words, I was looking for homo romanticus. I was not acquainted with everyone I interviewed, but because I began with Facebook I had friends in common with all the interviewees. The interviews were conducted by Skype or in person and lasted from one to three hours. In many ways, the interviews were like a date in 2017: two relative strangers, aided by technology, discussing some of their deepest desires and dreams.

The interviewees were mostly white (15 white, 1 Latina, 1 black woman, and 3 "others"), mostly female (14 women), and mostly straight or at least straight-ish, with many people looking for a heterosexual relationship but identifying as "heteroflexible" or "straight/occasional queer."[49] They had all had been in some sort of long-term relationship in the past. Their previous relationships had lasted anywhere from two to twenty-five years. My interviewees ranged in age from 24 to 63, with the average age being 34. They all had at least a bachelor's degree, but several had master's degrees and one had a PhD. This is hardly representative of anything, but these are exactly the sort of people for whom Love, Inc., exists. White and educated Americans are the most likely to be married (even "gay married") and the least likely to get divorced.[50]

There were some differences by age, with older people saying they missed earlier, pre-internet dating practices like "seeing someone in a bar" and "feeling that connection instantly." There were also differences by sexuality, with heterosexual respondents experiencing somewhat sticky gender roles: men initiating contact in most cases, with some expectation that the man would both plan the activity and pay for the date. As one young woman told me: "I always offer [to pay], but in my mind I think if I have to pay I am really annoyed. I don't think I've ever had to pay for a date."

All the interviewees were using or had attempted to use online dating services or dating apps and, in one case, a professional matchmaker.[51] And they all believed that their future happiness hinged on finding some sort of long-term relationship. As a sixty-three-year-old white gay man told me:

> I would love to have another long-term relationship. I do better in long-term relationships. [These three years] is the longest I've been single since I was fifteen years old, but it's become apparent to me that I do better in a couple.
>
> I am better with another person; I'm better being seen like that ... as a boyfriend.

Although those I interviewed were looking for love, they were also very clear that the technologies of the present, like dating apps, and the economy in which we live, which makes leisure time more and more scarce, make looking for romance a lot easier, but actually finding it far more difficult. In what follows, I consider the themes that came up in my interviews. Not surprisingly, the people I interviewed were both cynical and optimistic, pragmatic and impulsive. They were also all, like many of us, rather depressed about the historical moment in which we find ourselves and found romance's claim that it is always possible to find the one, to connect, to find stability and happiness in the future together a compelling fairy-tale. They also knew that fairy-tales are not real.

SOME ENCHANTED EVENING

> Don't treat your heart like an action figure wrapped in plastic
> and never used.
>> Amy Poehler, graduation speech to 2011 graduating
>> class at Harvard

When I asked my subjects, "What is a romantic date?," the answers were never about the perfect dinner out or even a hot sexual encounter, but rather human connection, particularly "talking." Ava, a thirty-two-year-old straight Brazilian woman, told me:

> I think the best date was this one guy. I met him for a drink in a bar on a weekday and we met up at seven and we just stayed talking till the bar was closing. And we had been talking for about five hours. And then I put him in a cab and said it's midnight, gotta go to work in the morning. We did it again two times. And finally on the third date I said screw it and kissed him.

A white twenty-seven-year-old man who describes himself as pansexual also found talking the most romantic of interactions:

> Dates I enjoy most are the ones in which I can feel relaxed and comfortable and it is a lot of laughter and interesting intense discussion about whatever ... the Muppets ... The last date I went on, that's what we talked about and the fucked-up relationships the characters on there have. Miss Piggy? Kermit? ... It's talking; I like talking.

A twenty-four-year-old white gay man: "The best first date was with [this guy]. It was great conversation and long, even though we went to a really horrible restaurant. An Irish Pub! And we sat there for three hours and as a vegetarian I was starving." Whatever dating used to be—a movie, a fancy dinner, a subway ride to Coney Island to go on the Cyclone—today the "perfect date" is less about consumption and more about connection. This makes some sense in the second decade of the twenty-first century, when nearly 80 percent of US adults are on Facebook and people check their social media accounts seventeen times per day.[52] Americans now spend five hours a day on their phones (including swiping through dating profiles).[53] Which is not to say they don't want other things, like movies and dinner, too. As one twenty-four-year-old white woman told me:

> Sometimes I think about my best date as in most exciting being my first date ever when I was fourteen or fifteen years old. It was my freshman year of high school and this boy, he and I went to the movies and I remember holding hands with this person and being out and just the two of us ... I think we went to see *Happy Feet!*

But for all of the people I interviewed, what they craved was actual human interaction. It is not that sex is not part of contemporary dating. It is. It's just that sex is not necessarily the point of dating.

SEX AND THE SINGLE GIRL/BOY

Everyone I interviewed had sex with people they met online, some more than others. A white fifty-year-old straight woman, who had been married until a few years ago and thus was new to the world of online dating, met all sorts of sexual partners through various sites and apps. Some of these sexual encounters were one-night stands, others regular hook-ups, and still others developed into potential relationships. According to this woman: "Ninety percent of the men I've encountered are not looking for anything long term ... My first date was actually with a couple." But this woman was also clear about her limits. She was not interested in certain forms of kinky sex: "Men send me messages all the time and ask me to send a photo of my feet and I'm like NOOOOOOOOOOO! Go on FetLife if that's what you want."[54] Still, she was very much enjoying the sex she was having, separating it from romance by saying: "I don't need to be in love with a person to have sex with them, but I need to *like* the person."

A sixty-three-year-old white gay man had a similarly pragmatic attitude toward sex and technology. He too had recently exited a long-term relationship and was somewhat new to the world of Grindr and other dating apps for men seeking men. "You have to have ten hook-ups to have one good sexual encounter. Six will be OK and three will be awful. One of the things is you have to have a lot of bad sex to have one good [encounter]." Despite the numbers game he had learned to play, he increasingly believed that "it's not worth it" and was hoping to find a long-term partner, something he believed was possible on sites like Grindr since he knew gay couples who had met that way. Of course, not everyone is having sex with no strings attached. A sixty-two-year-old white lesbian told me she was not interested in certain dating apps like Tinder because she thought it was too focused on sex and not focused enough on relationships. She had even turned to a professional match-maker service in hopes of avoiding the endless choices available online, but did not find it any more helpful than some of the online dating sites she was already using.

Surprisingly, sex might be less popular with younger people than it is with baby boomers. According to a 2016 survey of 5,500 singles by the online dating site Match.com, if you were born between 1982 and 2004, you are 51 percent more likely than those born between 1946 and 1964 to have no interest in dating just to find sexual partners. At the same time, millennials are far more likely to have sex before a first date (48 percent), perhaps as a way of determining whether or not they want to spend more time with that person or perhaps because that is the way hook-up culture moves bodies into relationships: first sex and then possibly a date.[55] According to this survey: "Millennials are diligently using technology to find love—and building new dating rules and taboos along the way [like] ... skip the flowers, leave your cell phone in your pocket." In 2017, millennials were 30 percent more likely than those in other age groups to want to find a relationship.[56] A twenty-seven-year-old white male who slept with both men and women told me he stopped using dating apps that are too focused on anonymous sex. "I don't really want to have sex with someone on the first date. I'm not really interested in that." It makes sense that a lot of people are using dating apps and sites to find emotional connection. After all, as one thirty-three-year-old Latina woman told me, "if I want anonymous sex, I can walk outside my door." But finding emotional connection with strangers takes time, and that is one thing Americans do not have.

TIME IS MORE PRECIOUS THAN LOVE

In the face of an increasing time famine, organizations and policymakers could move beyond their focus on promoting financial affluence to promoting time affluence as well.

Ashley V. Whillans et al., "Buying Time Promotes Happiness"

Americans work a lot—about 25 percent more than Europeans. They haven't always worked so much. Forty years ago, Americans worked about the same number of hours as Germans or Italians.[57] But something changed. Maybe it was that most of us started to feel more economic precariousness as wealth was transferred upward around the world and the social safety net was slashed in the US. Whatever the reasons, Americans have less and less time for leisure activities like dating. This time crunch came up again and again in my interviews.

A white man in his twenties told me that online dating is "a huge time suck," so much so that he deleted all the apps from his phone, which he had been checking multiple times a day. A white straight woman, fifty years old, told me about a relationship she thought was developing, but the man was so busy at work that it never seemed to go anywhere. They had great sex and felt very emotionally connected, but between her scheduling conflicts as a single mother with a demanding job and his scheduling conflicts as a busy academic who left the country regularly for research, not to mention the hour drive between their two homes, it was just impossible to find time to see each other regularly. Not that they discussed this in person. It all played out in text messages since, as she told me, "no one picks up a phone anymore or talks in person. It all happens on text."

My interviewees came up with various strategies to not "waste" time on these sites. They became experts at performing romantic triage. They made up rules to narrow the field. Never swipe right if they are shirtless (narcissist); took a selfie in a mirror (no friends); have a photo of their dog or cat (wants children too much); or have anything to do with dolphins as décor or background (too tacky). They never went out for a meal the first time (too time-consuming and awkward if you don't like them) and instead met for a drink, or better yet, coffee. If a meal is required, let it be lunch on a workday so it doesn't take more than an hour.

One young Latina woman, who had hit the big 3–0 and been single for a while, decided it was time to get married. She tried a few apps, but settled on Tinder because it uses Facebook, so you can see your common friends, and both parties have to match. In other words, no random strangers who you definitely do not like contacting you, which is a "waste of time." In order to be as efficient as possible in finding a husband, she developed what she termed a "Tinder strategy." Like a conquering general, she surveyed the field and looked at her competition (the other women in her age range and geographic location) and then wrote a profile that made her stand out. She also clearly stated she was not interested in casual sex. "Men are still the gatekeepers of relationships; women of sex … Why do I want to go online for casual sex?" That would not be a good use of her time. For her, finding a husband was a numbers game. For every hundred swipes right, she matched with about thirty. Of these, fifteen would contact her (she, like most women who use Tinder, never contacted the men first). She went on three (short) dates per week for months and months. Sometimes she fell in love, but she quickly realized the man was not marriage material.

> Tons of people on Tinder are what I call the walking wounded. Just out of divorce or whatever. They're on there for affirmation of their attractiveness.
>
> I was so attracted to this guy [I met on Tinder]. It was like that soul mate feeling that I've never had before in my life, not even as a teenager. We met and it was total love at first sight. We had three more dates after that and they were all magical and enticing, and it turns out he wasn't through processing his former relationship.

She ended it immediately upon learning this because she did not want to "waste time." She was going to win this battle and the prize would be a wedding—or at least a marriage. Actually, she wasn't that interested in the fairy-tale romance of a white wedding. She told me that the older she gets, the more she hates weddings, but she wants to give marriage a try, even though "it turns out badly for most people." She likes the idea of the stability and constancy of it.

One of the more interesting ways people deal with the "time suck" that is contemporary dating is by ghosting each other. Ghosting, according to the *Dictionary of Social Media*, is

> withdrawing from participation in a social gathering or a social networking site without offering any explanation or making an issue of it: this may be interpreted as a dramatic exit. In social media such a withdrawal may be temporary and does not necessarily involve deleting the account.[58]

This sort of "dramatic exit" from a dating relationship is so common that nearly everyone I interviewed had been the object of ghosting and a few had ghosted dating partners themselves.

One man I interviewed, white and in his twenties, told me that he just deletes people and any message stream when he feels too busy or decides they're not worth his time. "If I don't want to talk to someone I just delete the message stream. It's totally out of mind and if you don't see it, then it doesn't exist." A white woman in her fifties who had a very strong and "romantic" connection with a man she was dating suddenly found that he didn't respond to any of her messages. Another young white man who was ghosted felt devastated at first since he thought they had a real connection and then nothing, no response. He blamed this sort of bad behavior on the new technologies and the fact that "people are really busy."

> I think it's a strong by-product of technology. So easy to [ghost] now. In a culture where we are just swiping, you can get swiped at any point of the process. You've been swiped. I guess I was hurt by it ... I was more shocked by it ... to think that this is within the scheme of someone's self to stop talking to people without providing a reason. Once that happens [ghosting], it's like discovering someone's infidelity and wondering if you had no clue the whole time. A total breach of trust.

Such strong emotional responses to ghosting do not seem overwrought in the context of the hope that any date could in fact turn into love and a long-term relationship. Psychotherapist Jennice Vilhauer argues that ghosting can hurt as much as physical pain, causing people who have been ghosted to question themselves—what they did wrong, how they didn't see it coming.[59] So whether it's one date or months of dating, ghosting is yet another emotional landmine laid down by the contemporary technologies of love.

Not only did many of the people I interviewed get treated badly, but they also admitted to behaving badly themselves. Part of it was that dating apps meant there were always other options. As one young white man told me, "I'm just not good with too many choices." As anyone who has ever tried to buy toothpaste in a US supermarket knows, choice is not necessarily a good thing. Choice can make us far less happy. As sociologist Barry Schwartz has argued, more choice can lead to far less satisfaction.[60] Or as one twenty-four-year-old white gay man told me, these dating apps make "people seem so generic now, so interchangeable." A middle-aged straight white woman said,

> I've disabled my OKCupid account so many times because you're looking at these pictures and ... Sometimes a face will pop up and you're like, "Oh,

that's so unattractive." And then I think: "Oh my god!" I don't want to be that person who treats human beings like commodities because I don't feel good about the way I'm feeling about people right now. I feel like the lowest common denominator when I treat people like they're just how they look.

All of my interviewees wished dating were different, that people were different, that they were different. But in real life, wishes don't make dreams come true. And so, as if an evil fairy has cast a spell on them, they are glued to their phones, swiping right and left, waiting for the magic of romance to set them free.

HAPPY ENDINGS

> Oh ... I just love happy endings.
>> The fairy Fauna at the end of *Sleeping Beauty*, 1959

Dating is, metaphorically, the forest of thorns that Prince Phillip must cut through to get to Sleeping Beauty. But now, just when he's defeated the evil Maleficent and reached his one true love, she turns out to be a jerk and ghosts him. What choice does he have but to go back into that forest of thorns and swipes and wicked villains? To not return to dating is to give up on the hope of a happily ever after, and no one I interviewed had fully given up on that, no matter how much they might be skeptical of romance's claim that there is only one person and only one forever and ever. Of course, my interviewees fantasized about a world where they didn't have to use Tinder to meet Mr. or Ms. Right. As a sixty-two-year-old white woman put it,

> I would like to see more skill in dating. It used to be ... People are too ... risk averse in some odd way. They're willing to take all kinds of risk in terms of meeting strangers, but not really in terms of *emotional* risks ... [Dating's] an art form that's dying and I'd like to see it resuscitated.

It's not that everyone wants dating to lead to marriage, per se. In fact, many of my respondents spoke of marriage as a set of legal rights, not a fantasy about happily ever after. A young white queer woman said she and her partner were considering marriage because of "legal security, especially if Trump's president." A sixty-three-year-old white gay man is legally married to his ex-partner for "insurance reasons" even as he searches for true love. A fifty-year-old straight white woman said she would eventually like a long-term relationship since "I can't imagine being in my sixties and just having friends with benefits, although maybe that would be OK." Most of my interviewees, however, left open the possibility of marriage as something that would be a good thing *if* they met the "right" person, since it certainly seemed better than dating.

If they do decide to get married, then dating has prepared them well for what must come next: a spectacular engagement. In the next chapter, I consider how homo romanticus moves from the liminal state of dating into the sacred realm of "engaged to be married." In the same way that technologies and the economy have radically changed the way we date, they have also changed the way we get engaged. No longer a private affair, proposals are increasingly online. Like a successful dating profile, a successful marriage proposal relies on "likes" in order to feel the love.

CHAPTER THREE

Marry Me?

The first question your girlfriend is asked when she announces her engagement is, "How did he propose?" Every girl dreams of the day when she will finally be asked that question and we make sure you give her a story she is proud to tell over and over again.

The Heart Bandits, professional proposal planners

THE MOST SPECTACULAR DAY OF HER LIFE

A man by the name of Tom BetGeorge spent half a year figuring out how to surprise his girlfriend with "the best proposal ever." The proposal involved a volleyball game, a palanquin on which his girlfriend was carried from the volleyball game through the streets of their town and into a church, and gymnasts back-flipping down the aisle as she was led onto stage, where a large choir appeared, joyfully singing praises not to God, but to their romance. BuzzFeed described Mr. BetGeorge's proposal as a victory in the competitive sport that is contemporary marriage proposals: "Go Home, Everyone, This Is the Most Elaborate Marriage Proposal Ever." BuzzFeed crowned Mr. BetGeorge as the winner of the proposal game with a mixture of prose, GIFs, and video links.[1] This strange mix of extreme competition and highly publicized private emotions is how many couples get engaged in the twenty-first century. No longer satisfied with a private ritual, young couples now want a "spectacular engagement," a set of extremely theatrical gestures that are then translated into highly produced images consumed by millions of onlookers through new media like BuzzFeed and YouTube. In nearly all of these spectacular engagements, the denouement is still the man dropping to one knee, pulling out a diamond ring, and "popping the question." In the past century or so, despite the myriad changes in the role of men and women in society, three waves of feminism, and the advent of same sex marriage as both legal and widely accepted, the proposal remains a space where men ask and women answer.

Yet what has changed is the very public and reproducible nature of marriage proposals. A hundred years ago, such spectacular proposals would have been unrecognizable as the path to marriage. In the late 1800s and early 1900s, people entered into marriage in ways that were private and conversational even if just as emotionally weighty. In a book published in 1890 on engagements, the authors write:

> There comes a moment in the life of almost every man when, with his heart beating like a … hammer, with faltering voice, and his brain in a whirl, he takes fate in his hands, and tremblingly asks one of the gentler sex to be his—wife.[2]

In the book's nearly nine hundred pages of literary proposals—from Leo Tolstoy's *Anna Karenina* to Charles Dickens's *David Copperfield*—men ask and women answer in a way that is both similar to and also extremely different from what we imagine today as the necessary markers of a successful proposal.

The high emotional stakes of nineteenth-century proposals are clear in the stories. The term "popping the question" comes up regularly to signal that the woman does not know if or when the question will be asked, and the man does not know what her answer will be. It is the surprise beginning and ending of the proposals that create a familiar tension for the reader. These earlier engagements also reinforce the notion of active male agent (the one who asks) and passive female object (the one who answers). Indeed, today in the US, men propose to women 95 percent of the time even though 75 percent of those surveyed say it would be OK if the woman proposed. Not only that, but the practice of men asking women is stronger among younger respondents.[3]

Perhaps the most recognizable aspect of this nineteenth-century collection of fictional engagements is that large numbers of people consumed them and then expected to experience some version of these proposals in their own lives. In the US, where 90 percent of the adult population was literate by 1900, fiction became the site for the production of various sorts of cultural scripts about gender and love that shaped the lives of the ordinary people who read them.[4] As more and more people were reading about how people got engaged, they could imagine their own lives playing out like a novel just as today's couples often imagine their own engagements as a movie.

Despite the similarities, fictional proposals a hundred years ago were really quite different from today's spectacles of romance. For one, there is almost never a ring, and certainly not a diamond one. In R. D. Blackmore's *Lorna Doone* (1869) there is a ring, but without description. In Hawley Smart's *From Post to Finish* (1884) the protagonist asks his beloved, Dollie, to wear a little "half-hoop ring" to remember him. In the story "Kenelm Chillingly," by Edward Bulwer Lytton, there is a "trumpery little ring" of turquoise. And in *The Splendid Spur* (1899), by Sir Arthur Quiller-Couch (aka Q), it is the woman who gives her lover the ring.[5] In addition to the absence of the diamond ring as fetish item, there is also an absence of the bodily ritual of getting down on bended knee. There are moments when men fall to their knees, but those moments make up just a few examples out of hundreds of proposals. In Samuel Warren's *Ten Thousand a Year* (1841), Titmouse does indeed fall to one knee as he begs Lady Cicely to be his wife and she agrees, but in Walter Besant's *Dorothy Foster* (1892), it is Dorothy's rejection of her Lord's proposal that brings him to his knees. In Jane Porter's *Thaddeus of Warsaw* (1844), Thaddeus drops to his knees not to ask her to marry him but because he fears he has offended his beloved Miss Beaufort.

What is perhaps most striking about marriage proposals a hundred years ago is just how lacking in ritual they were. The literary engagements of the late nineteenth century are conversations, not gestures. As marriage moved from "arranged" to "companionate" in the 1800s, the work of deciding on a mate moved from parents to the groom. As Stephanie Coontz points out, marrying for love was a radical idea at the time:

> For most of history it was inconceivable that people would choose their mates on the basis of something as fragile and irrational as love and then focus all their sexual, intimate, and altruistic desires on the resulting marriage ... People have always fallen in love, and throughout the ages many couples have loved each other deeply ... But only rarely in history has love been seen as the main reason for getting married.[6]

When marriage became a "choice," young men had to, for the first time, screw up their courage and ask. No wonder "his heart beat like a hammer" given how new it was for young couples to decide for themselves on a mate. And women, liberated from being exchanged between parents and in-laws, understood that the ability to say "no" was a new power indeed.

The evolution of the engagement from a highly gendered conversation without ritualized gestures or mandatory fetish items into the now nearly universal practice of bended knee, diamond ring, and increasingly elaborately staged and public displays is a story of commerce, romance, changing yet sticky gender roles, and perhaps most importantly, shifts in forms of communication, which seep into our most intimate moments. All these changes have moved the question of "marry me?" from a private conversation to a semiprivate ritual to a highly public and increasingly spectacular event.

A DIAMOND IS FOREVER: DEBEERS AND THE INVENTION OF ETERNAL LOVE

What you call love was invented by guys like me, to sell nylons.
    Don Draper, *Mad Men*

The transformation of marriage proposals from a discussion between potential spouses to a highly ritualized event over the course of the past century happened for a variety of reasons, both ideological and commercial. For one, as marriage became primarily understood as a "match made in heaven," it moved from the profane world of everyday life into the sacred world of a nearly religious belief in the divinely preordained nature of a good marriage. It is not surprising that as young couples entered this newly sacred space, new rituals were invented for it. As Émile Durkheim wrote more than a century ago, that is what rituals do: they move us from the profane everyday world to the sacred.[7] But if modern love demanded a ritual to usher couples into the magical space of "engaged," why does the ritual consist of bended knee and diamond ring? And how did this ritual then become a highly public and staged event consumed not just by the couple's family and friends, but thousands and even millions of strangers?

The answer is, of course, capitalism. There was an emotional longing for a ritualized threshold into the world of a love match, and capitalism came along to sell us exactly what we needed to cross over. The best part is, people know this and yet they insist they still have to buy the diamond ring and get down on bended knee because it is "tradition." Yet this tradition of marriage proposals was invented by advertisers about seventy years ago thanks to a diamond-owning family by the name of DeBeers.

In 1888 when the DeBeers corporation began, they understood that for diamonds (which in fact are not rare) to have value, they had to control both supply and demand. Supply was relatively easy at first, when diamonds were only widely available from South Africa. The DeBeers corporation formed a cartel. But controlling demand required instilling the desire for diamonds into consumers. Struggling to replace customers lost during the Allied boycott of South Africa as an Axis state, DeBeers hired the Madison Avenue advertising firm of N. W. Ayer and Son. A brilliant young copywriter by the name of Frances Gerety came up with the "a diamond is forever" campaign, and the history of love was forever altered. The campaign came with a lot of advertising aimed primarily at men as "savvy" consumers, and even some payments to the burgeoning film industry to put diamond rings into their scripts. In addition, stories and photographs were sent to newspapers and magazines of celebrities and their engagement rings. According to a 1948 DeBeers strategy paper, "We spread the word of diamonds worn by stars of screen and stage, by wives and daughters of political leaders, by any woman who can make the grocer's wife and the mechanic's sweetheart say 'I wish I had what she has.'"[8]

Despite all this glitzy propaganda, diamonds were still associated with industrial uses, not love. This is why DeBeers went so far as to invent a ritual to mark the engagement as a sacred event, separate from everyday life and also from the uneventful agreements between young couples that had dominated much of the 1800s and early 1900s. The bended knee ritual came with a display of the now standardized Tiffany-style diamond engagement ring, sparkling in its crushed velvet box.[9] DeBeers then invented the "tradition" of spending a certain percentage of a man's annual salary on an engagement ring. At first a man was told tradition demanded that he spend one month's salary on a ring, but in the 1980s DeBeers doubled that with an advertising campaign that asked, "How do you make two months' salary last a lifetime?"[10]

The high cost of diamond engagement rings is a textbook case of manipulating the price of an item with almost no intrinsic value. As Rohin Dahr points out in *Priceonomics,* a diamond is neither a fungible nor a liquid asset. You cannot easily compare one diamond to another. Despite the claim that a diamond's value is determined by the 4Cs—clarity, color, carat, and cut—the actual price of a diamond in a jewelry store is based more on metaphysics than logic. "Diamond engagement rings are a lie—they're an invention of Madison Avenue and De Beers … Diamonds are not actually scarce, make a terrible investment, and are purely valuable as a status symbol. Diamonds, to put it delicately, are bullshit."[11] But by convincing couples that diamonds are both necessary and valuable, DeBeers managed to create an $11 billion market in selling engagement rings.[12] DeBeers pushed engagement rings from 10 percent of all proposals in the US in the late 1940s to 80 percent by the

A diamond ring and the Statue of Liberty, Tiffany's, New York. Photo by Willa Cowan-Essig.

end of the century.[13] In a recent study of 2,174 American college students at a large midwestern University, most respondents reported that in a strong relationship, marriage proposals will incorporate elements like the man asking the woman to marry him on bended knee and presenting a diamond ring. These "traditional" elements were identified as necessary signifiers of a couple's compatibility.[14] In other words, today more than ever, an engagement proposal demands a diamond ring, the average cost of which is now somewhere around $5,000.[15]

SPECTACULAR PROPOSALS: FLASH MOBS, NEW MEDIA, AND HIGHLY PUBLIC ENGAGEMENT RITUALS

> A marriage proposal is something that people look forward to all their lives ... When friends and family ask how you proposed, you can have your own version of a show and tell if you've taken steps to preserve the moment.
>
> The Heart Bandits, professional proposal planners

Thanks to DeBeers and Madison Avenue, men have dropped to one knee and presented a diamond ring for about half a century. This "traditional" practice, however, exploded into something far more spectacular about fifteen years ago as new technologies like handheld and inexpensive video cameras and social media platforms became widely available. The proposal, which had been a fairly private ritual, morphed into a highly public one. Popping the question began to require not just bended knee, but highly choreographed displays that were then shown not just to friends and family, but to "the world" through a variety of new media such as YouTube and Facebook.

This is not to say that the change in proposals is about money. Marriage proposals have been embedded in economic relationships for about as long as humans have bothered to record the history of their intimate relationships. In Genesis 34, Shechem wants Dinah and offers whatever bridal payment her brothers demand.[16] As Viviana Zelizer points out in *The Purchase of Intimacy,* "The twenty-first century may well bring terrifying changes in social life, but they will not occur because commodification in itself generally destroys intimacy ... Across a wide range of intimate relations ... people manage the mingling of economic activity and intimacy."[17] What has changed is not the commercialization or the commodification of intimate relationships, but the ability to display the purchase of intimacy in ways that create new forms of consumption, like engagements on BuzzFeed that are consumed by millions of people.

In one of the few academic studies of these highly public and completely new forms of proposing, Phillip Vannini turns to Guy Debord's classic *Society of the Spectacle.* In that book, written long before the advent of the internet, Debord argues that "the spectacle erases the dividing line between self and world ... it likewise erases the dividing line between true and false, repressing all directly lived truth beneath the real presence of the falsehood maintained by the organization of appearances."[18] Vannini sees these proposals as spectacular because they are "illusionary displays of signification of love through representation and consumption."[19] As in the film *The Matrix*, these spectacular proposals are copies without an original.[20] Not only do they play out the rituals invented by Madison Avenue and DeBeers, but they also play out contemporary notions of the self as constructed in and through social media, a space where views and "likes" are necessary for the construction of self. As Vannini points out,

> Romance ... must follow the logic of both spectacle and consumption because the ethos of interpersonal relationships has been increasingly intermixed with the ethic of consumer culture ... the [groom-to-be] becomes an entertainer, a representation of himself, and proposes to his girlfriend while playing the role of a Hollywood actor and that of a singer. The front becomes credible and real when the setting is magic, the appearance and manner illusory, and drama "movie-like."[21]

Yet there would be no drama at all in these spectacular proposals if the woman did not sometimes reply with a very public "no." Spectacular proposals are like a Formula 1 race, where the boredom of watching cars go around in a circle is relieved by the rare but inevitable crash and burn.

Because no groom wants to undergo the public humiliation of refusal, these new engagements have raised the expectations for how much time and labor are demanded. They have also increased the emotional and financial costs of an engagement, which now requires not just the diamond ring and bended knee, but "accessories" like flash mob dancing, a live band, a large number of community members, a highly edited video uploaded onto social media, and strangers' views (likes) in order to be "perfect." A recent survey found that one in four women were disappointed with their proposals.[22] Given the huge shifts in what is expected from men when popping the question, it is no surprise that what people want and what they actually get are often mismatched.

A lot of young men, faced with the stress of figuring out how to propose in some way that is both "unique" and "traditional," "intimate" and "public," turn to professional proposal planners. According to one report, proposal planning runs between $5,000 and $50,000.[23] At The Yes Girls proposal planners, men are told that it is time to think of something better than "over a romantic dinner."[24] In Boston you can hire The Heart Bandits to put together a proposal for you like the "romantic picnic marriage proposal" for $590 and then add some upgrades like a personalized proposal sign that says "Will You Marry Me?" for an extra $99. If the groom wants a "personalized professional poem," that will cost him an extra $155, a guitarist $365, a photographer $575, and a videographer $900, adding up to a whopping $2,684. Or how about a flash mob for $1,951, to which he could add himself ($209), family and friends ($365), and additional performers ($549)—not to mention the photographer and videographer. For this package plus extras, a young groom would spend $4,768.[25] Since same-sex marriage became federally recognized in 2014, gay and lesbian couples have also been invited to consume proposal planning. Although few of the major proposal websites list services for gay and lesbian clients, same-sex proposals also demand spectacle.[26] These spectacular proposals are not just highly produced and expensive, but edited, set to music, uploaded, and then, most importantly, consumed.

The twentieth century saw the ritualization of engagements in response to both capitalism and a shifting marital landscape that moved the decision from parents to young couples. The twenty-first century has seen a further transformation in which proposals, no longer a private ritual, have become a spectacle of romance for a variety of reasons: profit, the continued importance of marriage for full citizenship in the US, the decreasing numbers of Americans getting married, and changing technologies. There are so many more necessary products for an engagement today: engagement planners, multiple camera operators, professional editors, dancers, singers, gymnasts, and more. There are also so many more ways to express and consume romantic ideals, including new media like YouTube, BuzzFeed, Tumblr, and Facebook. There are also new technologies that allow for new forms of organizing bodies in space. For instance, a central component of many spectacular proposals is the "flash mob," something that only developed in 2003 when email and text messaging became widely available and could be utilized to assemble large numbers of people in a particular place.[27]

The incredible investment in staging proposals in the twenty-first century is the result of the contradictions of our time. As marriage rates decline, we spend more and more money and time on making the rituals of marriage perfect. If white weddings are getting bigger and bigger and require both more money and more planning, then proposals, as the entrance into the wedding, also require something bigger, more expensive, more elaborate, and far more spectacular than going to a nice restaurant and getting down on one knee. In order to trace the explosion of the spectacular proposal, I interviewed young couples about how they got engaged. I also watched the most popular wedding proposals on YouTube, all of which have millions of viewers. Finally, I looked at the darker side of spectacular proposals: failed proposals and failed promposals, that is, highly elaborate ways of asking someone to go to prom. It is not just successful proposals and promposals that draw millions of viewers on YouTube and other social media sites. That many of us are attracted not just to the "thrill of victory" in the competitive sport that is getting engaged, but also to the "agony of defeat," is some indication that our feelings about romance and its rituals are complicated and contradictory.

HOW DID YOU GET ENGAGED?

I had some friends hike into the woods ahead of us. They brought a chandelier, white table linens, crystal champagne glasses, candles. So when we hiked around the corner, it was all there waiting for her.

A friend describing how he proposed to his girlfriend at the end of a three-day hike

I interviewed sixteen couples at wedding expos in North America about how they got engaged. A few couples told me that it happened organically. One person simply asked the other whether they should get married. Yet most had some sort of elaborate and highly ritualized form of entering into the increasingly sacred space of betrothal. I interviewed a young white couple (he thirty-six and a physical therapist; she twenty-eight and a speech therapist) who love to run ultramarathons together. At an ultramarathon in 2014, he worked with race organizers so that her bib had "marry me?" on it rather than numbers. Unfortunately for him, her competitive nature overruled any inner romantic— she did not want to start the race late. Rather than letting the photographers take pictures of their engagement, she rushed off to the starting line. The couple laughed about how their big moment was not documented in any way that they could share. He shrugged his shoulders and said, "At least it's a good story." Another young man planned his proposal with tickets to Disney in his pocket. He popped the question and they were on a plane to Florida a couple of hours later to celebrate in style. One man proposed in the Magic Kingdom. On Christmas Eve of 2010, he brought his girlfriend out onto the balcony of their hotel. As they looked out at Cinderella Castle, the Christmas tree shimmered and the giant toy train set whirred by as he dropped to one knee. Other proposals took place on romantic weekends, at the site of their first date, on top of a mountain, during a Christmas Eve slideshow of their love, in Washington Square Park, on the steps of the Philadelphia Museum of Art, and during a scavenger hunt in a park.

At a Philadelphia bridal expo, a young white woman told me just how romantic her proposal was. Her fiancé invited her and her family and friends to an ice rink. After about a half-hour of skating, he pulled her out into the middle of the rink as everyone else moved to the side. "It was just one of those Hollywood moments where everyone stopped and stared and he told me that he loved me and asked me to marry him," she gushed. One of the few black couples I interviewed at a wedding expo also had Hollywood on their minds, or at least he did. Describing himself as the true romantic in the relationship, a man who loves Disney movies and happy endings, he told me how he arranged to have her entire family at a restaurant so they could witness his proposal, complete with a slide show of their love, and live music.

During one wedding expo in Tacoma, Washington, I actually got to witness a spectacular proposal. It went like this: Heidi, the twenty-five-year-old bride to be, was told by her boyfriend's sister, a makeup artist, that she had to show up at the wedding expo early to help her with her booth. Unbeknownst to Heidi, her fiancé, who is twenty-two and like her, white, camped out all night so he could be the first inside and win her a free wedding gown. When Heidi arrived at the expo, he not only popped the question with both their families and some local news media there, he also presented her with her wedding dress. When she walked out of the changing room in it, she was radiant. Blond hair swept up in a bun, she told me she could not be more excited to be marrying her best friend. Her job as a flight attendant keeps her away a lot of the time, but she had no doubt that although they were young, he was "the one." Because they were both devout Mormons, marrying for them meant marrying "for life."[28]

These young couples, although not able to stage the spectacular proposals seen on YouTube or BuzzFeed, know that even among regular folk, it is no longer sufficient to just get down on bended knee. A man must surprise the woman with something unique that shows some amount of planning and emotional work. A man should spend money not just on the ring, but also on the presentation of the ring in order for it to be special. Engagements that are public and witnessed not just by family and friends, but a larger group of people—like participants in a marathon or people at an ice rink or a crowd at Disney—are fairly common. Most importantly, a man must create a "story" out of a romance novel or at least a romantic comedy so that the couples can retell the story of their engagement over and over again. In this ritualistic retelling, their love is performed as magical, enchanted, and fated. Yet the proposals of the people I interviewed were poor imitations of the spectacular proposals on YouTube. On YouTube, proposals have flash mobs, marching bands, gymnasts, dancers--and are viewed by millions.

In order to map what an ideal proposal looks like, I analyzed YouTube's twenty most popular proposals as well as the five most popular lesbian proposals and the five most popular gay proposals. The most popular proposals had fairly high production values, had tens of millions of views, and elicited a large number of viewer responses. Many of the viewers were hopeful that they too might one day experience a similarly spectacular proposal.

MAKING THE MOVIES JEALOUS

I know nothing of life except through the cinema.
  Jean-Luc Godard, interview, 1962

In the "Greatest Marriage Proposal EVER!!!," which has nearly 33 million views and 215,000 likes, Matt Still sends his girlfriend to the movies. When the movie trailer starts, it is a film of Matt asking Ginny's father for her hand in marriage. With a slight southern drawl, Matt (seen from the shoulders down) says, "It might be old-fashioned and it may be unnecessary, but I'd like to ask you anyway ... may I have your permission to marry your daughter?" Once the father gives his permission, the video shifts into several different cinematic styles: action, romantic comedy, and so forth, till the denouement, when he appears in real life in the theater and gets down on bended knee to say, "Since our second date I've been telling you we'd be making the movies jealous."[29] This spectacular proposal even got the young couple on the Ellen show.[30] Although their wedding video received far less interest, with "only" 775,000 views, it too is told in romantic fashion, with scenes of Matt writing his vows of eternal love in cursive mixed with scenes of Ginny walking down a lush country road in her wedding gown.[31]

In a remarkably similar cinematic proposal, this one staged in Australia, a man also lures his girlfriend to the movies for a trailer of himself in a musical comedy, begging her father to let him "marry that girl" to the Magic song "Rude." The lyrics play in the background as a variety of comedic scenes are staged of the young man asking and the father refusing. Although the Australian proposal video does not have quite as many views, it still has garnered 9.5 million.[32]

Other cinematic spectacular proposals include a film made up of 365 days of a man asking his girlfriend to marry him (27 million views),[33] a staging of Peter Pan and Wendy on a "pirate ship" (over 3 million views),[34] and two documentary-style proposals. In the documentary-style proposals, one with 12 million and the other with nearly 2 million views, the couples narrate the story of their relationships and how he popped the question. This talking head footage is interspersed with scenes of the actual proposal.[35] Far more popular than the cinematic proposal is the music video spectacular proposal. Of the twenty most popular proposals online, three-fourths were done as music videos.

DANCING IN THE STREET

> I love music videos, I really do. I think it's kind of sad
> that it's a dying art form.
>   Adam Levine

One of the most popular music video proposals, "Isaac's Live Lip Dub Proposal," has nearly 31 million views. In it, Isaac stages a proposal as a music video for his girlfriend. While she sits in the back of a moving van and Bruno Mars's "Marry You" blasts from nearby speakers, a cameraperson films from behind the seated girlfriend to give us her point of view. What she witnesses is a whole community of family and friends (all white) dancing behind them on what appears to be a leafy but deserted suburban street.[36] The lyrics of the Mars song are perfect. Mars admits he wants to marry the person to whom he's singing. Perhaps it should come as no surprise that five of the twenty most popular YouTube proposal videos use this song. As one commenter pointed out, "If I had a nickel for every time someone used this song for their proposal I'd have enough to cover the cost of my ... engagement ring."

Other music video proposals occurred during sporting event halftimes or included flash mobs. One music video proposal (with more than 12 million views and 54,315 likes) features a man tricking his girlfriend by telling her that they are going to be in his cousin's music video. As the cousin's band sings, the man gets down on bended knee and breaks the "fake" video with his "real" emotion, saying, "We've been through so much over the years and it's gotten us to this perfect moment."[37] In another proposal video, an a capella show culminates in the "pitch perfect" proposal, in which the fiancée is tricked into coming up on stage. Once there, she is subjected to a surprise proposal with lots of a capella singing by a large choir and some highly choreographed dancing.[38]

Nothing is more spectacular than tricking a woman into a musical proposal unless it is tricking her into a surprise wedding staged as a music video. In one YouTube proposal, with 21 million views and 100,000 likes, Justin proposes to Nikki in ways that are cinematic and involve a lot of people dancing in the streets. The video begins with an actor—an attractive young white woman—throwing a drink into Justin's face, setting the scene for a highly emotional Nikki to be left alone while he goes to change. The entire video switches back and forth between the director, giving orders through a headset and watching the action on multiple screens, and the "actors" themselves. As a handsome young security guard interviews a sobbing Nikki, he rips off his uniform and breaks out into a song and dance number, part music video and part male stripper. A flash mob enters. Then the groom returns in a tuxedo. At this point poor Nikki is crying so hard her mascara runs down her face, but it is far from over. After Justin gets down on bended knee and presents her with the ring, he suggests they get married right there and then. The flash mob grows with what look to be hundreds of dancers, fountains flow, and her family appears as part of the flash mob as someone slips a dress over her head. The ceremony ends with the officiant asking the hundreds of dancers and family and friends gathered to congratulate "Mr. and Mrs. Davis." Although some of the comments express concern that this was just too much effort and money on a proposal, others see it as "genius. "You go from proposal, to marriage, to honeymoon without wedding planning stress for the bride. You get one of the most popular weddings in history with over 20 million views." Only one person dares to say, "Imagine if she said no."

Whether cinematic or musical, the most popular proposals I analyzed all shared certain qualities. The most popular proposals were disproportionately white (as is marriage in the US), with all the grooms white except for two and sixteen of twenty brides visibly white. In addition to the whiteness of popular proposals, all the participants were young and normatively gendered. For instance, nearly all the women were thin and had long straight hair. The only heavier bride is "ideal" in other ways in that she is blond and blue-eyed, and several of the comments described her as looking like Taylor Swift. Finally, nearly all the popular proposals demonstrated significant investment of time and money. In other words, men who could afford to hire professional filmmakers, flash mobs, marching bands, and more were the most likely to have popular proposals. The only two cases where this is not true is when a man proposed to a professional cheerleader, which did not require personal expenditure as much as it did personal connection to the team and the other cheerleaders, something we might call social capital.

The gay and lesbian proposals followed somewhat similar patterns. The most popular gay and lesbian proposals were also predominantly white (eight of the ten proposers and eight of the ten proposed to). Like the straight proposals, the gay and lesbian proposals evidenced high levels of planning, filming, and distribution for consumption by strangers. The gay and lesbian proposals tended to be primarily musical and used many of the same songs as the straight spectacular proposals. Finally, the ritual of bended knee and diamond ring was incorporated into all of these proposals, showing the flexibility and continued importance of this twentieth-century practice for the twenty-first century.

One interesting pattern was that the gay proposals were far more popular than lesbian ones by a factor of about 14 to 1.[39] Perhaps lesbian proposals were less popular because animus toward queer-identified women and girls is higher than it is toward gay men. A survey of fifteen thousand adolescents published in *Pediatrics* in 2010 revealed that non-heterosexual-identified girls were at the highest risk for being stopped by police or being punished at school.[40] Or perhaps it is just that our culture views proposals as emotional work that belongs to men and not to women.

The comments on all of the spectacular proposals—straight, gay, and lesbian—reveal several patterns. I read the most popular fifty comments on each video for a total of fifteen hundred comments. I could read this many comments because many consisted of a single word, like "love," a short acronym like "OMG," or just an emoticon like a heart.[41] I divided these comments into the sort of emotions they expressed, which I marked as "desiring a similar proposal/romance," "moved," "anxiety for self or for others failing at such proposals," and "critical."

Many of the comments seemed to indicate the viewer's desire for a similar proposal in his or her own life. For instance, one young viewer said, "I am 10 and have a girlfriend. Hopefully it works out like this." Another young viewer remarked: "I hope my boyfriend does that someday, when I'm old enough and have a boyfriend. Lol." Not that all such comments were by very young people. One viewer commented: "Sooo happy for them I cried ... here I am, 29 and single. Hoping this can one day happen to me too." Many viewers translated the ideal proposal they saw on YouTube into expectations for their own lives: "I have high expectations for my proposal now." "WHAT THE ACTUAL FUCK! WHO THE FUKING [*sic*] HELL IS GONNA DO THIS TO ME. LIKE NO ONE!!!!!!" and "CRYINGINACORNER cause no one ever would do something like that for me." This sense of self-pity was usually paired with happiness for the couple, like "congrats that was lovely" or with heart emoticons.

Some viewers did not express a desire for a similar proposal, but did seem to feel genuine emotion in response to watching one: "Grrrr ... Thanks Matt and Ginny. I'm in some coffee place and it's abnormally busy ... and I'm Literally trying Every Trick in the Book ... to NOT be spotted 'Crying like a Hungry Baby' ... ?!? Annnnnnnnnd ... FAIL!!" Another viewer asked,

> omg was that real?? Was a real proposal or wtf??? It took me to ... i don't know where, but it was so special ... the best 26.59 minutes spent and lived in my whole life ... the video ended 3 minutes before, and i'm just returning to the real world.

One viewer suggested that consuming these spectacular proposals was a great survival strategy, saying they are worth watching "everytime you need a bit of cheering up in life!" Yet another said, "Sometimes when I feel really sad, I remember/watch this video and feel better." Often the emotion was expressed in shorthand as "tears" or "crying" or even "stop slicing onions." This feeling of a strong emotional response was usually marked as a good thing, the "right side of the internet," and a necessary space of feeling good in a tough world.

Not all the responses were positive, however. A small number of comments were actually critical of spectacular proposals more generally. One woman asked, "Am I the only one that dreams [of] a super low-key romantic proposal? Like in a garden with nobody else looking." Many expressed disdain for what they viewed as the lack of authenticity of such spectacular proposals. For instance, one woman said she absolutely does not want "a fake life that only means something if filmed and broadcast on YouTube." Another viewer posted, "If this [proposal] was that spectacular, then the divorce is going to be epic!"

In fact, fear and anxiety, not desire, were the most common emotions expressed in the comments section. Viewers expressed fear that they would never experience romance of this sort and also the fear that if the woman said "no" it would be "funny" but also "fucked up": "I would feel bad for the guy but my god would I want to see that honestly who wouldn't," and "I'm always iffy about big proposals. It puts a lot on the receiver to say yes and if they don't they look like an ass." Men often expressed anxiety that they would never have the money to create this sort of proposal and therefore maybe never get married: "It's actually about who has money to do big stuff like this! I bet most of the cases, boys/men want to impress their lovely girlfriend/wife but they can't cause they are poor or whatever," and "Nice:o but damn, these kinds of proposals make it harder to the next guy to propose."

These anxieties reveal that the proposals are not merely doing the work of convincing us that romance is magical and can save us from uncertainty; they also increase anxiety about the future as "impossible" to achieve. Romance is always a double-edged sword, and comments on spectacular proposals trace the razor-thin line between total emotional and financial security and total collapse. Perhaps that is why there are other sorts of videos that haunt the space of spectacular proposals.

THE DARK SIDE OF OUR EMOTIONS

"Will you promise me that some day you'll be my wife?"
"I-I can't" ... There was [a] pause—so long and so dreadful that Anne was driven at last to look up. Gilbert's face was white to the lips. And his eyes—but Anne shuddered and looked away. There was nothing romantic about this. Must proposals be either grotesque or—horrible?
    L. M. Montgomery, *Anne of the Island*

Spectacular proposals make sense for reasons both economic and emotional. They increase the emotional weight of moving from the profane space of dating into the sacred space of engagement. Spectacular proposals allow the gendered nature of marriage to stay in place, at least symbolically, where men are active agents who ask and women passive subjects who say yes or no. They also very often allow for the playing out of even older gender roles, where young men ask fathers for "permission," and thus young women become that which is traded between men, but again only at a symbolic level and all in "good fun." Spectacular proposals developed in response to changing gender roles, the decreased importance of marriage, and a staggering number of technological developments like smartphones and social media platforms. A variety of businesses emerged to make a profit by selling such proposals, like diamond rings before them, as a necessary part of getting married. Yet there is a dark underbelly to these spectacular proposals, where emotions are not about love and the promise of a bright future, but about failure and mimicry. The concluding part of this chapter considers how the emotional work that spectacular proposals perform can be undermined and subverted by other genres of romantic asking that are available on YouTube: proposal fails and promposals.

PROPOSAL FAILS

> You have never loved me as I love you—never—never!
> Thomas Hardy, *Jude the Obscure*, 1895

Marriage proposals have always faced the risk of failure. When a man proposed marriage to a woman's father, the father always had the power to say no. When a man proposed directly to a woman, starting in the 1800s, a woman often had the right to say no. But with increasingly publicized private lives through a variety of social media, failing at a marriage proposal has now become an event that millions of strangers can watch and even comment on. Indeed, "proposal fails" is an entire genre of YouTube videos as well as the subject of various BuzzFeeds, Tumblr sites, and even Twitter feeds. Proposal fails are not as popular as spectacular proposals, but still have millions of views. These are fairly high numbers for videos that are usually not well edited (often caught on a passerby's phone) and thus do not lure the viewer in with good lighting, multiple camera angles, and background music.

I looked at the ten most popular videos under "proposal fail" on YouTube to figure out what these "cringe worthy" moments have in common. They were mostly highly public events, often in sports stadiums with tens of thousands of direct viewers and then played during a game's halftime for even more views before someone actually uploaded them to YouTube, where even more people could consume them. The people involved in them did not look remarkably different from the people who had highly successful spectacular proposals on YouTube. They were mostly young, white, and normatively gendered. Although these proposals could have been successful, they did seem to lack the sort of planning and family and friend involvement that structured many of the spectacular proposals. Often "proposal fails" just featured the couple in a crowd somewhere like Times Square. Also, failed proposals did not involve very large displays of wealth and consumption, like flash mobs or renting out an entire restaurant, that some of the more successful proposals involved. Still, the only real difference between a spectacular proposal and a proposal fail was that she (and it was always the man proposing) said no, or more likely, ran off crying as a crowd of strangers expressed dismay, but also glee that they were witnessing such a private loss in such a public setting.

A lot of the comments on YouTube's failed proposals blame the men for the failed proposals. "Never propose like this unless you talk to your partner first. Or you know 100% that they are fine with it and will in fact say yes." Or: "Never put someone on the spot like that ... It should never be a complete surprise." Several comments point out that the proposals are often at sporting events, marked as not sufficiently romantic. For instance, "I would be pretty fucking pissed if someone proposed to me at a game." Another fairly popular failed proposal involves a man proposing at a food court. Again, comments marked this as an inappropriate site for a proposal. "What kind of love drives a man to propose in a food court? Who wouldn't say no to that shit?" A few of the comments were critical of the women for saying no. One man suggested that the women would say yes if "moments before the men were Lotto winners," and another asked, "Will any kind soul please remind me of what good comes to a man in a relationship?"

Comments on the failed proposals often reflected a larger critique of the rituals and fetishes associated with marriage. In other words, they were sites where Love, Inc., was called into question.

"Eradicate the stupidity of marriage NOW and we'll all be better off."

"Shout out to all people who will never fall for that marriage crap."

"He's watched too many rom coms."

These comments are representative of those found on "proposal fail" videos. For instance, in one compilation of top proposal fails, with nearly 11 million views, 13 percent of the first hundred comments were critical of marriage more generally. In comparison, there were no comments that criticized marriage or romance more broadly on the spectacular marriage videos.[42] Additionally, "proposal fails" did not induce the desire for "perfect proposals" in viewers. Instead, the proposal fail sites served as a place to express anxiety about marriage, about women as only interested in money, and about men as emotionally clueless oafs who put women on the spot.

Another YouTube genre, the "promposal," functions as a sort of rehearsal to the spectacular marriage proposal. Promposals don't offer the promise of a happily ever, though; they reduce the scope of the question of "Will you marry me and can we be together forever?" to "Will you go to prom with me?" Unlike white weddings, high school proms are not seen as promising us a happy and secure future. In fact, many of the most iconic films about proms are more nightmare than fantasy. *Carrie* (1976 and remade in 2002 and 2013) shows a prom gone terribly, murderously wrong, but even less horrific prom films like *Never Been Kissed* (1999) and *Pretty in Pink* (1986) show that proms are often more about teen angst than enchanted evenings.

PROMPOSALS

MISS COLLINS: Hey, Tommy. Um, don't you think you're just gonna look a little ridiculous when you walk in the prom with Carrie White?

SUE SNELL: We don't care how we look. Do we?

TOMMY ROSS: Well...

From the 1976 horror film *Carrie*

Proms have been around for almost a hundred years, but their popularity has waxed and waned. Not surprisingly, the popularity of proms went down in the 1970s, as youth counterculture and feminism moved high school students away from institutionalized forms of heterosexuality. Proms started to get popular again in the more "romantic" and less critical 1980s. Like white weddings, proms are disproportionately white and increasingly require both time and money.[43] As a sort of wedding rehearsal for high school students, proms play an important role in producing us not just as romantics, but also as romantic consumers. In 2015, the average US family spent about $919 on prom for things like dinner, fancy clothes, and even limo rides to the event. According to one survey, "Families with a total household income below $50,000 a year plan to spend $1109 on the prom. Disconcertingly, those families making under $25,000 will spend a total of $1393 for the prom, while families who make over $50,000 will spend an average of $799." Today, elaborate ways of asking someone to prom make up about $300 of this total cost.[44]

In my Sociology of Heterosexuality course, I ask students to fill out a survey each year about their own proms. Starting about five years ago, many of the students started writing about their own elaborate promposals. This is consistent with Google Trends, which dates the appearance of "promposal" searches to 2011, with consistent growth thereafter. One young student in my class wrote about how he rented a backhoe to move a large boulder into his girlfriend's parking space. My student then painted "prom?" on it and waited for her to arrive at school as his friends filmed the entire event. A young woman wrote about a promposal gone wrong when a young man enlisted her father's help to spell "prom?" in fire on her driveway. At the appointed time, her father called her out onto the balcony and looked nearly as crestfallen as the young man when she informed them that she had already agreed to go to prom with someone else. Others wrote of promposal scavenger hunts, enlisting a teacher's help to show up in class with flowers and pop the question, and even writing it on a pizza box that was then delivered to her door. These promposals have found their way online and often receive millions of views.

Promposals exist somewhere between successful spectacular proposals and proposal fails. Because the people enacting promposals are children, they mimic spectacular proposals, but like all mimicry, simultaneously provide a space of vulnerability and failure of the sacred couple. Like spectacular proposals, promposals are highly public events. They are often filmed and then shared again through social media. Promposals developed alongside spectacular proposals as social media and inexpensive ways of filming an event made asking a classmate to prom a more public gesture. Like spectacular proposals, promposals are too new to have received much attention from researchers. In one of the few research articles on promposals, John M. Richardson describes them as a way of allowing high school students to reify traditional gender roles as well as stage what he terms "neoliberal selves" capable of both creativity and consumption and therefore ready to step into the adult world. Yet Richardson also points out that in his research, which included focus groups, a survey of high school students, and an analysis of online videos, "one word was notably absent … 'love' … little heed was paid to the emotion that one might assume was sometimes at issue."[45] For some observers, that is what makes promposals "sweet." In an article in the *New York Times,* Amanda Hess finds promposals touching because there is no promise of a happy future. "Marriage is forever. Prom is just a dance," she points out. Yet the amount of time and resources poured into promposals begs the question of why teens bother with such things. In part, the answer is that promposals have become a necessary part of going to prom, like getting a new dress or renting a tuxedo. The other part of the answer is that these promposals, like the new dress, demand resources and thus make prom an event that only certain sorts of students can participate in: those with more money and supportive adults, usually teachers or parents, who will help them have a "perfect prom." Finally, promposals, like spectacular proposals, publicly play out the gendered, classed, and racialized nature of successful romance: boys ask and girls answer and nearly all the boys and girls are white and well off.[46]

I looked at the ten most popular promposals on YouTube for what they revealed about promposals as a site of spectacular sexualized and gendered display devoid of romance. The teens in the most popular promposals were nearly all white, and all were normatively gendered. In one of the most popular promposals, with 2.2 million views, a young man writes "prom?" on hundreds of ping-pong balls and then puts them into her school locker. When she opens her locker, the ping-pong balls tumble out. All of this, as well as her reaction (an emotional "yes"), are filmed and set to music.[47] In another popular promposal, a young man makes a film that is shown to the entire school through in-class televisions; the promposal then switches to "real life" as he enters her classroom to "prompose."[48] In a promposal with over 3 million views, a young man and his mother stage a highly elaborate drama that involves pretending that he has been in a horrible car accident and showing up at the girl's house in an ambulance, where a stretcher of "dead" Hayden is rolled up to her front door so he can pop up with a "dying to go to prom" with you sign.[49] These promposals evidence a fair amount of adult participation (either teachers or parents), a fair amount of resources (access to the "stuff" of the promposal, but also access to cameras, computers, editing tools, etc.), and a noticeable lack of the future tense. In other words, these promposals are not staged because the young people involved like to imagine a future in which they are engaged and then married. To the contrary, none of the most popular promposals mentioned the future at all.

Although promposals might provide a certain affect of "hope" among those who consume them (e.g., "I hope my boyfriend does something like that for me"), they also elicit a lot of worry that too much time and money is being spent on them. Although many news stories about promposals talk about the sweetness of such gestures, just as many news stories express concern over the economic cost and rising social pressure of promposals. In one promposal that made international news in 2016, a senior from Tempe, Arizona, bought his girlfriend a trip to Hawaii as part of his promposal.[50] As an ABC News report put it, "The promposal stunts have gotten millions of views, shares and 'likes,' but this quest for social media fame is leading some teenagers to lay out elaborate amounts of time and money in an escalating game of one-upmanship."[51]

The most popular promposal by far, with nearly 14 million views, is one that very nearly failed. In it, a young man, Daniel, sets up road signs on a country road asking his girlfriend to go to prom. Not realizing the signs are meant for her, she blurts out, "That's a shitty way to ask someone to prom," before she realizes that the signs were placed there by Daniel. She then cries, feels terrible, and after a short camera break, says yes (of course).[52] This awkward promposal was so popular that it spawned a parody video with 145,000 views.[53]

Why the most popular promposal is also simultaneously a near failure has to do with the power of mimicry to both uphold the way things are and simultaneously subvert them.[54] In the case of promposals, young people who do not yet have access to the fantasy of a safe and secure future through romance enact romantic-like gestures in ways that can be read as "cute" and "harmless." These gestures do the work of romance as an ideology by ensuring that those with the most access to imagining a happy future are also those with the highest levels of racial, gender, and economic capital. But promposals also subvert romance's claims that it can ensure future well-being because the young bodies on which it plays out are clearly not yet part of the adult world and cannot yet speak in the future tense. Indeed, to imagine prom as happily ever after would so thoroughly undermine notions of "good marriages" that it would be laughable. Teenagers should not get married, but they can playact what getting engaged would look like in ways that are read as both harmless and harmful. In other words, because we cannot imagine these teenage couples riding off into the sunset, yet because they manage to stage their own promposals as similar to spectacular engagements, we are left with all the ideas of who deserves love, but none of the promises of a happily ever after.

SPECTACULAR PROPOSALS, FAILED PROPOSALS, PROMPOSALS, AND THE FUTURE OF LOVE

It's romantic. And romance is what telenovelas are about.
A pornography of emotions.
Jaime Camil as Rogelio De La Vega, *Jane the Virgin*

YouTube can certainly bring financial rewards, although direct payments are only about $2,000 for every million views.[55] But popular spectacular proposals can also pay off in less direct ways. *Jane the Virgin* star

Justin Baldoni staged and filmed a complex spectacular proposal that involved a series of faux comical proposal fails followed by the "real" proposal. He had his girlfriend watch the film while he prepared "backstage" (visible to the viewer). The faux proposal fails include asking live on air from a radio show, but there are technical problems and he is cut off; a dancing flash mob in a public square where they forget to bring the bride; and a variety of music videos that are "too cheesy." These spectacular but proposal fails then morph into a much more serious documentary of their relationship that culminates in him appearing in front of her to ask her to marry him.[56] This video, like most, allows the producers (Wayfarer Entertainment) to advertise their services, but it also increases the visibility and perhaps likability of a rising young star. Besides the million-plus people who watch *Jane the Virgin*, nearly 11 million now get to swoon over his "real life" romance.[57] Such spectacular proposals benefit many different players—production companies, the venues in which the proposals took place, or even a side business of one of the "protagonists." For instance, one proposal video with nearly 10 million views features a dancing flash mob and a large marching band—plus, the bride-to-be, Allison, announces her "new business designing beautiful home textiles and helping artisans in third world countries!"[58]

Even promposals, promposal fails, and proposal fails can be monetized, since they are usually connected to someone's YouTube channel and a button to click and subscribe. Also, some of the most popular promposals are part of teen entertainment sites, like *Seventeen*'s promposal series, sponsored by Covergirl, starring Becky G.[59] Money alone cannot explain why people are proposing in spectacular ways and why millions of us are consuming those proposals. Nor can money explain why we watch promposals and proposal fails. In order to really dig into what is going on, it is worth asking what cultural work is being done by these spectacular proposals.

On the one hand, we have some very important gender maintenance going on at a time when gender roles are in flux. Women make up half the workforce and are far more likely than men to enroll in and complete college. Furthermore, young women now place more importance on having a successful career than young men do.[60] Part of the fantasy of romance in general and spectacular proposals in particular is that by leaning back into "tradition," we will find ourselves in a safe future. Even when this is not what young women and men are doing in their actual lives, consuming it as a fantasy online provides relief from the anxiety about that future in the same way that consuming pornography can give momentary relief from the burdens of real relationships.

In all of the popular forms of popping the question, there is a clear maintenance of racial boundaries at a time when white privilege is increasingly questioned. Keeping romance for white people (mostly) and perfect proms for (mostly) white kids is a way of making the future not just bright, but also white. Of the twenty most popular spectacular proposals on YouTube, only three contained a nonwhite person. One is a flash mob proposal in downtown Disney, with nearly 14 million views.[61] Another is a proposal with nearly 4 million views featuring the black boyfriend of a Chicago Bulls cheerleader (aka a Luvabull), who is also black. Perhaps this video is most notable not for the sporting event theme, since spectacular proposals often take place during sporting events, but because the first comment underneath the video announces that "they divorced."[62] The other top-twenty spectacular proposal that is not white takes place through a series of notes leading to a room at a Hilton. Interestingly, the comments in this video also speak of the couple's supposed divorce, the woman's supposed sexual promiscuity, and how she wore too much makeup. Overall, the comments on these non-white spectacular proposals were far more negative than the comments in the other, whiter videos.[63]

Spectacular proposals do the work of making gender and race hierarchies appear in ways that make them seem desirable. The ones we watch are those where the man proposes, and the woman is proposed to. We watch when she is white and young and thin and feminine. We watch when he has spent huge amounts of money to signify that he is wealthy and therefore desirable because being rich is a good thing. It is possible that many of us who watch spectacular proposals do not want these things in our actual lives. The women watching might want equality; the men watching might want to be valued as human beings and not for the size of their bank accounts. Certainly we are, as a nation, increasingly unlikely to be white or married. Yet these facts are beside the point. The point of an ideal form is to induce both desire and compliance in us: a desire to become the ideal and a willingness to comply with whatever rules we must follow to get there. Yet few us will achieve this ideal. The vast majority of Americans are no more likely to be part of a spectacular proposal than they are likely to find a stable and secure future. These truths cannot stop us from dreaming that we will escape the grunt work of our increasingly precarious lives. To paraphrase Snow White, we might as well whistle while we work and dream that someday our prince will come. And as we dream of this magical future, millions and millions of us will continue to watch spectacular proposals on YouTube and plan for the most spectacular event of all: the white wedding.

CHAPTER FOUR

White Weddings

As you may have recognized, it's my mother's engagement
ring so of course it's very special to me and Kate's very special
to me now as well, and it's only right the two are put together.
   William explaining the diamond and sapphire
   engagement ring he gave to Kate

On Friday, April 29, 2011, even London's weather was in the mood for a wedding. The day dawned warm and sunny and stayed that way. I made my way down to Westminster Abbey a little before 7 A.M. to witness the wedding of Kate Middleton and Prince William. As I moved through the crowd, I was struck by how festive the mood was at such an early hour. People were popping the champagne as well as downing good old English pints at an alarming rate. The pungent smell of marijuana wafted through the air. The crowd was dressed in outlandish costumes, mostly comprised of Union Jacks: Union Jack hats in the shape of three-tiered wedding cakes, Union Jack capes, socks, shirts, and even baby blankets competed with red, white, and blue hair and the ubiquitous plastic "fascinators" that sat atop women's heads. As the morning wore on and we awaited the arrival of the beautiful bride and the lucky groom, the crowd swelled to over a million people. In a sea of humanity that large, there is nothing to do but go with the flow. I drank to the royal couple and the Queen, to true love and marriage, and to a variety of other things about which I am in fact quite ambivalent. But that is the power of a hegemonic ideological formation like romance.

Romance, like any ideology, disguises the material world in a smoke-screen of immaterial symbols. In the same way that US geopolitical interests are disguised as "making the world safe for democracy," romance makes race, class, gender, nation, and the sexual ruling elites disappear in a puff of fairy-tale weddings and happily ever afters. As Chrys Ingraham points out in *White Weddings,* the heterosexual imaginary is a sleight of hand to make us look away from what's really important and focus instead on fetish items and rituals, like engagement rings and vows.[1] This ideological sleight of hand, whereby the material world is ignored for the symbolic world, was nowhere more evident than at the royal wedding of Kate and William. Billed by the media as one of the most important events of the twenty-first century, an event that would unite rather than divide us, the royal wedding operated behind a magical screen of true love even as whiteness, heteronormativity, and the resurgence of the supposedly dead British Empire were at the heart of the affair. In some ways the wedding seven years later of William's younger brother Harry to Meghan Markle subverted some of these messages. After all, Meghan's mother is black (and her father white). American Episcopalian bishop Michael Curry's sermon was, according to Twitter, the blackest thing to ever happen to the royals. Meghan's position as nonwhite, a commoner, an American, and a divorced woman certainly made her ascension into the British royal family unusual. It allowed many of us to believe that any little girl, regardless of race, can marry a prince.[2] Yet this fantasy of the wedding becoming more "democratic" must be constrained by the fact that Meghan and Harry's wedding was watched by far fewer people than watched Kate and William's. Maybe the world just wasn't as romantic in 2018 as it was in 2011; maybe the more democratic nature of this royal bride also made her wedding less "perfect."[3]

Kate and William's wedding also engaged in a fantasy of "democracy" since it allowed us to believe that any (white) girl, even a commoner, might marry a prince. The event was billed by the palace and the press alike as "every girl's dream come true" and simultaneously an event watched by everyone. *InStyle* gushed that the royal couple got married "in front of the world!"[4] The *Daily Mail* told us that a crowd of a million "roared with excitement" as the two exchanged vows at Westminster Abbey.[5] Over 2 billion people around the world watched television coverage of the wedding. That is nearly one in three people alive today. What other event can we say that about? The Apollo lunar landing in 1969 had about five hundred thousand people watching out of a population of nearly 4 billion. Of course, a few sporting events have come close, with the 2012 London Olympics and the 2010 World Cup gathering nearly as many people around TV sets. Not to mention the funeral of Prince William's mother, Princess Diana. Still, as weddings go, this one was surely one of the most important to ever take place.

Yet even if a third of the world's population was watching the event, not everyone watched it with equal enthusiasm. Although the royal wedding was in fact a globalized event, it was never a universal one, a singular set of signifiers that were interpreted in lock step. A huge number of people around the world watched the event, but there is little evidence that the primary emotion they were feeling was love. It was in the crowd that day where the global circulation of the wedding as "for everyone" ran up against the truth of who actually showed up. Nearly everyone at the wedding, inside and out, was white. I noticed this almost immediately. On the Tube on the way over to Westminster Abbey, the crowd had been more racially diverse, more like the City of London, where more than a third of the residents are nonwhite and over three hundred languages other than English are spoken. Such diversity was not evident in the crowd of a million that showed up for the wedding. They were white; and with the exception of a handful of French, Italian, and Spanish speakers, they were Anglophones. To a man. Or I should say woman, because the crowd was predominantly female as well.

By examining the contradiction between the claim that "all the world loves a wedding" and the fact that the crowd that showed up at the wedding was far from universal, I hope to show that the wedding of

Kate and William, like all extravagant white weddings, furthered the interests of the sexual ruling elite, who also happen to mostly be the national, racial, and class ruling elites. The royal wedding worked to convince us, even those of us excluded from such weddings, that their love story was accessible to all. I also hope to show how even among the enthusiastic crowd at the royal wedding, there was some acknowledgment that a fairy-tale romance is not very likely for most people—not because we are unworthy, but because such a romance requires wealth, whiteness, heterosexuality, and a perfectly gendered and youthful body. Or to put it another way, without a magical fairy godmother able to transform us and our surroundings into something brighter and whiter, most of us are not expecting our dreams to come true. Instead, we consume these events in contradictory ways: sincerely and cynically, with tears in our eyes and a drink in our hands. In the postromantic and hyperromantic moment in which we live, we don't just love white weddings; we hate them too. And Kate and William's was no exception.

ALL GIRLS DREAM

> Every girl dreams of her wedding day since she a little girl.
> Pinterest Board post by Meaghanleigh13

The most common phrase I heard from people at the wedding of William and Kate was that "all little girls dream of their white wedding." In my fieldnotes the phrase appears twenty-two times. I interviewed nearly a hundred people in three days of wedding hoopla, and almost a quarter of them said the same thing. This is a sign that we are carefully following cultural scripts. Those are the scripts for little girls, anyway.

I typed the phrase "all little girls dream of perfect wedding" into a search engine. There was a news story about a nine-year-old girl, dying of cancer, who gets her "dream wedding" as her final wish.[6] An online game lets little girls choose their makeup, hair style, and wedding gown and then see themselves on the cover of a fictional wedding magazine.[7]

White Weddings is an app for planning weddings that's available for your iPhone. It tells us,

> Every girl dreams of her perfect wedding day, when she is a princess for a day in a beautiful white gown, walking on rose petals and dancing with her prince charming. Make all your wedding dreams come true with White Wedding! Plan every tiny detail of this special day.[8]

There are other apps you can download, like Wedding 101 or Wedding Dresses. All there to help little girls and grown women dream of their perfect day. According to recent news reports, six out of ten single women already have their weddings planned, and most start thinking about their dream weddings in elementary school.[9]

And who wouldn't want their little girl to dream? After all, everybody loves a big, white wedding. What's not to love? Dancing, outlandish costumes, cake, and booze. The white wedding is a perfect ritual. But before we rush into the big day, it's worth popping the question: Why do we do what we do when we say I do? Where did the white wedding begin, how did it spread, and why does it cost so much more money and labor than ever before?

TWO WEDDINGS, A QUEEN, AND A LITTLE PERSON

> When I think of a merry, happy, free young girl—and look
> at the ailing, aching state a young wife generally is doomed
> to—which you can't deny is the penalty of marriage . . .
> I feel sure that no girl would go to the altar if she knew all.
>   Queen Victoria

The white wedding as we know it probably began with Queen Victoria's.[10] The wedding of Victoria to Prince Albert on February 10, 1840, was, by all accounts, a magnificent one. Unlike Kate and William, Albert and Victoria awoke on their wedding day to grim and terribly English weather. Still, large crowds gathered at daybreak to watch the royal procession. Victoria wore a dress of white to signal her purity and

Weddings require research. Photo by Willa Cowan-Essig.

virginity and on her finger sparkled a diamond and emerald engagement ring shaped like a snake.[11]

Albert and Victoria's wedding and subsequent life were thoroughly infused with modern love: the virginal bride, the white dress, the engagement ring, the companionate partnership, the children, and the creation of an ideal that no one could live up to without spending some serious money. Even more modern was the fact that Victoria's wedding was a highly publicized event. As one of the first weddings to travel the globe via telegraph, Victoria's wedding became an ideal form for ordinary people in England and the United States. Victoria's wedding happened at the same time consumer culture, advertising, mass media, and popular culture were born and was probably the first "celebrity wedding," a highly iconic wedding that was represented through a variety of media so that it could be imitated at all levels of society.

Just two decades after the wedding of Victoria and Albert took place, another royal wedding occurred: this one in America. The prince of popular entertainment, General Tom Thumb (Charles Stratton), married the beautiful Lavinia Warren. The couple, standing at thirty-six and thirty-two inches, respectively, were so important to America's sense of itself and the creation of the ideal wedding that famous people fought to be on the guest list, and President Abraham Lincoln invited the couple to spend their honeymoon at the White House. The groom's best friend, P. T. Barnum, sold tickets to the reception and for a brief moment a nation torn by Civil War was moved to tears by the love story of two of its most beloved stars. Soon after the wedding, Americans began staging "Tom Thumb's Wedding" as a pageant, church fundraiser, and general good time, using children to play the roles of the little bride and groom.[12]

These two weddings, one of a Queen, the other of a popular entertainer, were signs that the white wedding was about to become the most important ritual of our time. From the Victorian era on, we would look to the weddings of the rich and famous for clues about how to lead our own lives. White dresses, diamond rings, large receptions, and a story about romance and true love (not property or commercialism) would be at the center of our dreams. Celebrity weddings, royal weddings— even fictional weddings in films and books—took hold of our collective imagination and moved us to act like movie stars and princesses in our own lives. Since then, there has been no such thing as a traditional wedding, which was, after all, both a church affair and an exchange of property. Instead, we have the celebrity weddings of the past century and a half as well as the representations of weddings in film to guide us in our own quest for the perfect way to say "I do."

THE DRESS AND OTHER FETISH ITEMS
OF ROMANCE

Who dreams of sifting through the thousands of dresses
at Kleinfeld's Bridal with me?
  Randy Fenoli, from *Say Yes to the Dress*

As the Victorian era faded and the twentieth century took hold, a whole host of changes took place that moved the dream weddings of queens and freak show performers into the lives of average Americans. First, the industrialization of the wedding dress. Before the early twentieth century, most people could not afford a white dress and so got married in their "Sunday best," usually somber frocks in dark colors. All that changed with the rise of department stores that could hold rack after rack of white dresses, mass produced and therefore more affordable. Spending money on a dress that could only be worn once became a popular, if not universal, practice that then spread throughout much of the world, so that in many countries two ceremonies are held, one in traditional garb, the other in a white wedding gown.[13] In addition to white dresses, as chapter 3 explained, Americans were sold diamond engagement rings. Since then, diamond engagement rings have spread around the world as "necessary" items. In Japan, DeBeers was able to convince newlyweds that diamonds were necessary in near record time; fewer than 5 percent of brides had diamond engagement rings in 1968, and nearly all of them had them a short fifteen years later.[14] Now diamonds are necessary for weddings in China as well. A wedding consultant in Shanghai recently told the BBC: "Ten or 15 years ago, if you asked people what diamonds were for they would tell you they were used in power tools. Now China is one of the biggest markets for

Wedding dresses rarely have prices on them. Photo by Willa Cowan-Essig.

diamonds—especially for engagement rings."[15] So it is that the rather commercial beginnings of the diamond ring and the white wedding dress got lost behind the frothy dreams of brides- and grooms-to-be. As for the labor used to bring these items to us at an affordable price and how that labor is "cheap" because of centuries of empire and racial exploitation, that too was disguised by the belief that these items are both necessary and traditional for our big day.[16]

In our time, for a wedding to be good we *must* have a white dress (average cost $1,500), a diamond ring (average cost $5,764), and even fresh flowers (average cost $2,379). Not only do we need to spend lavishly on the perfect wedding, but we also must have the perfect reception. Interestingly, because we are not usually given access to celebrity wedding receptions, we have mostly learned about what we need at a reception from films and, more recently, reality TV. The reception must have dancing with a DJ or even a band. It must also have an elaborate wedding cake (average cost $540), and certain rituals must be performed, like the bride and groom cutting the cake and smashing it into each other's faces. This particular "tradition" was, at least according to historians of weddings, learned from 1980s romantic comedies. Apparently, with the introduction of videography to weddings, the bride and groom increasingly imagined the videos of their weddings as if they were in a romcom, and shoving cake in each other's faces became a part of portraying themselves as lighthearted and in love.[17] The cost of all that filming and photographing: $4,542. In 2017, the total average cost of a wedding, not including the engagement ring or honeymoon: a whopping $34,000—and this number can be doubled or even tripled in large cities.[18] People may claim that weddings are "just about love," but the fact that they are a $55 billion a year industry in the US and $300 billion worldwide means weddings are also about how economy and culture can work together to produce real emotions.[19] And no wedding worked better to produce real emotions than the $33 million dollar wedding of Kate and William, a ceremony that probably cost the British economy something like $60 billion, all of which was reframed as "priceless."[20]

A REAL LIFE FAIRY-TALE

Checkmate, Kate—you've taken the King!
> Sign in the crowd at the royal wedding
> of Kate and William

On the plane from JFK to Heathrow, I spoke with six women, Americans, mostly from the Midwest, mostly middle-aged, all white, who told me the same story: the love between Kate and William was "the real thing." As one woman put it:

> You could tell by the way he looked at her, not at all like his father, Prince Charles, who never really did love his mother. After all, he was calling his mistress, Camilla, on the way to his wedding with Diana. Of course Charles loves Camilla. Why would he have married her if he didn't? She's not young anymore. Not much to look at. It must be a real love between them. It's romantic in its own way. But William, he's going to do it right. Marry the woman he loves the first time.

All six women agreed with the basic story of love, which was articulated by one of them as follows:

> William first noticed Kate at college, when she appeared in black lingerie in a fashion show. The two were friends and then lovers, but then they broke up for a while to make sure being in the royal family was what Kate really wanted, how they knew each other and knew themselves and were therefore going to last forever.

These women knew the inside story about Kate's social-climbing mother, Carole Middleton, who forced Kate to enroll in the University of St. Andrews because that was the college William was attending. These women knew all about the romantic proposal in a remote cabin on Lake Rutundu and how William had given Kate the beautiful sapphire and diamond ring that had been his mother's.

These women, diehard fans of "Kate and Wills," according to the buttons on their lapels, knew every single detail of their story because it had been told and retold over and over again in the press. A fairy-tale in the making, one celebrity rag at a time.[21] Romance is a successful ideology because of the habitual, almost addictive nature of telling love stories to one another over and over again. If whiteness is a bad habit, one that must be enacted over and over again, as Sara Ahmed tells us, then romance is a drug habit. We are addicted to these stories, to their narrative arc, to the eyes meeting across a crowded room, the immediate knowing that this is your fate, your beloved with whom you will share your life.[22] We must hear love stories and read them, but more importantly, it is necessary to tell and retell them. If love is a drug, then the telling is the syringe. When these women read the "true" story of Kate and William's romance in various magazines, they felt as compelled to repeat it as a drug addict feels compelled to repeat the high.

This story of true love was certainly the dominant one in the press and among the crowds at the wedding. A young American woman camping out the night before the wedding told me that the fairy-tale romance of Kate and William was more important to Americans than to Brits because we Americans really needed some good news to distract us from the wars and the crumbling economy. "That's how it is for me," she told me, flipping her long blond hair. "If I pick up a book to read or go to a movie there damn well better be a happy ending. And this wedding damn well be the love story we're all looking for … But I think it is. I think their love is real." A sixty-year-old white woman from Nottingham at a traffic barricade the next day told me that although she herself had never been married, the romance of Kate and William gives her hope that someday "my prince will come." Then the woman sighed and admitted to me, rather wistfully, that this wedding was not nearly as romantic as Charles and Diana's. I was surprised to hear this, but throughout the day I heard it over and over again, especially from the older women. "Diana," she explained, "was so young and so pure. And Charles was older and so powerful. Kate and William, well, they've lived together, she's older than he is and just as educated as him." Apparently, at least for an older generation, romance still needs an older, powerful man and a young, virginal princess to work. That makes sense given how Disney and other cultural scripts shaped the early romantic consciousness of these women.

But for women under fifty, women whose childhoods intersected with Second Wave feminism as well as Disney, there was nothing romantic about the power inequities between Charles and Diana. Instead, they saw Kate and William's equal education and similar ages as a sign of true partnership—and that was a "real fairy-tale." A white twenty-two-year-old student from Germany told me that she wasn't sure if Kate and William's was a real love story, but she certainly hoped it was.

> Charles was way too old for Diana. Kate and William are more modern. She talks back to him. It's not important to me to marry a prince. I want to take care of myself. I don't want to have to rely on someone. I would like to rely on them, but not have to be dependent on them, you know?

A forty-something white Englishwoman with a professional job told me, "Charles and Diana were brought together. These two met out of the public eye. Kate's not like Diana. She's thirty. She's got it together. She has her own mind." A few hours later another middle-aged white Englishwoman, this one a small-business owner engaged to a much younger man who worked in construction, told me,

> This relationship [between Kate and William] really is so much more solid [than Charles and Diana's] and it's going to last. At the time, I thought Diana and Charles would last, but you can see now they wouldn't. But Kate and William? You can just see that they're going to make it. Whereas Diana was hanging on Charles's every word. Diana was trying to please him. Kate and William. There's equality.

As I moved through the crowd, or more accurately, as the crowd pushed me along, I eventually got shoved into a group of Australian women. They were part of a tour organized by a radio station in their small city. It was advertised as "the ultimate hen party," and this bachelorette party from down under sold out almost immediately. These women were in their thirties and forties, mostly married, all white, with mostly white-collar jobs. For them, this wedding was far more romantic than Charles and Diana's. According to the radio host who had organized the hen party, her own life was a fairy-tale because she got married at twenty-one, "just a couple of kids with a white wedding in a house we were renovating," and has been married for twenty-six years. It's the partnership with her husband, the lifelong commitment that makes it a fairy-tale, just like the relationship between Kate and William seems to be. "Kate and William have a mature relationship, whereas Charles was a father figure and Diana was a rabbit caught in the headlights."

One of the women on the tour agreed. Dressed to the nines, in high heels and a tight-fitting white skirt and lacy blouse, makeup and hair done to perfection for the big day, she jumped into the conversation: "This is way more romantic than Charles and Diana because Kate and William are not a fantasy. They're more normal." She herself is married for the second time, this time the "right" way. Her husband had given her the trip to the royal wedding as an anniversary present because he knew how much she wanted to go; he himself had stayed home with their six children, from this marriage and previous ones.

But as they talked about the present, the ghost of Diana appeared as if on cue.

> I think Diana was in love with Dodi. I do. I couldn't believe it when I heard she died. I was doing a radio show and word came through that she'd been in a car accident and she was dead and I said no it can't be; she'll be fine.

Her friend nodded her head in what seemed to be disbelief that Diana was really gone. "My ex–mother-in-law was a huge Diana fan—had all those Franklin mint commemorative plates, you know? And I didn't know what was going on and I went over to her house and she was sobbing. I thought someone in the family had died." And in a way, someone had. Diana so thoroughly represented the perfect bride, the perfect mother, and the perfect royal that her death nearly destroyed our belief in fairy-tale romance. Support for the monarchy slipped, and it was difficult for anyone to believe in romance after the truth of her relationship with Charles was revealed.[23]

Fortunately, Kate and William had come along and everyone could get excited about the "commoner marrying a prince" part of the fairytale. A young black student from the US studying at Cambridge said, "It's a true life fairy-tale, isn't it? A commoner marrying a prince." Two white thirty-something stay-at-home wives from Huntington who had taken the train to London for the big day said the same. As one of them put it,

> This girl is becoming a princess today and that's part of it. I wonder what she thought this morning when she got up and shaved her legs—like, "Oh, I'm becoming a princess." Kate grew up normal. Everyone dreams of marrying a prince ... We all dream about it even though we know it's not true.

"But if we know it's not true, then why is it romantic?" I asked. The woman pointed to some friends who had come down with them. In the group were two little girls, seven and nine years old, dressed as fairy princesses, tiaras and all. "See them? That's why it's romantic," she answered. The girls were literally jumping up and down with excitement. "I want to see William kiss Kate. And her dress," one told me. "That's why we're here," her mother told her.

MARRYING ROMANCE AND EMPIRE

> The monarchy is finished. It was finished a while ago,
> but they're still making the corpses dance.
> Sue Townsend, English writer and humorist

It's not too much of a stretch to claim that weddings have always been central to state power, whether through royal weddings or the more recent insistence that political leaders confine their sexual practices to the conjugal bed. For many in the crowds at the royal wedding, the event was about the nation, not the heart. The night before the wedding, among the hundreds of diehard Will and Kate fans who were camping on the sidewalk, I met a man and a woman from Buckinghamshire who described themselves as Royalists. They shared their seemingly endless supply of beer and thoughts with me. Both were unemployed at the moment, but the woman had worked as a security guard over the years. They were not interested in the wedding per se, but in the royal family.

These two were decidedly not under the influence of romance. Although the woman had once had a white wedding, with a former partner, she did it for her family, not for herself. "Like Diana," she told me. "I even had a dress like she did." Indeed, these two pushed the love story aside as "made up" and, ultimately, "unimportant." She said, "We don't know a lot about their love story. We didn't hear anything about that till after the engagement. I think to be honest a lot of stuff in the press is crap. Who knows?"

The point wasn't the love story, but the reinvigoration of royalty and by extension all of Britain. She said,

> I love royalty. Mum and dad were very royalist. Anything to do with royalty I loved. I can remember when Diana and Charles got married. I was seventeen and working as a nanny so couldn't come down for it and had to

watch it on TV, and it was not what I wanted to be doing, watching it on TV while I got the kids supper...

This wedding is a good thing coming from bad [meaning Charles and Di]. A bit of safety for this country. The Queen is in charge of their own soldiers. If it weren't for them we'd go down this path where we'd have no rulers. She has her say. The Queen has her say about important matters, and has her advisors but she does what she thinks needs to be done...

We all protect [the Queen] because who would be in charge? Politicians?

Here the woman literally spat on the ground in disgust with the idea of elected officials being rulers of the state. But then she looked up again, her eyes shining with love for the royals, especially Diana.

I worked at Wembley Stadium with security, and royals would come to concerts. Diana came and they put me in charge of the royal box and I remember her coming back to the box and she was even more beautiful than you could even imagine. Even more beautiful than you could see in photos of her...

I came down for her funeral. We were just remembering her funeral... We need this couple. I don't know much about Kate.

Her male companion interjected, saying that Kate's "bringing some normality back to the royals—she's just kinda Joe Public." Then the woman swerved back to the people's princess:

Because Diana was such an average person when she died, they [the royals] missed her. They needed her. Harry and William will say hello to anyone. They were raised by Diana to be like that. Of all the girls he could have chosen he chose her. She's a real commoner. She has family who worked as miners. Her cousin runs a fish and chips shop. Things like that.

These two were hardly alone in their assessment of the wedding as a chance to reinvigorate the royal family. One family of Royalists told me that their religion is "God, Queen, and Country." Not surprisingly, this family had working-class accents and working-class jobs; being a Royalist in England is primarily associated with lower levels of education and income.[24] That's not to say that support for the royal family isn't high more generally. It is. About 80 percent of Brits support the monarchy according to most polls. But as an article in the *Economist* the week of the wedding pointed out, asking Brits whether they support the monarchy is too easy a question. Public resentment toward the royals rises when it appears they are too wealthy. The reason Diana was so popular is that she eschewed much of her upbringing—horses and hunting—to do "normal" things with her sons, like going to theme parks and beaches.[25] Of course I did run into some upper-class Royalists in the crowd. One thirty-something woman, stuck in a crowded fenced-in area alongside me and another couple of thousand people, told me that if there was one thing she hated more than the royal family, it was crowds. Asked why she was here, she pointed to her boyfriend and his family. "They love the royals." Her boyfriend's family were highly educated, consisting of a psychologist, an advertising executive, and a fund-raiser for a charity. The mother, in her late fifties, told me that she loved the royals so much that when Diana and Charles got married, when her children were young, they camped out to see it.

Typical of the love/hate relationship with fairy-tale weddings felt by many, the crowd expressed contradictory attitudes about the royals. On the one hand, there was a lot of love and support and a sense that the royal family was good for Britain. A twenty-something white Englishwoman in a cowboy hat with a bottle of open champagne told me, "It's a good day for the country because it gives everyone something to look forward to with the recession and all bringing us down." Just a few feet away in the crowd, a middle-aged white Englishwoman in a polka-dot dress expressed some class resentment, telling me that all the articles in the press describing Kate Middleton as a commoner were utter garbage. "You should watch *Meet the Middletons*," she told me conspiratorially. "A commoner? Humph." I asked her to explain what she meant. After all, *Meet the Middletons*, a Channel 4 series, was meant to show the class mobility of the Middleton family by giving us a glimpse into the future Queen's family tree, a tree that includes a lot of working-class sorts from hairdressers to grocery store managers. The point, the woman said, was that although she may have distant relatives who are commoners, Kate's family is rich, very rich, and she went to all the right schools and her mother practically raised her to marry William. Another middle-aged white Englishwoman solved the contradictions this way:

> A wedding is hopeful. It's good for us. It gives us something to feel good about. But the royals have to be approachable. Really, after Diana's death I didn't care about the royal family at all. But now with Kate and William, I think they'll be more approachable. More normal.

In other words, if the royal family can act as if they are just regular people, there is less class resentment, regardless of the actual income inequality that exists in the UK. But the moment the British get a whiff of elitism, support for the royal family and the royal wedding became much more shaky.[26] For the Americans I met, the display of extreme wealth merely signaled the celebrity status of the royal family. The royals were like our celebrities except they had crowns and tiaras. Or as one white woman, an American college student, put it, "The royals are just like our celebrities, but they're not douche bags the way celebrities are."

About a third of the more than one hundred people with whom I spoke in the wedding crowd said they were there because they wanted to support the royal family. They seemed less interested in the romance between Kate and William than in how their wedding would bolster support for the royals. The people who were there solely to support the monarchy—as opposed to being caught up in the fairy-tale romance of the couple—were much more likely to be working class than the ones there for the couple. They were also much more likely to be men or have men in their group.

This is not to say that the people there for the romance were not supportive of the monarchy. They were. In fact, during the entire day I only met one staunch republican who thought the monarchy should be abolished. Everyone supported the monarchy either as true believers who invested the royal family with the ability to bring Britain and even the world out of the mess it's in or as hardheaded pragmatists who saw the royals as good for tourism and good for Britain's reputation abroad. For a lot of people in the crowd that day, their love affair was with the royal family, and especially the idea of the British Empire, rather than with Kate and William. Support for the monarchy is at an all-time high in England and Wales, although it is strongest among Conservative and older voters. It is also extremely high among Americans, according to recent polls.[27]

All of this was crystal clear in the crowd. Nearly everyone there loved the Queen and the flag. People oohed and aahed as military regiments rode by on horseback. The palace itself was festooned with so much red, white, and blue that it made the crowd look drab in comparison. Just as soon as the now iconic kiss on the balcony took place, the crowd was treated to a display of British military prowess. Three planes from World War II—the Lancaster, the Spitfire, and the Hurricane—flew over. Then more modern fighter jets—the Typhoons and Tornadoes—roared through the sky. I didn't know any of the names of the planes, but a white Englishman standing next to me was explaining it to his towheaded sons, telling them what a great country they live in and that they should be proud.

HAPPILY EVER AFTER AND OTHER CONTRADICTIONS

> Why should we care to know that the naggingly persistent contradictions of the romantic sentiment have assumed the cultural forms and languages of the market?
>
> Eva Illouz, *Consuming the Romantic Utopia*, 1997

Modern love is far more contradictory than a Disney film would have it. Modern love, like the ongoing struggle between our inner cynic and our inner romantic, is a bit of a mess. It goes off on tangents, undermines itself, and even falls back in love with itself again. Even at the royal wedding of Kate Middleton and Prince William—the most iconic and highly choreographed wedding ever—there were undercurrents that not all is as it seems. There were two aspects of the royal wedding that complicated its telling. The first was a queering of the event; the second was a kind of

British snarkiness, what Eva Illouz or Max Weber would call disenchantment, that made even the most diehard fans of royalty and romance smirk.

Royal Queers

I am not the first to point out that there is a strange relationship between gay men and white weddings. As Chrys Ingraham argues in *White Weddings,*

> The use of the gay character as cipher in the service of heterosexuality is a theme prevalent in many films and television shows. As battles over the legitimacy of homosexuality and human rights for gays ... are fought out in a wide variety of political arenas today, the contradictory use of gay characters speaks to a state of ambivalence about the institution of heterosexuality and the legitimacy of homosexuality.[28]

That was certainly true for Kate and William's wedding. Although the crowd was overwhelmingly female, about 20 percent or so of the crowd were men. Some of these men were husbands or sons who seemed to be there not out of their own interest, but for their women. Some of the men were avid supporters of the royal family and saw this marriage as a way to solidify the importance of the royals and by extension England. Some were just there for a party. But of the men I interviewed, about a third were gay, and they were there for the wedding.

A thirty-something white lesbian from Leeds pointed to her white gay male companion when asked why she was here. "He forced me to come down. Gay men are loving this." She herself had had a big white wedding with her ex-partner and didn't want that again. Of course, so did he with his ex-partner, and he was not interested in staging that sort of event for himself again either. But he couldn't wait to see this wedding, and especially the dress. One young white gay man I interviewed told me that he shouldn't be there at all and that I was absolutely honor bound not to use his name since he was a Catholic from Northern Ireland. He laughed and said, "My family would kill me if they knew I were here, really, my dad would actually kill me. But I want a big white wedding . . . I'd like to marry Prince Harry actually."

The entire event was brought to American audiences on TLC by two gay icons, Clinton Kelly and Randy Fenoli. Fenoli is famous for his role as wedding expert extraordinaire on the reality TV show *Say Yes to the Dress* and about as gay as two grooms on a wedding cake. Kelly and his husband, Damon Bayles, are often mentioned in celebrity publications. It is not unusual for openly gay men to play the role of telling us what is stylish and what is not. But for gay men to narrate, to make meaningful, a set of events like the royal wedding for an American audience also undercut that very wedding because gay men could not yet get married in the United States. Although a handful of states, like Massachusetts and New York, allowed same-sex marriage, the Defense of Marriage Act meant that no such union could be recognized at the federal level; it would be another four years before the Supreme Court would recognize gay marriage. Americans were, having been subjected to nearly two decades of protest and litigation around same sex-sex marriage, acutely aware of this. To watch as gay men gushed about a wedding, a wedding in which they themselves could not participate, made clear to all the viewers that love is not all you need. You also need legal rights. It was a lesson that dreams can come true, but not for everyone.

The Disenchantment of Snark

Although the gay men I interviewed and the gay men on screen were genuine in their love for weddings, all weddings, much of England was in a more impertinent mood. Londoners walked around in T-shirts that said, "Just another bank holiday." The *Guardian* had special updates for royal wedding "haters." The *Guardian* also ran a sarcastic op-ed claiming that despite their long support for ending the monarchy, seeing the movie *The King's Speech* had changed their mind since

> there are times when only the calming leadership of a hereditary monarch will do; and as the MPs' expenses scandal illustrates, it can be dangerous to

trust power-hungry elected officials, who lack the security provided by land ownership and immense wealth... The marriage of a prince to a commoner—a true bridging of class divides, if ever there was one—represents the perfect moment for progressives to commit again to the promise of hereditary monarchy.

Of course, the article was run on the first of April, and was part of a much broader cultural impulse to mock the royal wedding.[29] A series of TV shows continued the national mockery of the wedding and the royals, including *The Royal Wedding Crashers* and even that week's *My Big Fat Gypsy Wedding*, a reality show that follows "travelers" from Romany and Irish backgrounds (broadcast on TLC in the US).

The day after the wedding I decided to go to some anti–royal wedding burlesque; I had several different ones to choose from. I went to the one billed as "Not the Royal Wedding Night." I paid my money at a small box office on Oxford Street and descended into a black box theater with a bar. Among a crowd of about a hundred of London's hippest hipsters, I listened as act after act sent up the wedding hysteria. The line that stuck with me most, perhaps because I was seemingly the only Yank in the theater that night, was this:

Well at least the Americans are happy. That's really who we did the wedding for. The Americans think we live in a Medieval Theme Park. Women are all dressed as serving wenches and the men are eating big chicken legs that they throw over their shoulders.

But it wasn't just the Americans that were happy. So was everyone else that day at the royal wedding, all million of us, plus or minus a few thousand. And that is in fact the point.

WHAT'S LOVE GOT TO DO WITH IT?

The totality of beliefs and sentiments common to the average members of a society forms a determinate system with a life of its own. It can be termed the collective ... consciousness.
Émile Durkheim, *The Division of Labor in Society,* 1893

Claiming that the royal wedding of Kate Middleton to Prince William was an assertion of privilege embedded in race, heteronormativity, and empire is a sociology of the obvious. But here's a less obvious claim: that's not all it was about. The royal wedding was also about authentic human feelings of connection. Indeed, even as privilege depends on ideologies like romance and nationalism to erase the violence and exploitation upon which it rests, privilege cannot erase the authentic human emotions that its own propaganda produces. In other words, just because romance is an ideology that privileges whiteness and wealth doesn't mean that it isn't also experienced as real emotion, often by the very people excluded from its rewards. This was certainly the case at the royal wedding. That's because authentic human emotion doesn't exist in some power-free plane, but rather right here in a world where racial, national, and sexual hierarchies produce not just romance, but the very real feelings of happiness and well-being that so often accompany it.

The crowd seemed unanimously happy about the wedding of Kate and William on that particular day. People were genuinely moved by the service, which was broadcast along the route on loudspeakers and on large TV screens in nearby parks. A lot of the wedding-goers bought programs and sang along with the hymns. Real tears flowed from most people's eyes as they listened to the young couple's vows to love one another. By the time the carriages came along the processional route to Buckingham Palace, people were not just waving flags, they were genuinely happy for this couple, for England, but more importantly, for love and marriage. As the carriages roared by and the crowd cheered, I too felt happy and hopeful. It was impossible not to. There is something about a million people believing, a million people sensing something positive and true and real that *is* real. It was greater than adding up the wishes of all those individual well-wishers. It was something sociologist Émile Durkheim described as an excess of energy, something more than the sum of individuals, something bigger, a collective consciousness.[30] And this collective consciousness of happiness and optimism and romance seeped into my body like tear gas thrown into a crowd.

Interviewing a retired schoolteacher from London, I was struck by the way this sixty-year-old white woman, equally well versed in political philosophy and romcoms, understood romance as a necessary human emotion in conditions of postmodernity. She told me that Karl Marx had it wrong when he said religion was the opiate of the masses. It was celebrity. Celebrity distracts us from the material reality of our lives.

> I've met little children who want to be rich and famous. These days there's no glamour left. We don't know anything about the Queen, do we? She's managed to stay above it all. I hope they will too. They say they're going to keep them out of the public eye for a while.

Unlike celebrity, romance makes us feel better.

> When we watch those [romantic] films we do feel better, don't we? We're bombarded day in and day out with so much bad news ... Such a lot of bad news in the world and this was good news.

This woman, a socialist to her core, was very aware and critical of the structural inequalities that make the perfect white wedding possible. As was I. But sitting on a bench in the sun, drinking a pint, and toasting the young couple, she and I were also genuinely moved by the experience. It was, at that moment, a happily ever after.

Sadly, happiness is always a fleeting emotion. And by the end of the summer, there was a definite sense that even Kate and Wills couldn't keep our spirits up. The US was not a very happy place compared to other countries.[31] We had been given our royal wedding, the one to imitate for the next twenty years, the very image of perfection, and still we moped. We had our perfect bride, so thin and beautiful that she looked exactly like a Disney princess. We had our groom, so handsome and charming in his red military uniform that he looked like a Disney prince. We had a love story that fit our newer, more egalitarian notions of the perfect match, more Mulan than Cinderella. And yet there was something about the days after the wedding that felt like a letdown. All that perfection for the big day, but then Kate and William were forced to delay their honeymoon because of security concerns. And really, maybe the bride's sister, Pippa, her Royal Hotness according to the tabloids, was more beautiful? And like every big party, there was the sickening realization the next day of how much the whole thing cost. Although the wedding probably generated an extra $80 million in revenue for London (with extra hotels, souvenirs, restaurant meals, etc.), it also cost about $35 million in extra policing alone. Not only that, but because of the extra days off created by the wedding, it probably cost the British economy about $50 billion in loss of productivity, or a quarter of a percent of the GDP.[32]

Somehow, by the time I arrived back in the states, the sense of endless romantic possibilities that the royal wedding seemed to evoke was nowhere to be found. It felt as if we were already jonesing for the next big celebrity wedding to inject us with happiness, romance, and the promise of perfection. But all we had were some D-list celebrities to keep us going. Kim Kardashian, who married NBA star Kris Humphries, tried her best to feed our addiction to fairy-tale weddings with, according to *People* magazine, "three couture gowns, 50,000 flowers and $15 million worth of diamonds." Words like "perfect" and "fairy-tale" infused the press coverage of the August 20 event. But Kim Kardashian is no Kate Middleton. At that time, Kim was best known for a reality TV show based on America's obsession with the superrich, *Keeping Up with the Kardashians*. Rather than making us feel optimistic and as if we too might marry a prince, or at least an NBA star, Kardashian's wedding served as a reminder that since 1980 most Americans have been getting poorer.[33] As of 2011, the top 1 percent of the population controlled 40 percent of the wealth.[34]

Part of it was that the Kardashian-Humphries relationship seemed doomed from the beginning. She didn't like his dogs; he hated paparazzi.[35] But Kardashians exist to be photographed and dog-people, when forced to choose, generally pick Rover over Beloved. Yet there was something deeper, more depressing, about the lavishness of the affair. The Kardashian-Humphries wedding made us realize that we are far less likely to be able to afford a perfect wedding now than our parents were. Not just because we're poorer, but because the cost of a perfect wedding itself has risen exponentially. Now one gown isn't really enough. We need two or three, like Kim. A groom's cake is added to the reception. Certain cosmetic procedures, like teeth whitening, are de rigueur. Other cosmetic procedures, like Botox or even boob jobs or Kim's rumored butt implants, are increasingly part of normal wedding expenditures. This fact was driven home with the airing of *Bridalplasty,* a reality TV show on E! that ran the same month that William and Kate announced their engagement. On *Bridalplasty,* primarily working-class, white, blond and blue-eyed brides competed for different cosmetic procedures, from nose jobs to breast implants, and for the ultimate prize of a $200,000 dream wedding. As contestants got eliminated, they were told, "You're still getting married, your wedding just won't be perfect."[36] What cruel words for the contestants and for us, the viewers. These words signaled to the viewers that our weddings, too, are unlikely to be perfect unless we can spend hundreds of thousands of dollars on everything from flowers to going under the knife. And if our weddings aren't perfect, how can our marriages be?

As if *Bridalplasty* weren't enough to bring us down, seventy-two short days after Kim Kardashian staged her perfect wedding, her marriage to Humphries was over.[37] Maybe Kardashian was suffering from what is now labeled postnuptial depression, a condition that may affect as many as one in ten brides.[38] Postnuptial depression is that flat feeling that just won't go away on the morning after what is supposed to be the happiest day of our lives. I was pretty sure I had it in spades. Drinking coffee out of my royal wedding mug one day, a few months after the royal wedding, it hit me. What I really needed was a break from the monotony of real life and the debt I had gone into to be part of that most perfect day in London. I needed an excursion into a fairy-tale land. What I needed after the wedding of the century was the honeymoon of a lifetime. And so I decided to go on a research trip to the most magical place on earth, the place more Americans choose for their honeymoons than anywhere else in the continental US, the place where dreams are made. I decided to go to Disney World.

CHAPTER FIVE

The Honeymoon

Our honeymoon will shine our life long; its beams will only
fade over your grave or mine.

Charlotte Brontë, *Jane Eyre*, 1847

Whether it's a royal wedding or a commoner's, the ritual requires large
expenditures of time and money. Since at least the 1920s, the wedding
industry has convinced engaged couples that a "perfect" wedding is a
necessary part of romantic well-being.[1] Although the standards for that
perfection have changed dramatically, the manufactured demand to
have a "perfect" wedding remains, with 63 percent of brides in a 2016
survey saying they felt pressured to do so. In order to have the perfect
wedding, you have to plan, with most engaged couples (mostly the
women) spending hundreds of hours to research everything from venues to caterers to dresses.[2] In fact, brides-to-be are often so pressured
to plan the perfect wedding that they steal hours from their employer.
In one survey, nearly 90 percent of brides admitted to wedding planning at work, and nearly a third said their wedding planning negatively
affected their work performance.[3]

So much planning can apparently leave the young couple completely
exhausted and stressed. Fortunately, capitalism and romance have
invented the perfect antidote to wedding burnout: the honeymoon. The
theme of the honeymoon as the reward for all that wedding planning is
evident in nearly all of the bridal magazine websites. *The Knot* insists that

"after months of wedding planning, your honeymoon is the time to sit back, relax and let it go," and "the honeymoon is your hard-earned reward after months of wedding planning."[4] *Brides* magazine echoes similar concern for the poor, unfortunate newlyweds. The honeymoon allows you to "enjoy each other with all the planning and stress behind you."[5] In fact *Brides* is so worried about the horrors of wedding planning that they encourage couples to take a honeymoon before they ever even get married, an "earlymoon," because "when it comes to weddings, everyone always talks about the honeymoon you're going to take after the ceremony. But, with all the stress involved in the planning process, wouldn't it make sense to take a break before walking down the aisle?" Kate Middleton's sister, Pippa, apparently took an earlymoon with her then fiancé James Matthews.[6] Although there is little evidence of this public health epidemic of "wedding planning stress" in *Black Brides* magazine, it is evident in *Equally Wed,* an online magazine for LGBTQ couples. In fact, *Equally Wed* created yet another "moon" vacation, telling couples that when they get engaged they should go on an "engagementmoon," since "planning a wedding can be very stressful." So, "before jumping into the planning, go away with your new fiancé."[7]

Nearly 100 percent of straight couples and 57 percent of same-sex couples who have weddings go on at least a honeymoon, if not an earlymoon. That's about 1.4 million US couples per year.[8] After the royal wedding, Kate and William spent ten days on North Island in the Seychelles in a $5,000/night beachside bungalow.[9] The average honeymoon takes months to plan, and the average couple in the US spends $4,000 on their honeymoon, or about 11 percent of the $37,000 total wedding cost.[10] That is more than twice what the average US household will spend on a vacation, which makes sense given that a honeymoon is marked as "sacred" and "once in a lifetime," whereas a vacation can happen every year, at least for the 45 percent of Americans lucky enough to be able to take one.[11] All this honeymooning, engagementmooning, and earlymooning is part of the global trade in tourism, the sixth largest industry in the world, accounting for about $7.6 trillion a year. To put that in perspective, global tourism produces about the same amount of global trade as agriculture.[12]

All this money is meant to produce the pure bliss and pleasure that is in the very name "honeymoon," a period of "unusual harmony," according to standard usage. Yet we seem to have some cultural anxiety about honeymoons. Movies about honeymoons often feature a less-than-happy ending. In the 1942 film *Once upon a Honeymoon,* Ginger Rogers's character, Kate O'Hara, marries a fabulously wealthy Austrian baron. Unfortunately, the baron is involved with the Nazis. The bride accidentally kills her husband and ends up with the always-dashing Cary Grant, as American reporter Pat O'Toole. The ending saves democracy, but not the marriage plot. In the 1953 film *Niagara,* Marilyn Monroe plays a honeymooner who is trying to make her husband appear mad so that her lover can murder him and make it look like suicide. Many other honeymoon-themed movies contain some seriously rough patches, like 2003's *Just Married,* where the star-crossed lovers find that their class differences split them up during the honeymoon (they are reunited later). The 2014 horror film *Honeymoon* imbues this most beautiful of times with "groomicide" when the alien-infected bride drowns her beloved.

If honeymoons make us anxious as a culture, perhaps it is because we know that the honeymoon magic always comes to an end. And when it does, some people even experience "postnuptial depression." So many people, especially women, spend months and even years planning the perfect day and then going off onto the perfect vacation that many arrive home after the honeymoon to find that the magic of being "engaged" or being a "bride and groom" has disappeared and all that is left is the "void in their lives when it comes to an end."[13] Perhaps this anxiety about the honeymoon ending is why one of the most popular honeymoon destinations is also "the happiest place on earth," Florida's Disney World.[14] Disney World is the most popular vacation resort in the world, with 52.5 million people visiting annually. It includes the Magic Kingdom as well as Epcot, Disney's Hollywood Studios, and Disney's Animal Kingdom.

In order to figure out why newlyweds would be so drawn to a place marked as "for children" and therefore not obviously a site of eroticized leisure, I traveled to Disney World in the summer of 2012. There I interviewed thirteen couples about their weddings, but also about their hopes for their honeymoons. As more than one person told me, going to Disney for their honeymoon was a way to "keep the magic going." In other words, Disney, as the primary propaganda machine for the ideology of romance, is a safe place, a happy place where the future is always bright as long as we find our true love. The romance of Disney disguises real material relationships like labor conditions for the workers and the environmental impact of the resort, replacing them with enchantment and excitement. In order to get to Disney, though, we have to take short detour through the Poconos and Niagara Falls.

NIAGARA FALLS, THE POCONOS, AND DISNEY WORLD

Niagara Falls, Honeymoon Capital of the World.
   Infoniagara.com

In the Pocono Mountains, we know a thing or two about romance.
   Pocono Mountains slogan

The most magical place on Earth.
   Magic Kingdom slogan

Many people imagine that the honeymoon has been around since the invention of marriage. The honeymoon seems so obvious: a time for couples to get to know each other as lovers, in an erotic and magical space in which the new Mr. and Mrs. can explore each other's bodies as well as new landscapes. Nothing could be further from the truth. Like most things that Love, Inc., convinces us are "natural" and "traditional," honeymoons are a fairly recent invention. Nothing like the current honeymoon existed until well into the nineteenth century and, even then, it only existed for wealthy couples. These posh newlyweds spent their honeymoons in the most unsexy way imaginable: traveling to different relatives accompanied by an entire retinue of family members. It was only at the end of the 1800s that newlyweds started going off on their own. As Kris Bulcroff et al. put it in their look at the cultural production of honeymoons,

> The honeymoon, as we know it today as a private retreat from social contacts and obligations, is a relatively modern invention. Although there have always been customs surrounding the wedding night ... the emphasis on the private nature of the honeymoon is only a little more than one hundred years old.[15]

This shift from family affair to a private time for the couple occurred alongside the shift in marriage from arranged to companionate. It also occurred alongside increasing anxiety about the ignorance of virgin brides and their need for sexual initiation.[16] Still, a very small number of people tying the knot could actually take a honeymoon, which became a more widespread practice only in the 1920s. As more and more Americans had access to automobiles, newlyweds often had the ability to drive to a rustic cabin or a hotel near Niagara Falls for a few days.[17]

Even in the Victorian era, Niagara Falls was a highly eroticized location, with the pounding water as a (bad) metaphor for heterosexual intercourse. Perhaps it was the erotic charge that moved so many people to not just take the plunge and get married, but to literally plunge over the falls. Annie Edson Taylor was the first person to go over the 170-foot falls in a barrel in 1901, although she was moved to take this plunge for purely financial, not romantic, reasons.[18] As Karen Dubinsky points out in her account of honeymooning at Niagara Falls, the space became even more sexualized in the 1920s as heterosexuality itself became more celebrated.[19] During World War II, Niagara Falls became the "spot for brief and affordable honeymoons for servicemen and their brides," and after the war it became a popular destination for those looking for a honeymoon on a budget, a place where many couples experienced their "first hotel stay, their first restaurant meal, their first glass of wine."[20]

Even when honeymoons were fairly simple affairs like a drive to upstate New York, the politics around them were always complex. Whether in a cabin in the woods or at a hotel in a city, there were always both racial and financial barriers to taking a honeymoon. Most resorts did not allow blacks or Jews to stay at them for the first half of the twentieth century.[21] Over time, however, as jet travel became more accessible and racial barriers were lowered, more and more newlyweds found the time and money for a honeymoon.

No longer looking for just natural beauty or a restaurant meal, the restless honeymooners of the 1950s and 1960s wanted an all-inclusive experience in which they could enjoy being recognized as "newlyweds" and having constant activities and entertainment. In the postwar years, honeymooners wanted not just to escape, but also to be entertained. This production of honeymoon as spectacular and also widely available was invented in a heart-shaped tub in the Poconos, the most popular honeymoon destination during the middle decades of the twentieth century. The Poconos resort "The Farm" was the first honeymoon-themed resort in the post–World War II marriage boom. At The Farm, Christian, white, and, of course, heterosexual couples could be with other couples just like them for their honeymoon experience. There they could enjoy a variety of activities, from horseback riding to tennis, and then take in a show in the evening. As Cele Otnes and Elizabeth Pleck point out, this gathering of honeymooners prepared them for their new life in the newly forming suburbs: "It was time spent with married couples of one's own age, education, and social status ... also ... mainly white, Christian clientele, since resorts in the Poconos discriminated against both blacks and Jews."[22]

The Poconos resorts invented the honeymoon as a particular sort of vacation, one marked not just by the sacred state of "just married" and time together, but by being with other couples for constant entertainment and activity. The Poconos honeymoon resorts also invented the "all-inclusive" price, thereby relieving couples from having to think about the dirt of money while enjoying their postnuptial bliss. A

Poconos honeymoon was a mass-produced experience, one that removed all the surprises of a journey and replaced them with a highly rationalized and highly produced "experience." As Bulcroff et al. put it: "Honeymoons have long been fantasies. Yet, society has only recently been able to mass produce and market honeymoon fantasies, thereby making them a more depersonalized set of expectations and symbolic representations that are necessary components of the fantasy."[23] Since then, many newlyweds have been drawn to this highly planned and produced experience. Today's honeymooners book all-inclusive packages at Caribbean honeymoon resorts like Sandals or drive to the Poconos, where honeymooners can still enjoy a heart-shaped tub. As this sort of experience has become more democratized, many wealthier newlyweds seek extremely unusual locations for their honeymoons. Whether camping in Alaska, taking a safari in Kenya, or taking a bubble bath in a heart-shaped tub in the Poconos, honeymooners continue to want to create, consume, and record "memories." These honeymoon memories are meant to be, like true love, once in a lifetime and magical.

And although elites might go off the beaten path to memorialize their honeymoon, the most popular destinations by far remain Hawaii and Florida, especially Disney World. Disney World, alongside Las Vegas, became the most popular domestic US honeymoon destination in the 1990s, attracting about one in six newlyweds. In part, this was due to a Disney advertising campaign exhorting adults to "remember the magic" as well as the company's ability to provide a honeymoon of manufactured memories with no or at least very low risk. At the Disney "honeymoons" website, an engaged couple can fantasize about how "on a magical Disney honeymoon, you'll dine like royalty, dream in luxurious accommodations, sit together on thrilling attractions and enjoy spectacular firework shows. Get ready for a honeymoon filled with wonder and delight—where every day has a fairy-tale ending."[24] As Otnes and Pleck put it,

> Many couples preferred the excitement, the shopping, and the restaurants of Disney World ... They wanted a supercharged version of the Internet-, media-, and image-driven world they inhabited, but one that was safe,

clean, festive, and friendly and offered restaurant dining … A few hours spent at Epcot provides tourists with the experience of a trip abroad without lost luggage, rude cab drivers, or strange food.[25]

Not that Disney World is for everyone. After all, it is not cheap. A room for June 2018 cost $150 a night at the All-Star Sports Resort and nearly $700 a night at Disney's Polynesian Village Resort. Then there's the price of theme parks (which is about $80 per person per day), as well as meals, drinks, and the romantic fireworks cruise (about $350 per hour).[26] Disney theme parks and resorts rake in about $4.3 billion annually, with a good chunk of those visitors on their honeymoon, engagementmoon, or celebrating a wedding anniversary or having a destination wedding at the Wedding Pavilion.[27]

Getting married and honeymooning in the same place has grown in popularity, more than doubling since 2000, with one out of four weddings now a destination wedding.[28] In 1991, Disney World began offering destination weddings in their specially designed building, situated to have a view of Cinderella Castle and offering everything from the groom riding in on a white horse to the bride arriving in a "glass" carriage. When I arrived at the Wedding Pavilion on a hot and steamy day in July—planning the perfect wedding as part of my research—it was under construction. Like much of Disney World and certain Catholic cathedrals, it felt like a work in progress, a place where perfection was always eternally delayed. Inside, the building was all polished wood and decorative flourishes There were no crosses or signs of any religion other than romance, consistent with the fact that fewer than a third of American weddings now take place in a church, synagogue, or other religious space.[29] The Wedding Pavilion is especially popular since guests can marry at any time of the day that suits them. Couples can also get married inside Disney World itself, but it has to be while the park is closed—before 9 A.M. or after 9 P.M.

At the Wedding Pavilion, I learn that for about $30,000, a couple can have seventy-five to a hundred guests. According to the staff, most of their weddings run between $25,000 and $30,000. If you exclude the cost of flying to Orlando and staying in the park, a Disney wedding is certainly within the national average and, conveniently, the couple (and their wedding party) are already at one of the world's most popular honeymoon destinations. Of course, weddings can run as high as $100,000 at Disney, but such weddings typically involve a lot of extras like the wedding party arriving in horse-drawn carriages and having Disney characters at the reception. Flipping through the wedding photographs in a book sitting on a table in the Wedding Pavilion, I note how all of couples pictured are white and straight. And young. I ask the women working there if they ever have older brides, since I am in my late forties at this point. They assure me that lots of women in their fifties and sixties have their weddings at Disney and that many of them want to arrive in Cinderella's coach as well. I forget to ask about same-sex couples, which is strange since I am a lesbian, but when I go to the Disney Weddings website later that night, I find that it is easy to plan a same-sex wedding with two brides or two grooms.

My imaginary Disney destination wedding would cost about $35,000, and that includes all the magic of fireworks over Cinderella Castle and special fireworks in the shape of Minnie and Mickey Mouse. But as I walked to my rental car in the sweltering heat of a July day, I could not help but wonder why anyone would want to get married there. Admittedly, I am a sociologist and a gender theorist by trade. I make my living keeping a certain ironic distance from highly produced and commercial spaces. I realize there are many writers much smarter than I who embrace the unrealness of the place, the fact that Disney is, in the words of philosopher Jean Baudrillard, a copy without an original. For Baudrillard,

> Disneyland is a perfect model of all the entangled orders of simulation. To begin with it is a play of illusions and phantasms ... Disneyland imaginary is neither true nor false: it is a deterrence machine set up in order to rejuvenate in reverse the fiction of the real ... It's meant to be an infantile world, in order to make us believe that the adults are elsewhere, in the "real world," and to conceal the fact that real childishness is everywhere, particularly among those adults who go there to act the child.[30]

But it was exactly this childishness that gnawed at me. Why would adults staging their wedding, a ritual that has always marked entrance into adulthood, want to arrive in Cinderella's carriage from an animated film for children based on a fairy-tale? Why would they pay extra to have a wedding where they could see Cinderella Castle, which is also a copy without an original? In my fieldnotes, I wrote: "Why infantilize weddings? Isn't wedding about become adult?" Understanding why Disney World is one of the most romantic spots on Earth is a mystery that can best be solved by situating this very unreal place in the reality of US culture and history.

ROMANCE AS REAL

> Disneyland exists in order to hide that it is the "real" country ... Disneyland is presented as imaginary in order to make us believe that the rest is real.
>
> Jean Baudrillard, *Simulacra and Simulation,* 1981

The reasons couples spend thousands of dollars to honeymoon in a crowded park full of crying small children and the heat of hell are complicated. Partly it is, as others have suggested, the manufactured and highly controlled experiences at Disney, experiences that can be collected, documented, and brought home after the excitement of a wedding to remind couples of the special magic that enchants their own relationship. Partly it is that Disney is contained in ways that make anyone too different from the paying customers invisible. Poor people cannot get into the park, except as workers, and even they are kept from showing the signs of their labor with an elaborate system of underground tunnels that can hide the "dirt" of making the park run and thus keep the "magic" alive. Even when minimum-wage workers are close to passing out from the heat of wearing the heavy costumes of various Disney characters, they are forbidden from taking off the heads of their costumes and must instead just collapse and hope the Disney-fied ambulance crew, also in costume, takes them down below to cool off and rehydrate.[31] In this way, Disney is *like* a wedding: the couple gets to be special and to avoid being exposed to anything or anyone that would upset them, like workers passing out from the heat or evil and cynical villains trying to destroy their love. Disney is also like a wedding in that it is a symbolic representation of whiteness—both literal and figurative—as clean, pure, and innocent.

Disney as a franchise creates nostalgia for an imaginary past and a longing for a highly technical future that is closely intertwined with whiteness. Louis Marin described the space of Disney parks as replaying "the ideology of America's dominant groups."[32] Disney can take a minstrel figure like Uncle Remus, turn it into one of its most iconic (if now largely censored) films, *Song of the South* (1946), and then morph this minstrel show into one of its most popular rides, Splash Mountain. Despite the fact that Disney pulled the movie from circulation more than twenty-five years ago, Splash Mountain uses the characters from *Song of the South,* including Br'er Rabbit, in a way that both replays the minstrelsy of the original film and washes it clean of its blackface origins.[33] Splash Mountain, according to Jason Sperb, reflects "the state of race relations in America over the last sixty years ... a racially sanitized commercial venture ready for popular consumption."[34]

It is not just Splash Mountain, however, that engages in a project of white forgetting. Disney's reconstruction of "Main Street" in its parks as both safe and innocent requires an erasure of Jim Crow segregation and the white violence that kept it in place in the real Florida. The racialized origins of small-town America are a rewritten at Disney World as clean, innocent, and safe. As James Baldwin famously pointed out, white America always insists it is innocent, and it is this innocence more than anything else that "constitutes the crime."[35] At Disney, the crime of white racial innocence is turned into a spectacle mobilized to construct both childhood innocence and the innocence of the virgin bride. Needless to say, both the innocent child and virgin bride are already imagined as white.[36]

Disney produces whiteness as safety and "niceness" through representations of the past and the future. Epcot is meant to represent the future, a future made better through technology, not romance. The name itself means Experimental Prototype Community of Tomorrow. Built as if it were a world's fair, Epcot mixes displays of technological prowess in Future World with representations of world cultures at the World Showcase. Originally Walt Disney had designed Epcot as a planned community for twenty thousand actual residents, one where every aspect of daily life would be controlled, including who could live there and who could not. Walt Disney's Epcot community imagined the future as not just white and centered around nuclear families, but also young, since retirees were excluded as well.[37] Together, both Epcot and the Magic Kingdom, which focuses on childhood and magic, represent a fantasy about the future. At Epcot, tomorrow is made safe through modern technologies as well as a freezing of world cultures into contained and highly sanitized symbols that can be consumed without any danger of contagion.[38] At the Magic Kingdom, Mickey leads a parade down Main Street as fireworks explode over Cinderella Castle, and everyone, from young children to aging lovers, can imagine riding off into the sunset to live happily ever after.

All of this innocence and whiteness are on full display at Disney's Fairy Tale Weddings and Honeymoons *Ever After Blog.* An analysis of the site on three days in July 2017 revealed that nearly all the brides and grooms were white. For instance, on one day, of the first 52 images of people, 50 out of 52 were white (with one Asian American couple who got engaged at Disney). Ninety percent of the brides were white in the first ten images of brides. Not only is racial innocence played out on the blog, but so is what might be called "gender innocence." All the couples on the site were normatively gendered and there were no same-sex couples. Patriarchal gender roles—such as fathers giving away daughters to husbands, women bent over backwards being held up by men, women standing on one leg, and the infantilization of women by being compared to "Disney princesses"—appeared in nearly every image of weddings and engagements. Many of the suggested costumes, settings, and even wedding cakes play out childhood as a permanent state, for instance, a Peter Pan–themed wedding cake with "never grow up" written on it or a proposal based on the Disney film *Tangled*. Romance is told both through stories, like "Fraternity boy meets sorority girl—a classic story," to words like "magic" and "fairy-tale come true." Excluding "Magic Kingdom," "magic" came up five times in five stories about couples getting married or engaged at Disney World. The word "dream" also came up in each description of the young couples. Phrases like "always dreamed" and "dream come true" reinforce the sense that these couples had no choice but to play out the scripts of romance with each other and at Disney. It was fated like the love between Sleeping Beauty and Prince Phillip, who knew each other "once upon a dream." The blog also uses the symbols of romance—castles, rose petals, white dresses, candlelight, fireworks—to further erase how the romance of Disney, which is primarily a product to be sold, also sells the ideology of romance, an ideology of innocence and forgetting when it comes to both race and gender hierarchies.[39]

This visual representation of Disney World honeymoons is fairly consistent with the fieldwork I conducted. Yet, as is often the case, speaking with real people produced far more nuanced and complex narratives of the pleasures of honeymooning in the most magical place on earth. The pleasure for many of the couples I interviewed was not just about a nostalgic whiteness and rigid gender roles (although there were elements of this as well), but also about creating alternative models of masculinity where men can show emotion and deepening connections beyond the couple into larger networks. Over the course of three days in July 2012, I went to Disney World and the Epcot Center. I saw very few nonwhite people in the parks, especially Epcot. On one day, I saw only one black family in six hours. On another day, counting a crowd of one hundred, 80 percent appeared to be white. I saw a few same-sex couples, but did not see any same-sex couples visibly on a honeymoon. I did see a lot of mostly white and straight people celebrating either their honeymoon or their anniversary. They were, as fieldwork goes, fairly easy to spot since they wore various sartorial signifiers of their special status. Those celebrating anniversaries wore giant pins announcing the year of their anniversary, and newlyweds wore special groom and bride mouse ears.[40] The mouse ears, which sell at the Disney Store website for $21.99, come in black for him and white for her. The groom's ears feature a "playful Tuxedo" while the bridal ears feature a veil and a tiara.

What I did not see was the "magic" or the "romance." According to my fieldnotes, it was over 100 degrees Fahrenheit during the time I was there, and my clothes were melting into my skin. The parks were crowded and I had to be on constant guard to avoid being hit by parents pushing strollers or people on motorized scooters. Children were crying, parents were yelling, and the staff looked exhausted. The food I bought was pricey, but not particularly good, and the bathrooms were filthy. I could not imagine it as a space to have romantic memories with my partner. It was loud, crowded, child-centered, and manufactured. Yet, according to the people I interviewed, this was the most romantic place on earth. How to account for our radically different experiences of the same space? Perhaps the best answer to that question is that the promise of romance—that the future can be secure—requires the sense of control and familiarity that Disney offers, one magic moment at a time.

ROMANCING THE MOUSE

> Disney and romance go together ... You can't think of Disney
> and not be reminded of the beautiful love stories that weave
> their way into most every Disney animated classic, setting
> our hearts a flutter and making us swoon. It's no wonder then
> that Disney World ... is ... [so] romantic.
>   Kelly B. on the Disney Fanatic site, 2015

I interviewed thirteen couples, eleven of them on their honeymoons and two of them celebrating their anniversaries. All of the honeymooning couples were in their twenties or early thirties. They were all college-educated, some with advanced degrees. Except for one bride who was black, and one groom who was Asian American, they were all white.

Three couples identified as "very religious" (Christian Evangelical or Catholic). They were mostly from the Midwest or California. Their professions were highly gendered, with eight of the thirteen women being teachers (mostly elementary school) and seven of the men being either engineers or in IT. In other words, they were, statistically, exactly the sort of people who have big white weddings and go off on a honeymoon afterward.

Most of the couples I interviewed thought Disney World was so romantic because it allowed for an extension of both childhood and the "magic" of their wedding and engagement. They also found the ability to "travel" without actually leaving the US to be very appealing. As one worker at Disney told me, "Honeymooners love to go to Epcot in the evening because they can drink around the world. They start off in Canada and end up in China." Most importantly, what the couples found romantic was the connection between the physical space of Disney World, particularly its fantasy architecture and the ambience of "real-life" characters walking through the crowd, and the stories they had grown up watching. Everyone, including the men, had a favorite Disney movie—and all of those movies were about finding true love and thereby having a safe, secure, and happy tomorrow.

For all the honeymooners I interviewed, part of the "magic" of Disney World was how they were treated as "special" there. In this way, a Disney honeymoon allowed them to prolong the enchanted status of "being engaged" and the focus on them as bride and groom. A man in his twenties on his honeymoon told me that although most of his family and friends thought they should go to "the tropics" for their honeymoon, he was very glad they came to Disney instead: "It's a very romantic place. We get treated really special. We have already seen four other couples on their honeymoons here, with their ears on, and we all get treated special. Like at the photo stops we get special poses. We get special dinner." Another young white man in his twenties echoed this idea of being treated with "incredible friendliness and kindness ... getting all this extra attention ... being special. We always get bumped up in line." Another young white man admitted that at first he was not sure Disney World would be a romantic place for their honeymoon, "but we have had so much special treatment here that it's made it really romantic." His wife added that "we get special desserts at dinner and that kind of thing and that makes it such a romantic honeymoon." Another young white groom told me they chose Disney over the Caribbean in part because "they treat us really special. We were brought up on stage in a show; everyone greets us here. Everyone we pass who works here says congratulations." As if on cue, an older couple came up and handed them some tickets to an evening concert that they could no longer use. When I got back to my room that night, I looked up the price of the tickets: about $60 each. It does seem like serious magic when complete strangers hand you expensive gifts.

Another theme for many of the couples at Disney was adventure without the risk. As a young Asian American man in his twenties told me, "It's better to go to these countries all at once, rather than having to get on a plane." Another young black woman said she was aware that the geography of "the world" at Disney is not quite right since it goes Canada, UK, France, Morocco, American Adventure, Germany, Norway, African Outpost, Japan, China, Mexico, and Morocco. She started to ask why these countries and not others, and how is it "African Outpost" and not a country? Yet she stopped her critical inquiry midsentence, since she felt very strongly that authenticity was really not the point. Her stepmother was from Morocco and was very critical of Epcot's version of her homeland, but this young woman insisted that Epcot exists not to accurately represent the world, but rather "to create an experience. And create an experience it does." She added that she really did want to travel, particularly to Asia. At this point her husband said, "I don't really want to go anywhere." For him, a few acres in central Florida symbolizing the world was enough of a voyage. He was not unusual. Few of the couples I spoke to had traveled out of the country, with the exception of Canada or the Caribbean. One had been to Paris; two had been to Mexico. This is not that different from Americans overall. According to William D. Chalmers, although nearly 42 percent of Americans hold passports, fewer and fewer are actually interested in traveling overseas (as opposed to within the North American continent). Chalmers notes that traveling overseas for vacation is done by only 3.5 percent of Americans, leaving the vast majority back at home—and much more likely to see the world according to Disney.[41]

Many couples spoke of Disney World as a place where they could move through space, but also through time and "be a kid again." A forty-something woman celebrating her fourteenth anniversary told me that Disney World "is about having fun. Being a kid again." A woman in her early thirties who was on her honeymoon and had also come to Disney World for her engagement and planned to come regularly for anniversaries, echoed the fantasy of traveling back in time. She explained that at Disney World, "you feel like a kid again. Everything here is about love." Her husband also liked the idea of returning to childhood, so much so that he told me that when they had lunch at Cinderella Castle, "we were literally pushing two-year-olds out of the way to get to the princesses." For him, there was a connection between romance and childhood, noting that "of all the things we've done so far, lunch at Cinderella Castle was by far the most romantic thing we've done." A woman in her late twenties on her honeymoon said: "I came here in second grade and to come back here and relive all those memories is really magical."

There might seem to be a contradiction between the honeymoon as a highly sexualized space and the childishness of Disney World. As historian James Kincaid tells us, there is something particular about the relationship of modern Americans to childhood. On the one hand, childhood is a space of sexual innocence. On the other hand, there is something erotic about innocence: the blond hair, the large blue eyes, the full, red lips. We did not always find "innocence" erotic. Innocence became erotic about the same time capitalism developed.[42] As Hanne Blank points out in her cultural history of virginity, the virgin became a site of erotic desire at the birth of modernity, but the erotic virgin became a product to be bought and sold much later, during the late 1800s.[43]

Needless to say, the honeymooning couples who spoke with me did not notice the contradiction that the mixing of eroticism and childhood in a Disney honeymoon represents. Instead they talked about the "magic" and the "romance" of going on their favorite rides together, watching the parades at the Magic Kingdom, or seeing their favorite princess. Nor did they notice the racial hierarchies that "childhood innocence" embodies. As historian Robin Bernstein explains, "The cult of domesticity demands performances of sexual innocence [which] divided white and black children in much the same way it did white and black women."[44] What makes Disney World seem safe and clean and magical is the mythology of whiteness—particularly white femininity and white childhood—as pure. The real threats to women and children, particularly within patriarchal family structures, are erased, as are the real dangers of white supremacy to nonwhite bodies with the fairy dust of romance. And romance as an ideology was everywhere for the honeymooners at Disney World.

Nearly everyone I interviewed spoke about Disney movies and the landscape of Disney World as cocooning them in a sense of optimism about the future. As one white honeymooner in her thirties put it:

> Ever since you're a little kid you watch Disney and you dream that some day your prince will come. And everything here is about love, about how fairy-tales do come true … My favorite film is *Sleeping Beauty* because they know each other since they were little kids and they were meant to be together and at the end they are. They manage to be together.

Another newlywed, a thirty-something white woman, said she prefers to watch Disney films because "they are always hopeful. They always have happy endings." A white woman in her twenties told me her favorite film is *Pocahontas*, which, although it does not end in a white wedding or a castle, is "all about meeting Prince Charming." Then she points at her husband and adds, "He is my Prince Charming." A young black woman loved *Aladdin*:

> Jasmine was always my favorite character. From a narrative point of view, not to go all lit crit theory on you, but the growth she experiences, where

she starts and where she ends up. And although I love Mulan because she's so strong, well, when you think about it, she doesn't really end up with a partner, does she?

It wasn't just women who bought into the promises of romance. Men did too. All of the grooms had a favorite Disney film, with *Aladdin* being by far the most popular. Several of the men spoke explicitly about how seeing men in love on Disney allowed them to express their feelings for their wives. For instance, one white man in his thirties talked about how much he loved *Cinderella* because of the "whole love at first sight thing." Of his wife, he said, "Ever since I met her, it was love at first sight. I knew I wanted to be with her." A groom in his early thirties told me that he loved to watch Disney films because although "there's trial and tribulation, then there's a happy ending and that is what everyone wants. Well, not the trial and tribulation, but that's what life is. We all have them, but it's the happy ending we hope for." A thirty-year-old white honeymooner saw Disney films as a way to forge a different and perhaps less toxic form of masculinity:

> Disney for me—as a heterosexual male—is the *only* place I had access to socially acceptable role models for romance ... When I was a pre-teen, I watched *Aladdin* over and over again ... *Aladdin* is a door onto how to be a man ... How to be a man in love because it is redefining the hero as a man in love and so allows boys to experience romantic love.

The people who spoke with me did not just accept the ideology of romance lock, stock, and barrel. As a white woman in her forties celebrating her anniversary told me:

> We aren't into all the fantasy, fairy-tale stuff. We didn't have a wedding. We got married in a courthouse and that was fourteen years ago ... Love is not a fairy-tale ... it's a growing process, it's sickness and in health, for better and for worse.

A couple in their thirties, he white and she black, clearly had thought deeply about the ways in which both marriage and Disney can reinforce existing hierarchies of gender and sexuality. They wanted a world where love is love, and they turned to Disney for that world, not blindly, but knowingly. As the young groom put it:

> If I can be honest, among my friends there has developed a fear that by doing this, that by running around in our groom and bride outfits, that we are upholding all the traditional stuff here. Which we are not! Because for instance, if I'm standing next to a male friend someone will say "thank you" to us like we're together, me in my groom ears, they're congratulating us like we're making Disney gay.

He understood that Disney upheld many of the things he and his new wife and their friends were trying to resist: "There is ... a fear that we are accepting all the conservative things Disney stands for because of course Disney pushes 'family friendly' and it is in the South so they have to make sure that Southerners are happy." Like this young groom, the newlyweds I interviewed at Disney were both sharp-eyed and soft-hearted. It is clear that Disney gives them hope for a better future, a world filled with love and magic, not hate and violence. We all need a space of hope, especially as the future seems increasingly grim.

But this hope—or, more accurately, *ideology*—is exactly what stops us from seeing things as they really are. Global warming is happening twice as fast as scientists had predicted. Large swaths of Florida are at risk of being under water with increasing hurricane surges. Six of the ten American cities most likely to go under due to rising seas are in Florida.[45] Even if the newlyweds leave Florida after their honeymoon, they won't be safe from environmental change. Large chunks of the ice shelf in Antarctica are breaking off. Huge swaths of the Earth will be destroyed or at least highly inhospitable by the time these newlyweds grow old together.[46] Even if humans manage to survive catastrophic climate change, these young, middle-class Americans with a college education are still facing fairly grim economic prospects. Young people, no matter how perfect their white wedding or their Disney honeymoon or their spectacular engagement, are set to earn far less than older generations, and this is true for young people in nearly all of the industrialized world. Their income in the US is lower than for retired people. In the seven wealthiest countries in the world, young adults' disposable income has declined significantly.[47]

Faced with this future, these millennial newlyweds have decided to privatize their futures: find their one true love, get married, and ride off into the sunset. The sunset is supposed to be a magical life in a castle, or at least a split-level colonial in a nice suburb. But a privatized future will not actually save them. In order to understand why Americans, even the married ones, live happily *never* after, I spent a week in the most perfect suburb on earth: Celebration, Florida. Originally designed by Disney as the "American hometown," but later abandoned by the corporation, Celebration embodies both the promise and the limits of romance as an ideology as it became located in real space and time and intersected with real lives.[48]

Conclusion

Happily Never After

> The truth behind the lies the media spreads. There is no such thing as happily ever after apart from those who have wealth and power.
>
> Definition of "happily never after," urbandictionary.com

After learning to love, finding love, and having the most spectacular engagement, the most perfect white wedding, and the most romantic honeymoon, we have finally arrived at our happily ever after. Given how much money, time, and political energy we devote to romance, the US should be the happiest place on earth, a real-world Magic Kingdom, but that's not how things turned out. We Americans are pretty miserable, and we feel worse today than we did ten years ago. According to the 2017 *World Happiness Report,* Americans fall behind most industrialized countries in levels of happiness. One of the authors of the report, Columbia economist Jeffrey D. Sachs, argues that happiness is in free fall in the US *not* because of money worries, but because of a collapse in the social fabric of this country. For Sachs, the real issues are decreasing trust in both institutions and individuals and a decline in social support networks. According to Sachs,

> It is of course well-known that social capital in the United States has been in decline for several decades now ... In recent years, the evidence of social

crises has become overwhelming ... A small group at the top of the income distribution has continued to make striking gains in wealth and income, while the rest of society has faced economic stagnation or decline, worsening public health indicators including rising rates of drug addiction and suicide and declining social trust.[1]

Sachs writes that the data clearly show that "the United States offers a vivid portrait of a country that is looking for happiness 'in all the wrong places.'"[2] For Sachs and many other economists, more money is not the solution, but rather a sense of trust and community.

Throughout this book I have been arguing that we Americans are in fact looking for happiness in all the wrong places. It is our unshakable belief in the magic of romance that is making us miserable. The privatized future offered by Love, Inc., disconnects us from a larger sense of community even as it takes a lot of our time, energy, and money, which could be better spent creating a social safety net for all. The real danger to our happiness is to believe that love is all we need. Such a belief blinds us to the larger world around us even as it lulls us into a false sense of security.

In this chapter, I explore the "happily ever after" we imagine and locate that imaginary place in the very real space of suburbia. I spent four days talking with residents of the most perfect planned community on earth, one carefully designed by Disney to make our dreams come true. That suburb, Celebration, Florida, is both a microcosm and a metaphor for why we cannot privatize our futures. No matter how protected our own "castle," the future demands a collective set of actions. Yet Celebration is part of a long line of American fantasies that the future can be privatized. This particular fantasy of the future as individual and bounded from the outside world found its most iconic form in the 1950s and 1960s with the nuclear family living in a detached house in the suburbs. The first suburbs were, like Celebration, planned communities, built to house white and married soldiers returning from World War II, but also to create this new sort of family, detached from any historical or kinship ties.

SUBURBS, NICENESS, AND WHITETOPIAS

If we sell one house to a Negro family, then 90 to 95 percent
of our white customers will not buy into the community ...
We can solve a housing problem, or we can try to solve
a racial problem, but we cannot combine the two.
   William Levitt, developer of Levittown

Although suburbs have been around for a couple of centuries, they were
mostly for the wealthiest of families. In the mid-twentieth century, new
technologies like the standardization of design and prefabrication in
home construction, as well as the GI Bill's low-interest housing loans,
created a far more democratic suburb: Levittown. Levittowns and the
newly forming suburbs like them were instant communities. They went
up quickly and grew exponentially. These 1950s suburbs lacked any historical antecedents and were filled with young white families trying to
invent what it meant to be a nuclear family in the nuclear age. Between
1952 and 1958, Levittown, Pennsylvania, was transformed from twelve
hundred acres of potato fields to a community of over seventy thousand
residents. These brand spanking new communities came with churches
and schools built in. They were also TV ready, with a television console
built into the stairs. Watching TV shows that mirrored suburbia back to
them helped these suburban pioneers learn how to model their own
nuclear family.[3] These suburbs created a sense that a "real" or "traditional" family was white, straight, and separated from larger networks of
kin. The nuclear family was aided in its development through a variety
of state policies and Federal Housing Administration (FHA) regulations
that found its fullest expression in the detached, single-family home of
the suburbs, the ticky-tacky boxes that all looked just the same.[4]

   The invention of the family as isolated and separated from extended
families happened at different rates and in different ways depending on
class and ethnicity. Before the growth of suburbs, however, it is nearly
impossible to imagine a working-class family existing within the isolation of suburbia. In 1940, about one in four Americans were living in a

multigenerational household, but by 1960 that number had dropped to 15 percent as more and more young people moved to the suburbs.[5] Yet despite the mass exodus of young white families to the suburbs, they were always a minority of Americans. In 1970, at the nuclear family's peak popularity, nearly 40 percent of US households were married couples with children. Today that number is less than 20 percent.[6] The suburbs helped disguise the fact that living in a nuclear family was not the traditional family form. Instead, because suburbs were entirely comprised of married white couples, most often with children, they helped foster the lie that the nuclear family was "normal."

The nuclear family was more child-focused and also created a more mobile workforce, a necessity in the postwar economy.[7] The cultural desire to create family separate from larger kinship networks and existing alongside relative strangers, themselves in nuclear families, was in large part orchestrated by the state with laws like the federal Interstate Highway Act (1956) and the GI Bill, which extended homeownership to many blue-collar workers.[8]

Needless to say, to get a home mortgage, the young returning soldiers had to be married and white,[9] a category that in the postwar period included southern Europeans and Jews for the first time.[10] As historian Clayton Howard points out, the various state and federal policies that helped create suburbia not only discriminated against non-whites and women, but also policed sexuality and made sure that only those in white, heterosexual marriages would benefit from this national program. As Howard explains,

> Numerous scholars have illuminated the ways in which these government policies reinforced racial and gender restrictions on lending. FHA and VA programs largely excluded most people of color and women from the postwar housing markets ... they also reinforced the incentives for Americans to enter certain kinds of sexual relationships, but not others ... By explicitly offering married couples low-interest loans, the federal government implicitly encouraged whites to wed other whites.[11]

These government welfare policies facilitated the accumulation of equity and wealth among a large swath of Americans.

It is worth noting, however, that no amount of money or state regulation could have moved so many Americans to the newly forming suburbs without cultural changes that made romance more central to a new kind of citizenship. This citizenship was not just heterosexual and white, but also home-owning and engaged in the romance of a privatized future. As media expert Lynn Spigel explains, there was a direct relationship between how pop culture represented the suburbs and how people in the suburbs pictured themselves: "By purchasing their detached suburban homes, the young couples of the middle class participated in the construction of a new community of values; in magazines, in films, and on the airwaves they became the cultural representative of the 'good life.'"[12] In other words, the detached home in suburbia became the literal castle on the hill in the same years that Disney made *Cinderella* (1950) and *Sleeping Beauty* (1959), and television aired nuclear family romances like *Father Knows Best* and *Leave it to Beaver.* The promise of a happily ever after was sold to young families through cultural forms that modeled what a nuclear family ought to look like and how they ought to behave. In these romantic fairy-tales and TV sitcoms, gender roles were clear: father went to work, mother stayed home and took care of the house, and children focused on their own future nuclear family formation through dating and "crushes." And everyone, or at least everyone who was family, was white.

In other words, it was romance as much as low-interest loans through the GI Bill that moved white couples to the suburbs. To totally leave their neighborhoods and relatives behind and head to the newly forming suburbs, these couples had to believe that the future was bright and always and forever located in the romance of the nuclear family. For a generation who had gone through the Great Depression and World War II, a privatized future surrounded by others like them and away from anyone who was different must have seemed like a fairy-tale come true. As Steven Mintz and Susan Kellogg explain in their history of family life in the US, *Domestic Revolutions:*

> To a generation economically strapped in the depression and sacrificing for the war effort in World War II, the opportunity to have a family and buy a suburban house, with a backyard barbecue and a living room teeming with children, filled a deep emotional need. For two decades American families had experienced unprecedented strain and now they turned away from public concerns.[13]

Over time, the dream of riding off into the sunset to a split-level colonial and the most rigid of gender and racial segregation began to morph into other fantasies. Women (including the white, middle-class married women idealized in much of 1950s culture) entered the workforce in larger and larger numbers, nearly doubling their participation between 1950 and 2010.[14] And despite all the romance of being a stay-at-home mom, the suburbs were hardly a dream come true for many of the women there, creating a widespread disaffection that Betty Friedan famously called "the problem that has no name." The beginnings of Second Wave feminism helped to reshape suburbs from primarily feminized spaces to ones where both men and women left for work in the morning. Large and globalized economic forces also pushed women into the workforce. By the mid-1970s, 90 percent of Americans were losing ground economically. Increasingly most families needed two incomes to maintain the same standard of living they had once hoped for on one income.[15]

Despite all these structural and cultural changes, many Americans clung tightly to the dream of romance and the idea that the future should be both private and contained. As suburbs became more racially and economically diverse, those most invested in the promise of a white wedding and a happy future—white people with economic means— left the suburbs for gated communities. Gated communities are both whiter and more affluent than the rest of the country, including the increasingly racially and ethnically diverse suburbs.[16] As anthropologist Setha Lowe shows, gated communities do much of the work of earlier suburbs by isolating people who are more or less alike: straight, white, and middle or upper class. Like the residents of suburbs in the 1950s and 1960s, residents of gated communities describe them as "safe" and "nice" in opposition to cities and older suburbs, which are browner, queerer, and poorer. The "niceness" Low describes in gated communities "is about keeping things clean, orderly, homogenous, and controlled ... it is also a way of maintaining whiteness."[17] In other words, they are the proverbial "castle" that Love, Inc., has promised us and, like weddings, gated communities use images of white innocence as "nice" to lure whites to them.

Rich Benjamin describes these new dream communities, whether literally gated off from cities or separated through geographical barriers that make a car and a long drive necessary, as "whitopias." A whitetopia is

> whiter than the nation, its respective region, and its state. It has ... at least 6 percent population growth since 2000. The majority of that growth (often upward of 90 percent) is from white migrants. And a Whitopia has a *je ne sais quoi*—an ineffable social charisma, a pleasant look and feel.[18]

As Benjamin makes clear, the movement of white bodies into whitopia is more than economic; it is ideological as well. "The white-inflected rights-based outlook champions individuals and neighborhoods, withdrawn from the common nation, preoccupied by private interest."[19]

This private future in a gated community is not only white; it is also romantic. Moving to a gated community is not that different from how people imagine their white wedding or perfect honeymoon: an inalienable right and unrelated to the common good yet somehow bathed in goodness and light. In other words, Love, Inc., lures us into the white wedding, the white honeymoon, and the white gated community by promising us security, something it cannot deliver in a globalized economy experiencing global environmental crises. It is this misery that gnaws at the edges of our dream homes, even more than it does at our weddings. The "happily ever after" of married life that leaves us feeling alone together.

Most scholars who look at family formations agree that marriage can increase happiness, yet this depends to a great extent on whether a culture values alternative family forms or just marriage. Some of these studies also find that women are often not as happy with "family life" as men are and that children do not necessarily increase happiness.[20] Yet even if marriage tends to increase happiness in countries that denigrate those who are not married, happiness in the US is decreasing. Our increasing misery is not the result of declining marriage rates, but a declining sense that the world can be trusted and that the future is safe and secure.[21] Nowhere is this more obvious than in the town that Disney built: Celebration, Florida. I spent four days in Celebration doing participant observation in July 2012. I interviewed twenty people, mostly homeowners, but also a few employees who worked in town as well as three tourists there for the day. Most people I met in Celebration were just day trippers, people there to enjoy the rockers by the human-made pond or dining at a local restaurant. They had come to gawk at the way the world "ought to be," but a world they saw as "too expensive to live in" or not made for them.

IMAGINEERING HAPPILY EVER AFTER

> But if Disney World was meant to entertain and excite,
> everything within [Celebration's] confines was intended
> to be soothing to the eye and comforting to the soul ... It was
> a town of pretty buildings, neat streets, and smiling people,
> with an overall effect quite similar to the one we would
> have found ... in the Magic Kingdom. But Celebration
> was a real town.
>
> Douglas Frantz and Catherine Collins,
> *Celebration, U.S.A.,* 1999

Celebration was designed by the "imagineers" at Disney in the early 1990s. Although it was not the city of tomorrow that Walt Disney originally designed as Epcot, it did apply some of the principles Walt had developed for building a community out of thin air. Celebration also utilized many of the principles of New Urbanism, which shaped places like Seaside, Florida. New Urbanism looked to design elements of a pre-car America, like having porches that are at the same height as the people walking by and making the town more pedestrian friendly, with carefully designed sidewalks and paths. New Urbanism also hid the now ubiquitous car out of sight, dislodging it from its position front and center in the older suburbs. Suburbs like Celebration and Seaside were developed as an " antidote to the isolation of the suburbs ... [as their] ever-longer commutes and the rise of shopping malls and big-box stores fractured community life, as downtowns emptied and commerce shifted to the edges of highways."[22] Celebration utilized both Walt Disney's designs and New Urbanism to create what the town's website describes as "not a town, but a community." It is a community so highly designed that even the manhole covers were created to evoke "American small town" and to be "warm" and "nice."[23] Despite being known as the town that Disney built, the corporation actually sold its interests in Celebration in 2004, in part because it had always meant to withdraw from the town once it had sold enough lots to make it profitable.[24]

Driving into Celebration is like driving into a past that never quite existed. The houses have large front porches, the sidewalks are wide, the colors pastel but saturated. The unrelenting "hominess" is in stark contrast to the brutal architecture of mass consumption that surrounds it. Celebration is centered around a town square and all the shops seem local, or at least not global, except for the Starbucks. I write in my notes on my first day there: "No junk on porches or in yards—no bikes or boats or even a half-done gardening project. It's as if no one actually lives here—more of a movie set than real life." Later I learn that there are a lot of rules about what can and cannot be visible to the public in Celebration, but at the time it feels eerie, like a set from *The Twilight Zone* or even, as one commentator wrote, *The Truman Show*. Ed Pilkington, in the *Guardian,* described coming to Celebration as

> like stepping onto the set of *The Truman Show,* the film in which Jim Carrey plays a man trapped inside an invisible bubble ... But of course that's what

Disney's all about: the stitching together of reality and fantasy so finely that you can't tell where the one ends and the other begins.[25]

Many of the people I interviewed liked *The Truman Show* as a metaphor for their town and how it often felt like living inside a staged reality, referring to their town as a "bubble." Celebration is fairly isolated from many of the challenges that urban centers like nearby Orlando face, in part because it is physically, economically, and racially at a distance. Celebration is not a gated community, but large swaths of green surround the town, making it accessible only by car. It had a population of about 7,400 in the 2010 census and was 91 percent white (compared to 75 percent of Florida's population statewide). Not only are Celebration residents whiter than the surrounding community, they are about three times more likely to have a college degree and have a median household income that is nearly twice the statewide median income.[26]

Like other planned communities, including Levittown, Celebration was meant to foster a sense of community among people who are quite similar to each other. Also like other planned communities, Celebration erases the presence of those who are "other" through financial and spatial means, but also by creating an architecture that is not open to all. In the same way that not everyone feels comfortable at a big white wedding, walking into a space like Celebration—a space meant to model some Southern past without the explicit racism—can feel a bit creepy and even threatening. As now-disgraced comedian Louis C.K. once joked:

> Here's how great it is to be white. I can get in a time machine and go anywhere and it would be awesome when I get there. That is exclusively a white privilege. Black people can't fuck with time machines. A black guy in a time machine is like "Hey anything before 1980 I don't wanna go."[27]

Or as geographer Kris Bezdecny points out:

> Celebration symbolizes the use of nostalgia to return to the concept of knowing ... one's place ... The amnesia worked by imagineering tidies up

any unsavory vestiges: while a segregated community is being modeled, that pejorative aspect of small-town, early twentieth-century Florida is to be ignored or forgotten. This amnesia, however, becomes that much more telling upon seeing the town, modeled on a earlier time period, yet recreating similar socioeconomic dynamics of the type being forgotten in the nostalgic quest for community.[28]

Celebration is what "imagineers" created as our "happily ever after," and if the people living there are happy, they are also scared of what is going to happen in the future. Louis C.K. ends his joke about white time travel with this: "I don't want to go to the future and see what happens to white people though ... we are going to pay for this shit." The people I spoke with in Celebration expressed happiness at living in such a privileged place, but they also spoke of isolation and a deep and persistent fear that one day the bubble that surrounds them will pop.

LOVE AND FEAR IN CELEBRATION

TRUMAN BURBANK: Was nothing real?
CHRISTOF: You were real.
    The Truman Show, 1998

People in Celebration seemed to be friendly, regardless of where they came from. Lifelong New Yorkers, trained in the art of avoiding speaking to strangers, took time to talk to me as a researcher. Nearly everyone I spoke with in Celebration talked about the same things: the enchantment and romance of the place, a sense of community, and a feeling of loss as the town became increasingly invaded by problems from "the outside world." Like Jim Carrey's character in *The Truman Show,* Celebration's inhabitants were pretty happy in the bubble that was their life but also pretty miserable because they felt the bubble was starting to fray. Many of the Celebration residents I spoke with expressed a similar sense of knowing Celebration is not "the real world" and also not wanting to live in the real world. In fact, they spoke of Celebration in ways that can best be described as utopian, but like the *Truman Show,* this utopia was constantly under threat from the "outside."

Laura Poe, who worked in the media office for the town but could not afford to live in Celebration herself, still spoke of Celebration as a kind of classless society because of the "broad mix of housing styles that makes Celebration accessible to everyone, so a teacher might live next to a doctor." Several residents mimicked this dream of money not determining one's worth as a member of the community. One longtime homeowner told me,

> It's truly a melting pot here. Like my neighbors used to live in Italy and just keep a second home here, but now they moved into an estate house and just visit Italy. Or you have a conversation with someone and they're one of the founders of AOL and they're just regular people.

This sense of everyone belonging is, of course, not actually true. Media director Poe mentions how the homeowners' association makes sure all the residences are "kept up" so that "property values won't go down." Yet when people cannot afford the stringent requirements of "keeping up the façade" of a perfect community, they are often forced to sell their homes and leave the bubble. One person I interviewed told me about an architectural review board meeting where a man was fined $15,000 for having his hedges too high. A British filmmaker, Ryan Ruaidhri, who was in Celebration doing research on how film shapes our understanding of reality, found Celebration's external perfection disconcerting. "It's all so highly planned it can feel fake, and yet people are also actually living here, living their lives."

Even the highly planned nature of the place—the very thing that makes it seem fake—is beginning to show some very real signs of aging. Despite the community demand that houses be repainted every five years so they don't look like they're aging, twenty years after it was built, the architecture itself is starting to seem a bit dated. Walking through the town hall, designed by Philip Johnson, or the post office, designed by Michael Graves, I write in my notes: "Postmodern architecture seems, a few decades on, dated. The houses—the faux-Savannah and faux–New England styles—seem so out of context, like a late 20th-century dream of a place."

Yet none of the residents complained to me about the Community Standards Board's hyper-policing of all things aesthetic or the predictability of postmodern design. Instead, they found Celebration really and truly magical. They spoke about how moving to Celebration was "fated" and "meant to be" in the same way that Americans have been taught to speak about "true love." They described the "magic" of artificial snowflakes at Christmas or the pride they take in the Fourth of July parade. For them, Celebration was love at first sight. One white woman in her forties, very active at the school, both as a substitute teacher and on the Parent-Teacher Association, told me that when she and her mother looked at Celebration fifteen years earlier, she just knew it was where they were meant to live. She drove into town and saw the picket fences and

> was just like wow! ... I just knew this was the place. My mom always loved grapes and when I pulled into town and parked it was in front of a store called Soft as a Grape and it just had that small-town feel ... It was meant to be ... we went home to Connecticut where I had lived for twenty-nine years ... and we just knew, based on one afternoon, that we felt more at home in Celebration than in Connecticut ... My mom always said she would die here in Celebration and she did.

A man in his seventies who had lived in Celebration for twelve years told me that he and his wife had a similar experience of seeing Celebration and knowing it was the place they needed to be. "We were down here on vacation and my wife drove in looking for a mailbox and we were like 'what is this place.' It was so beautiful, but I also thought it might be some sort of religious community." This man had himself grown up in Levittown on Long Island. His father, a third-generation New Yorker, took advantage of the GI benefits and bought his family a brand-spanking-new home sixty years ago. But this man was fleeing

Long Island and its suburban sprawl. He wanted out. For him, Celebration is "much more upscale and not as blue collar" as where he grew up, and "not everyone's commuting on the train together."

A white woman in her late fifties, an ESL teacher at the town's Stetson University campus, loved living in Celebration. She had moved there from the New York metropolitan area eleven years before with her three school-age children. For her 9/11 was the

> straw that broke the camel's back ... I just love it here. It's such a peaceful environment and Celebration is perfect. It's a traditional New England town with a central square that you can walk to ... I wanted that small-town America kind of feel ... It's peaceful and tranquil and safe and secure.

For another white woman, Celebration's design as *walkable* reminded her of more urban spaces, but without all the crime. A gynecologist in her thirties with three young children, she told me, "I guess this neighborhood compares to where we used to live in Atlanta before we moved to the suburbs. We could walk to everything—stores, restaurants, the movies ... It's so safe here and the crime rate is ridiculously low." Another resident, a twenty-six-year-old hostess at a local restaurant, told me that she loved Celebration for the safety as well.

> The police are around, but they often wear regular clothes. So you don't know they're there. It's a really safe place to raise kids because they can wander around unsupervised ... And they even monitor the alligators in the lake and take them out when they get too big.

Celebration is about fifty miles from where Trayvon Martin was killed just a few months before I was in Celebration. No one I interviewed mentioned Martin, but his death hung there, a ghoulish reminder that this feeling of safety because of the presence of armed police in regular clothes makes certain bodies unsafe in the happily ever after of whitopias. Like the whitopias Benjamin explored, Celebration offers a more urban version of daily life without any of the "problems" that come with living in economically and racially diverse communities. It also ignores all the very real problems that happen in whitopias: domestic abuse, child abuse, sexual violence, economic downturns. And no one can hide from the effects of global climate change, even in communities as hyper-constructed and insulated as Celebration.

For most of the residents in Celebration who spoke with me, the problems always come from without. There was a pervasive sense of contagion from the outside world. It was not exactly a fear, but a deep mourning and nostalgia for the way things used to be there, a time when the outside world did not leak into their perfect space. Whether or not such a time ever existed is unclear, but many of the longtime residents believed there was a better world in some perfect time in the past. Perhaps this is the romantic's lament: another, better world is always possible. Perhaps it was a growing mood among white Americans that history had taken a wrong turn, leaving them less secure and less happy than they should have been. Whatever it was, there was a persistent narrative that Celebration used to be better before it was infected by the world with problems like homelessness, migration, and bank foreclosures.

THE WAY WE WERE

Everything seemed so important then—even love!
Tagline from *The Way We Were*, 1973

Often the very same residents who described Celebration in such romantic language as "perfect" and "meant to be" also expressed some sense that it was not as it used to be. As one middle-aged white woman told me,

> It's more difficult to be a resident now. I have to fight tourists to get a rocking chair by the pond ... It's changed since I came here. The high school has changed a lot since my daughter graduated. It used to all be in one building and now there's this huge high school and they're bringing people in from other places. The school is just too big now.

Another forty-something white woman also saw the local school as a place where the problems of the outside world invaded the space of Celebration.

Of course, the high school is a county high school now and it is not the same place it was when we moved here. And in our elementary school there are a lot of transitional families from Home Suite Homes—that's a residency hotel and they are all basically homeless. And we have some of those students here. They say we'll never have more than a hundred of them, but of course you never know. There are about 1,344 students at the elementary school, so 100 spread out over nine grades.

This woman was not ready to abandon or even exclude the children in need and told me that "we work together as a community to gather food for them because we found out these kids don't have anything to eat all weekend so we send food home with them on Thursday afternoons." Yet she said that "real life" came to Celebration too.

Real life happens here too. We call it the bubble and it's safe. When we have a murder, it makes national news ... But look, the real world interferes. Of course. [Highway] 192 is right over there. And on the sex predator list? There's an older gentleman in town who is on this list. And that man who was murdered recently? He was killed by a young man who he was paying for sex.

For her, having "real life" happen in Celebration was still better than having it happen back home in Delaware. Whether it was the poverty of some of the students or the personal losses she suffered when loved ones died, "real life would have happened anywhere, but I wouldn't have had the support I've had here."

Many residents, however, did not feel that sense of support. Although Celebration was designed to foster community, many residents did not in fact really experience life there as particularly connected to those around them. One longtime homeowner in his seventies told me, "You know, it's really transient here. I hardly ever see the same person twice ... I hardly know any of our neighbors ... There's a lot of international money." Another older white man, a self-described Disneyphile who moved to Celebration to be closer to the parks, told me:

There is a lot less community spirit since the withdrawal of Disney. They just kind of abandoned us ... The community has changed ... and I don't know what Stetson University does except teach a lot of Arabic speakers English as a second language. [He gestures toward a group of young women sitting outside Starbucks with drinks. They are all wearing black headscarves.]

A middle-aged white woman said rather wistfully: "I don't really know my neighbors. I live in a condo and there is not as much permanence in condos as in homes. A lot of people in the complex rent and there's a lot of turnover. I really have no idea who my neighbors are." Not that she missed living back in New York City, where "no one greets you. No one has a smile on their face. Everybody is just in the rat race and the subways are overcrowded and the streets and the buses."

Perhaps residents of Celebration are like any married couple, a decade or two in. They loved their town and felt, as in any romance, fated to be there, yet they also felt some nagging sense that things could be better. And they could. That's what this story, the story of romance and capital in the twenty-first century, is about: making things better. And what better way to start anew than with a big, white wedding, especially a mass, lesbian one?

LOVE TRUMPS HATE

> I want … an America where we build bridges, not walls.
> Where we prove, conclusively, that yes: Love trumps hate.
> Last words spoken by Hillary Clinton during her 2016
> presidential campaign

On a hot and steamy day in July 2017, I rode my bike up a steep hill to the Pilgrim Monument in Provincetown, Massachusetts. The monument, built in the early 1900s, is meant to mark the spot where the Pilgrims originally landed in 1620. It is large and granite and pushes more than 252 feet into the sky. I make my way through a large group of tourists and up the hill to the structure. There I find about 150 people milling about for the second annual Bride Pride. Bride Pride is the brainchild of Allison Baldwin and Ilene Mitnick, owners of a local inn.

They themselves have had a civil union and a wedding, but when they moved from Connecticut and left their community behind, they decided to renew their vows and "invite women from the entire planet" to join them. Their idea was "Bride Pride," a mass lesbian wedding that in its first year attracted 106 lesbians and was, according to the wedding-planning website The Knot, "the most joyful thing we've seen."[29]

The Second Annual Bride Pride, in 2017, was slightly smaller, with ninety-four brides, but no less joyful. The women gathered around were between twenty-five and seventy-five years old and from states as far away as Colorado, Florida, and Kansas. They were all women, since the organizers of Bride Pride ask that the participants identify as women, regardless of gender assigned at birth or genital configuration, although two of the brides also identified as genderqueer. They were mostly white (87 of the 94 brides), despite the fact that the organizers of the event offered to waive the $150 ticket cost for participants in Women of Color weekend as well as for women who were "locals." The brides had professions like book editor, physician's assistant, and social worker, although two women I interviewed had not completed college and worked in the retail industry. And they were mostly not poor, with nearly all of them on vacation in Provincetown or second homeowners there. In other words, the mass lesbian wedding was pretty similar to other weddings in the US, except for the mass and the lesbian part.

As an all-woman's drumming circle created a rhythmic pulse through the crowd and two young women dressed as Greek statues stood watch, the brides paraded through the monument. Most were not dressed in traditional wedding attire, although four brides had traditional wedding dresses on (one was barefoot, two were wearing Converse sneakers, and one had a full sleeve of tattoos). They were, however, fairly dressed up, often in matching ensembles, for instance white slacks and pastel shirts with matching sneakers or kaftans and head wraps. Kate Clinton, lesbian comedian, social justice activist, and minister for a day, married the brides. The wedding was part somber ceremony, with lines like "With these rings you offer each other your hand,

Matching bridal high top sneakers at Bride Pride. Photo by Laurie Essig.

your heart, and your soul," and part stand-up routine, with lines like "You may kiss your bride … NO tongue!" The actual ceremony took under an hour. After the ceremony, the brides piled into three trolley cars and one pedicab with cans tied to the back and rode through Provincetown to the cheers of at least a thousand townspeople and tourists.

There is no doubt that the women who gathered for this lesbian wedding extravaganza believe deeply in romance as an ideology. Of the sixteen brides and four guests I interviewed, all but one imagined that marriage would make the future more secure. One middle-aged white woman, dressed in a snazzy button-up vest, dress shirt, and pants, all in shades of purple, gushed like any good subject of romance about how from the moment she met her wife, in 2003, she knew she was the one. She even used to stand in the line at the store where her beloved worked, just to catch a glimpse of her. Another fifty-something white woman said, "Isn't it every girl's dream to have a wedding, wearing a white wedding dress?"

But people also said they got married because they were scared that the conservative turn in US politics might mean they would have no rights in the future, saying that getting married is particularly political right now, and that they saw same-sex marriage as a powerful tool in pushing back against a global right-wing agenda in large part because it could build "community" as well as transform heterosexual marriage into something more feminist and more egalitarian for all women. They also told me that marriage was hardly necessary to make a relationship real and that they wanted a world where everyone had access to health care and where they could define their own families without the state deciding. One six-year-old girl—in a white dress and a rainbow flag cape—explained the rainbow rule to me: a boy can marry a boy or a girl can marry a girl or a girl can marry a boy. But when I asked her if she wanted to get married, she said she didn't know. All the adults around her, including her lesbian grandmother, who was ambivalent about having a wedding herself, quickly and emphatically told her: "You don't have to!"

It would be easy to see Bride Pride as just another piece of Love, Inc. It has an official corporate sponsor, *GO Magazine*, as well as thirty local sponsors. It is a marketing tool of local business owners to bring more women to town. And marriage in no way solves, as one Bride Pride observer put it, "the need for health care for everyone and inheritance rights for everyone." But the more I spoke with people there and the organizers, the more I began to feel an optimism—not Berlant's cruel optimism, but an actual optimism that there could be a happy ending after all and that a happy ending could happen as feminism transforms marriage into something less oppressive for women, makes marriage an unnecessary option, and situates all relationships in larger structures than the couple or the family.

Infused with feminism, the ideology of romance that has bewitched us for so long might actually be turning into a good character, like Elsa in the 2013 Disney blockbuster *Frozen*. It is not that the participants in Bride Pride weren't romantics. They were. They believed in the power of love to make us safer. It is not that they were somehow not subject to romance as an ideology. After all, some amount of money and labor was spent to make it happen, although less money and labor than goes into most weddings. It is that these brides and the people surrounding them believed not in a private future that involves just the couple, but a collective future where we *all* have happy endings. According to the organizers of the event, the whole point of it is to build communities and networks of women who use love as a weapon. For them, even something as seemingly meaningless as a trolley ride ended up giving some of the women on board a romantic sense that the world could be different. Some of these women were from places where they cannot tell anyone that they're lesbians, but here in Provincetown, they see what the world could be. As Bride Pride organizer Mitnick told me, they are very aware of what's going on in the political realm, but

> after the election, we personally chose to focus on love ... to put love out there ... We cannot stay in fear. We cannot say if the waters rise ... if Trump takes all our rights ... we have to focus on what matters most. Love is what matters most.

Her partner in love and business adds:

> If you stay in the panic, if you stay there and become unable to function, they win. And if you stay there your individual behavior can go crazy. It can become lord of the flies ... I have to balance myself and focused on ... love.

These women believe that romantic love can build entire communities and that these communities can have a positive impact on the world. Bride Pride's organizers donate the profits to homeless youth, and many of the brides and the community members watching felt energized to fight for LGBTQ rights. And they all believed in something else too. They believed that things can get better. This is not the cruel optimism that is always a dead-end, the kind of optimism that ignores structural inequities and historical patterns in favor of fairy dust. This is the sort of optimism that moves people to act, to sit on buses and go on hunger strikes and make demands. When these women say that they really and truly believe that love trumps hate, they mean it as a set of actions as much as a set of beliefs.

As Bride Pride creator Baldwin told me, "Only the bitterest of souls could look at that ceremony and not see beauty." I am bitter. I am bitter that the world my children, everyone's children, will inherit is on the brink of environmental collapse and the political system of one of the world's richest countries is so dysfunctional we can no more fight climate change than provide health care or higher education for all. I am also feminist enough that there is no way that I could see marriage as the solution to anything. As Jill Filipovic writes, "The brutally misogynist history of marriage should have rendered it obsolete long ago." But as she also writes, "Marriage has evolved so much, especially with the expansion of marriage rights to same-sex couples, it's hard to argue that the institution itself is irreparably broken."[30] A big white wedding can never fix patriarchy, nor will marriage ever solve poverty, as many conservative scholars have argued. If there is anything my travels in the land of romance and capital have taught me, it is that love can be a dead-end that leads us to a privatized future and therefore no future at all. Love, Inc., can drain us of our resources, emotional and financial, and blind us to the work that needs to be done for our communities and the world.

If I am bitter, I am also deeply romantic. I really do believe tomorrow can be better than today, that we can find our way through the forest of thorns, fight the dragon—or better yet, be the dragon—and end up in a happily ever after that has nothing to do with the couple. But getting there requires a lot more than believing in magic. It requires political action. In December 2017, the organizers of Bride Pride told me they were suspending it for 2018 and instead gathering their community of romantics to work on the midterm elections. Sometimes you need a wedding to make the future seem possible; sometimes you need door-to-door canvassing.[31]

Yet Bride Pride shifted something in me. A mass lesbian wedding that is done as a political act, as a protest against the death drive that seems to be pushing this nation and the world to the brink, might in fact be a Trojan horse that enters Love, Inc., and then destroys it from within. The participants in the mass lesbian wedding at the Pilgrim Monument did not seem indifferent to the world around them; they were thoroughly located in it. This wedding and the people participating in it and the people cheering them on as they rode through town in their white dresses and lavender suits was further proof of what I've long suspected: romance is not just the problem, it's also the solution. Romance gives us hope in increasingly hopeless times. A belief in the power of romantic love is like a little bubble of oxygen, a space to breathe again, when hate and greed have taken all the air out of the room. If, in the words of Bride Pride organizer Mitnick, we can be "a sea of love rising up ... collectively as a community with love as our weapon of choice," then we might just be able to have a happy ending after all. And in that happy ending we ride off into the future not with our prince or princess to a castle on the hill, but with each other, all of us—married, single, straight, gay, old, young, white and black and Latino/a and more—fighting harder than we have ever fought before for a collective future. In the end—happily or not, in the Disney sense—we might just survive. As Rebecca Solnit writes, "To hope is to give yourself to the future and that commitment to the future makes the present inhabitable."[32] Romance can allow us the space to hope for a future—and having a future is the most romantic ending of all.

NOTES

INTRODUCTION

1. VanDerWerf, "How Hallmark Took Over Your TV Every Christmas."
2. Long, "The Feel-Good Hallmark Channel."
3. Cohn, "Love and Marriage."
4. "Single by Choice."
5. Peppers," How Much Would You Spend on Your Bridal Dress?"
6. Vasel, "Couples Are Spending a Record Amount of Cash to Get Married."
7. Rainie and Perrin, "Slightly Fewer Americans Are Reading Print Books, New Survey Finds."
8. "myRWA: The Romance Genre; Romance Industry Statistics."
9. Rich, "Recession Fuels Readers' Escapist Urges."
10. Negra and Tasker, "Neoliberal Frames and Genres of Inequality," p. 351.
11. Cohn, "Love and Marriage."
12. Actually, J. K. Rowling now says that Harry should have ended up with Hermione. Anderson, "J. K. Rowling Is Wrong."
13. Vella, "Apple's Latest Ad Is Probably Going to Give You Chills."
14. Covert, "Nearly a Billion Dollars Spent on Marriage Promotion Programs Have Achieved Next to Nothing."
15. Nancy D. Polikoff, *Beyond (Straight and Gay) Marriage.*
16. Bazelon, "Marriage of Convenience," p. 13.
17. Walters, *Tolerance Trap.*

18. Katz and Eckholm, "Anti-Gay Laws Bring Backlash in Mississippi and North Carolina."

19. Weber, *The Protestant Ethic and the Spirit of Capitalism,* p. 53.

20. Edelman, *No Future.*

21. Candiday, *The Straight State,* p. 2.

22. Callahan, "How the GI Bill Left Out African Americans."

23. McGee, *Self-Help, Inc.,* p. 177.

24. Kipnis, *Against Love,* p. 19.

25. Ibid., p. 19.

26. Illouz, *Cold Intimacies,* p. 5.

27. Ibid.

28. "Global Wealth Data Bank 2013."

29. Fry, "Four Takeaways from Tuesday's Census Income and Poverty Release."

30. Buchheit, "The One Percent Just Keeps Getting Richer."

31. "On this Day, 29 July 1981."

32. "Forget Kate's Dress."

33. "Disney Posts Record Profits."

34. Fraser, "Transnationalizing the Public Sphere," p. 21.

35. Berlant, *Cruel Optimism,* p. 3.

CHAPTER ONE. LEARNING TO LOVE

1. Fisher, "Biology."

2. *Bridezillas.*

3. Fisher, "The Forgotten Sex."

4. "Brothers Grimm."

5. Essig, "The Mermaid and the Heterosexual Imagination."

6. Bernstein, *Racial Innocence,* pp. 41–42.

7. McClintock, *Imperial Leather,* p. 162.

8. "Lady," *Merriam-Webster Dictionary,* www.merriam-webster.com /dictionary/lady.

9. Kincaid, *Erotic Innocence,* p. 52.

10. Wesley, "How Much Will You Spend for Valentine's Day?"; Stampler, "Americans Could Spend $703 Million on Their Pets This Valentine's Day."

11. Kaminetsky, "5 Biggest International Holidays for E-Commerce."

12. Radway, *Reading the Romance.*

13. Giddens, *Transformation of Intimacy,* p. 44.

14. Kipnis, *Against Love*, p. 22.

15. Although he wasn't speaking about romance, French social theorist Pierre Bourdieu called similar ideological formations "doxa," a set of ideas that seem so obvious that they cannot be questioned because we absorb them from birth like the air we breathe. "The ideology of natural taste owes its plausibility and its efficacy to the fact that, like all the ideological strategies generated in the everyday class struggle, it naturalizes real differences." Bourdieu, *Distinction*, p. 68.

16. Cott, *Public Vows*, pp. 77, 104.

17. See Somerville, *Queering the Color Line*.

18. See McClintock, *Imperial Leather*.

19. Rubin, "Thinking Sex," pp. 151–52.

20. For instance, see England, Descartes, and Collier-Meek, "Gender Role Portrayal in the Disney Princesses," and Giroux, "Are Disney Movies Good for Your Kids?"

21. Lugo-Lugo and Bloodsworth-Lugo, "'Look Out New World, Here We Come'?"

22. Giroux, *Mouse That Roared*.

23. Cokely, "Someday My Prince Will Come," pp. 167–68.

24. "Revenue of the Walt Disney Company."

25. For instance, see Fink, "Tween Romances You'll Love," and "Popular Tween Romance Books."

26. Simmons-Duffin, "School for Good and Evil."

27. Cook and Kaiser, "Betwixt and Be Tween."

28. Moraski, "Miley Cyrus' Booty-Shaking VMA Performance Gets Quite the Reaction."

29. "Chart History," Hannah Montana Billboard, www.billboard.com /artist/276390/hannah+montana/chart?f=395.

30. For more on the erotic virgin as a figure of the late twentieth century, see Blank, *Virgin*.

31. Mutch, "Coming out of the Coffin," p. 77.

32. "Box Office History for Twilight Movies."

33. Dirks, "All Time Top Box Office Major Film Franchises."

34. Meyer, *Twilight*, p. 175.

35. Church of Latter Day Saints website, http://mormon.org/beliefs/plan-of-salvation?gclid=CO2bs7_zm7kCFYyi4AodXlEAuw&CID=33481310&s_kwcid=AL!3737!3!23873314935!p!!g!!mormonism&ef_id=UHRu8QAACvRWPRAv:20130826200114:s.

36. Meyer, *Breaking Dawn*, pp. 87–94.

37. Ibid., p. 179.

38. Borgia, "Twilight," p. 6.

39. Ibid, pp. 8–9.

40. Ibid., p. 1.

41. "The Official Website of Stephenie Meyer," FAQS: Is Bella an antifeminist heroine? www.stepheniemeyer.com/bd_faq.html.

42. Baumgardner and Richards, *Manifesta*. Needless to say, the notion of "choice" has been thoroughly critiqued by many feminist scholars as oblivious to how choices are coerced within structures and to how a rhetoric of choice mirrors neoliberalism unwillingness to account for things like poverty, racism, and sexism. For instance, see Ferguson, "Choice Feminism and the Fear of Politics."

43. Romance Writers of America website, www.rwa.org/p/cm/ld/fid=1682.

44. Taylor, "The Urge towards Love Is an Urge towards (Un)Death," p. 35.

45. Radway, *Reading the Romance*. For information on the role of romance novels in American publishing see the website for Romance Writers of America, www.rwa.org.

46. A police officer's salary in Forks, Washington, is somewhere around $60,000 a year. www.lawenforcementedu.net/washington/washington-salary/.

47. See "Cullen Cars." The fashion blog *Inside Bella's Closet* outlines some of the ways Bella's wardrobe transforms after her marriage to Edward. https://insidebellascloset.wordpress.com/page/6/.

48. Holland, "High Economic and Social Costs of Student Loan Debt." Miller, "Simple Truth about the Gender Pay Gap."

49. "Romance Genre," Romance Writers of America, www.rwa.org/p/cm/ld/fid=582.

50. FAQs, E. L. James website, www.eljamesauthor.com/faq/.

51. Nazaryan, "'Fifty Shades of Grey' Tops Ten Million Sales."

52. James, *Fifty Shades of Grey*, loc. 1716.

53. Ibid., loc. 1042.

54. Roiphe, "Spanking Goes Mainstream."

55. Elliot and Pilkington, "New Oxfam Report Says Half of Global Wealth Held by the 1%."

56. "'Fifty Shades of Grey' Movie Mansion Part of Vancouver House Tour."

57. James, *Fifty Shades of Grey*, loc. 188.

58. E. L. James, *Fifty Shades Freed*, epilogue.

59. Abrams, "Sex Toy Shops Prepare for Tie-Ins to 'Fifty Shades of Grey.'"

60. "Fifty Shades of Grey Sex Toys."

61. "Fifty Shades of Grey Bear."

62. Dymock, "Flogging Sexual Transgression," p. 891.

63. The movie portrayed the fountain as being in Volterra, but they actually filmed in the nearby village of Montepulciano.

64. Author's interview, February 10, 2010.

65. Author's interviews, March 11, 2010.

66. Balk, "As Seattle Incomes Soar, Gap Grows between Rich and Poor."

67. Reuters, "Washington."

68. Author's notes, March 2014.

69. Sheftell, "Breathless 'Fifty Shades of Grey' Apartment Is No Work of Fiction."

70. About 63 percent graduate in four years. "Common Data Set."

71. "Project on Student Loan Debt," http://projectonstudentdebt.org/state_by_state-data.php.

72. Balk, "Census."

73. "New Ferrari Cars"; Pepitone, "Buy Edward Cullen's Twilight House."

74. "Annual Earnings of Young Adults."

75. "Living Wage Calculator."

CHAPTER TWO. FINDING LOVE

1. Department of Labor statistics show a general trend toward working more hours per week since 1990. One recent survey measured Americans working more hours per year than people in any other industrialized country with the exception of Ireland. Velasco and Turcotte, "Are Americans Working Too Much?" See also Schabner, "Americans Work More Than Anyone."

2. Wade, *American Hookup*, p. 240.

3. Ibid., p. 17.

4. Kuperberg and Padgett, "The Date's Not Dead."

5. Ibid, p. 245.

6. Traister, *All the Single Ladies*.

7. Cohn, "Love and Marriage."

8. For an excellent overview of early American courtship practices, see Adams-Campbell, *New World Courtships*. Of particular interest is her chapter on the "bundling" of young couples.

9. For instance, see Peiss, *Cheap Amusements*.

10. Finkel et al., "Online Dating," p. 11.

11. "GenePartner."

12. Smith and Anderson, "5 Facts about Online Dating."

13. Ibid.

14. Finkel et al., "Online Dating," p. 4.

15. O'Brien, "81-Year-Old eHarmony Founder on Gay Marriage and Tinder."

16. eHarmony "About" section, www.eharmony.com/about/eharmony/.

17. O'Brien, "81-Year-Old eHarmony Founder on Gay Marriage and Tinder."

18. As cited in Finkel et al., "Online Dating," p. 21.

19. The inverse relationship between class and obesity is well established; see "Socioeconomics and Obesity." Dental inequality in the US has been documented—114 million people lack any sort of dental coverage. Gaffney, "Devastating Effects of Dental Inequality in America."

20. Radford, "Sweet Science of Seduction or Scam?"

21. Finkel et al., "Online Dating," p. 25.

22. Pavlo, "Fraud Thriving in US Churches but You Wouldn't Know It." For a more amusing account of selling people religion for large profit, see John Oliver's "Our Lady of Perpetual Exemption" episode on HBO's *Last Week Tonight,* which aired August 16, 2015.

23. Finkel et al., "Online Dating," p. 11.

24. Sales, "Tinder and the Dawn of the 'Dating Apocalypse.'"

25. "Nosedive," *Black Mirror,* episode 1, season 3, first aired October 21, 2016.

26. Sindy R. Sumter, Laura Vandenbosch, and Loes Ligtenberg, "Love me Tinder," p. 67.

27. Mason, "Tinder and Humanitarian Hook-Ups," p. 824.

28. Kim, "Here's How the Dating Service Company That Owns Tinder Makes Money."

29. Reuters, "Match Group Revenue Up as Tinder Attracts More Paid Users."

30. "Introducing Tinder Online-Swipe Anywhere."

31. Illouz, *Why Love Hurts.*

32. Khoo, "Tinder Issues Lifetime Ban to Man Who Hurled Racist Slurs at Asian Woman."

33. Mason, "Tinder and Humanitarian Hook-Ups," p. 828.

34. Shaw, "Bitch I Said Hi," pp. 4–5.

35. Frankel, "Whitney Wolfe."

36. If it is a same-sex couple, Bumble assigns someone to contact first.

37. Tepper, "Bumble Is Finally Monetizing with Paid Features to Better Help You Find a Match."

38. For a more detailed analysis of these hierarchies, see Ahlm, "Respectable Promiscuity."

39. For instance, see "Douchebags of Grindr" on Facebook, www.facebook.com/DouchebagsOfGrindr/, or at www.douchebagsofgrindr.com/2017/06/douche-extreme/.

40. Zane, "Tough Love."

41. Brubaker, Ananny, and Crawford, "Departing Glances."

42. Yuknavitch, *Book of Joan.*

43. For instance, see Lapidot-Lefler and Barak, "Effects of Anonymity, Invisibility, and Lack of Eye-Contact on Toxic Online Disinhibition." For a more journalistic account, see Mapes, "Anonymity Opens Up Split Personality Zone."

44. Dredge, "42% of People Using Dating App Tinder Already Have a Partner, Claims Report."

45. For instance, see "Noel Biderman." See also Luckerson, "13 Most Controversial Super Bowl Ads Ever."

46. Whitty, "Anatomy of the Online Dating Romance Scam," p. 443.

47. For instance, see Edwards et al., "Physical Dating Violence, Sexual Violence and Unwanted Pursuit Victimization."

48. The interviews were semistructured, but I allowed the interviewees to go in whatever direction made sense to them. I took notes during the interviews, but did not record.

49. Interestingly, some of the people I interviewed looking for a same-gender partner did not identify as "strictly" gay or lesbian but used terms like "mostly gay."

50. For instance, see Aughinbaugh, Robles, and Sun, "Marriage and Divorce."

51. Interviewees used Tinder, Grindr, Bumble, Hinge, Match, JDate, and Scruff. Interestingly, none used eHarmony, perhaps because of its fundamentalist Christian founder; no one I interviewed identified as a practicing Christian (two identified as Jewish) and most identified as atheist or agnostic.

52. Greenwood, Perrin, and Duggan, "Social Media Update 2016."

53. Perez, "U.S. Consumers Now Spend 5 Hours per Day on Mobile Devices."

54. FetLife is, according to its website, a "Social Network for the BDSM, Fetish & Kinky Community." http: fetlife.com.

55. "Singles in America 2017."

56. Ibid.

57. Steverman, "Americans Work 25% More Than Europeans, Study Finds."

58. Chandler and Munday, *Dictionary of Social Media.*

59. Vilhauer, "This Is Why Ghosting Hurts So Much."

60. Schwartz, *Paradox of Choice.*

CHAPTER THREE. MARRY ME?

1. Bagg, "Go Home, Everyone."

2. *How Heroes of Fiction Propose and How Heroines Reply,* p. 3.

3. "Why Don't Women Propose to Men?"

4. Roser and Ortiz-Ospina, "Literacy."

5. Ibid. The book is available as a PDF, making it simple to search for terms like "diamond," "diamond ring," "ring," "knee," and "bended knee."

6. Coontz, *Marriage, a History,* p. 3.

7. Durkheim, *Elementary Forms of Religious Life.*

8. Friedman, "How an Ad Campaign Invented the Diamond Engagement Ring."

9. Otnes and Pleck, *Cinderella Dreams,* pp. 65–66.

10. At $4,000 average, it seems like men actually spend less than two months' salary on a diamond ring, but more than one month's, suggesting that the campaign did have some effect on amount spent.

11. Dhar, "Diamonds Are Bullshit."

12. Reuters, "2011 Engagement & Jewelry Statistics Released by TheKnot.com & WeddingChannel.com."

13. Cawley, "DeBeers Myth."

14. Schweingruber, Cast, and Anahita, "A Story and a Ring," p. 169.

15. Various studies address average ring cost. For instance, according to The Newlywed Report, the average ring is $4,758. *The Knot* estimates the average ring at $5,978. Deitz, "This Is the Average Cost of an Engagement Ring."Also see Bernard, "With Engagement Rings Love Meets Budget."

16. Genesis 34:12, Bible Hub, http://biblehub.com/genesis/34–12.htm.

17. Zelizer, *Purchase of Intimacy,* p. 40.

18. Debord, *Society of the Spectacle,* p. 153.

19. Vannini, "Will You Marry Me?," pp. 175–76.

20. As Catherine Constable shows in *Adapting Philosophy, The Matrix* is deeply indebted to the work of Jean Baudrillard.

21. Vannini, "Will You Marry Me?," p. 182.

22. Dunning, "1 in 4 Women Disliked Their Marriage Proposals."

23. Doll, "When the Proposal Costs More Than a Wedding."

24. "Marriage Proposal Packages."

25. "Boston Marriage Proposal Ideas."

26. For instance, see "21 Epic Same-Sex Wedding Proposals That Will Make You Cry."

27. Rebecca A. Walker, "Fill/Flash/Memory," p. 118.

28. Fieldnotes at wedding expos in Boston, Philadelphia, Tacoma, and Richmond, BC, conducted 2013–14.

29. "Greatest Marriage Proposal EVER!!!"

30. "Matt and Ginny on Ellen."

31. "Making the Movies Jealous."

32. "Aussie Guy Proposes to Girlfriend in Packed Cinema."

33. "Best Marriage Proposal of 2015."

34. "Sweetest Peter Pan Marriage Proposal."

35. "Her Fantasy Proposal That Exceeded Her Expectations"; "Wedding Proposal That Will Leave You Breathless."

36. "Isaac's Live Lip Dub Proposal." One interesting aspect of this video is that they seem to be visibly Jewish; a joke is made about this when the lyrics "Is it the look in your eyes / Or is it this dancing juice?" come on and some "dancing Jews" dance across the road.

37. "He Loved Her since They Were 10."

38. "AMAZING!!!"

39. The most popular gay male had over 13 million views, whereas the most popular lesbian did not have quite 7 million. See "Cutest Lesbian Proposal EVER!" and "Spenser's Home Depot Marriage Proposal."

40. Himmelstein and Brückner, "Criminal-Justice and School Sanctions against Nonheterosexual Youth."

41. To preserve the tenor of the genre that is YouTube commentary, I did not change the language or correct the spelling.

42. "Top 5 Marriage Proposal Fails."

43. Best, *Prom Night*.

44. "Practical Money Skills for Life."

45. Richardson, "The Promposal," p. 83.

46. In one notable exception to boys asking and girls answering, a young woman asks a young man to prom. It should be noted, however, that she is a cheerleader (as is he) and thus her status as "feminine" is firmly in place. In addition, they are both white and seem to have the full support of their coaches, who allow the promposal to happen during a practice. "Becky G. Plans the Perfect Cheer #Promposal—Ep. 2."

47. "Cutest Promposal!"

48. "A Just Incredible Promposal."

49. "Most Epic Prom Proposal."

50. Tempesta, "Proof That Promposals Are TOTALLY out of Control."

51. Chang, McAfee, and Effron, "Teens Stage Elaborate 'Promposals' to Score Dates, Social Media 'Likes.'"

52. "Daniels PromPosal."

53. "Daniels PromPosal Parody."

54. For example, see Bhabha, "Of Mimicry and Man," and Boym, "'Banality of Evil,' Mimicry, and the Soviet Subject."

55. Edwards, "Yes, You Can Make Six Figures as a YouTube Star ... and Still End Up Poor."

56. "Justin and Emily."

57. Rick Porter, "Monday Final Ratings."

58. "Surprise Ending."

59. "Prom Flashmob with Becky G! #Promposals Ep. 1"; "Becky G Plans the Perfect Cheer #Promposal—Ep. 2."

60. Patten and Parker, "A Gender Reversal on Career Aspirations."

61. "Jamin's Downtown Disney Flashmob Proposal."

62. "Chicago Bulls Luvabull Cheerleader Surprised with Marriage Proposal during Bulls/Heat Game."

63. "A Very Sweet Proposal."

CHAPTER FOUR. WHITE WEDDINGS

An earlier version of this chapter appeared in *QED: A Journal of GLBTQ Worldmaking* 3, no. 2 (Summer 2016).

1. Ingraham, *White Weddings*, pp. 12–14.

2. Essig, "In the US, Fairy-Tale Royal Weddings Clash with Reality."

3. Kelly, "Royal Wedding 2018 Viewing Figures."

4. "Royal Wedding Watch."

5. "Tents, Tiaras and a Few Tears as a Million Turn Out for Wills and Kate."

6. "Children's Wedding Dream Comes True."

7. "Bridal Magazine Girl."

8. http://itunes.apple.com/us/app/white-wedding/id422241465?mt=8.

9. "Bridezilla Britain."

10. The quote from Queen Victoria is from www.biographyonline.net /royalty/quotes/queen-victoria-quotes.html.

11. "Queen Victoria Wedding."

12. Benjamin, "America's Royal Wedding."

13. Otnes and Pleck, *Cinderella Dreams*.

14. Ibid.

15. Pressly, "Cost of Weddings Spirals in China."

16. Like all clothing, wedding dresses are often made in ways that are bad for both the environment and workers. Recently, there has been a movement for fair trade wedding dresses. For instance, see Eisenhart, "Fair Trade Wedding Dresses." The conditions for diamond production and trade are harsh enough that those from conflict zones became known as "blood diamonds"; the industry responded with the "Kimberly Process" to cut down on diamonds that fund war, but the process is full of loopholes, and even if the diamonds are conflict free, they are still mined, often by children, in grueling and often life-threatening conditions. Baker, "The Fight against Blood Diamonds Continues."

17. Otnes and Pleck, *Cinderella Dreams*.

18. Seaver, "The National Average Cost of a Wedding is $33,391."

19. Bourque, "Technology Profit and Pivots in the $300 Billion Wedding Space."

20. Carla Fried, "The Royal Wedding: What Will It Cost?"

21. For instance, see *Wedding of the Century, Royal Scandals and Shockers,* and *William and Kate: The Royal Wedding,* all April 2011. In addition to these special issue magazines, articles in *Us, People,* and many major newspapers, as well as a comic book series from Markosia Enterprises Ltd., all told more or less the same story.

22. Ahmed, "A Phenomenology of Whiteness."

23. In general, support for the monarchy in the UK remains quite high (above 70 percent) regardless of royal shenanigans. "Monarchy/Royal Family Trends."

24. For instance, see Grice, "Polls Reveal Big Rise in Support for Monarchy."

25. Bagehot, "Set the Royal Family Free."

26. For instance, see the CIA's "World Factbook."

27. Tom Clark, "Queen Enjoys Record Support in Guardian/ICM Poll."

28. Ingraham, *White Weddings,* p. 188.

29. "Magic of the Monarchy."

30. Durkheim, *Émile Durkheim on the Division of Labor in Society,* pp. 79–80.

31. Rosenberg, "Economics of Happiness."

32. Mark Phillips, "Royal Wedding Could Cost UK Economy $50 Billion."

33. For instance, see the University of California, Santa Cruz, web page "Who Rules America," http://sociology.ucsc.edu/whorulesamerica/power /wealth.html.

34. Stiglitz, "Of the 1%, by the 1%, for the 1%."

35. See www.eonline.com/on/shows/bridalplasty/index.html and Melander-Dayton, "Bridalplasty."

36. Sorren, "14 Times During Kim Kardashian & Kris Humphries' Wedding You Could Tell They Were Doomed."

37. Pous, "Top Ten Short-Lived Celebrity Marriages."

38. For instance, see Edward-Jones, "Bride and Gloom."

CHAPTER FIVE. THE HONEYMOON

1. Otnes and Pleck, *Cinderella Dreams,* pp. 18, 267–68.

2. "2017 Newlywed Report."

3. Casserly, "When Wedding Planning Becomes a Full-Time Job."

4. Jessee, "Your Inner Disney Princess?"

5. Romeyn, "Top 100 Honeymoon Destinations for 2017."

6. Lippe-McGraw, "Yes Couples Are Now Taking 'Earlymoons' before Their Weddings."

7. Rochotte, "Engagementmoon."

8. Sardone, "Wedding Statistics and Honeymoon Facts and Figures."

9. Sykes, "William and Kate Honeymoon Photos Published."

10. "2017 Newlywed Report," p. 17.

11. Garland, "Americans Spending Less Time, More Money on Vacation."

12. "Global Travel and Tourism Industry—Statistics and Facts."

13. Foster, "Deflated after the Big Day?"

14. Sardone, "Wedding Statistics and Honeymoon Facts and Figures."

15. Bulcroff et al., "Social Construction of the North American Honeymoon, 1880–1995," pp. 467–68.

16. For example, see Stopes, *Married Love,* or Russell, *Hypatia.*

17. Otnes and Pleck, *Cinderella Dreams,* pp. 135, 139.

18. "Niagara Falls."

19. Dubinsky, *Second Greatest Disappointment,* p. 155.

20. Otnes and Pleck, *Cinderella Dreams,* p. 142.

21. Ibid., pp. 141–42.

22. Ibid., p. 143.

23. Bulcroff et al., "Social Construction of the North American Honeymoon, 1880–1995," p. 483.

24. "Disney's Honeymoons."

25. Otnes and Pleck, *Cinderella Dreams,* pp. 155–56.

26. All prices from Walt Disney World website, https://disneyworld.disney.go.com.

27. "Fast Facts." According to the Disney wedding website, in the last twenty-five years, more than fifty thousand couples have married at Disney.

28. In 2000, only 11 percent of weddings were destination weddings. Otnes and Pleck, *Cinderella Dreams,* p. 158. Today, 25 percent are. Sardone, "Wedding Statistics and Honeymoon Facts and Figures."

29. Sardone, "Wedding Statistics and Honeymoon Facts and Figures."

30. Baudrillard, *Jean Baudrillard,* pp. 166–70.

31. Kuenz et al., *Inside the Mouse.*

32. Marin, *Utopics,* p. 241.

33. Lingan, "Bristling Dixie."

34. Sperb, "Take a Frown, Turn It Upside Down," p. 936.

35. Baldwin, *James Baldwin,* p. 722.

36. Bernstein, *Racial Innocence.*

37. Rika Houston and Meamber, "Consuming the 'World,'" pp. 179–80.

38. For instance, consider how the It's a Small World ride locks world cultures not just into stereotypes, but into an imaginary past that is always already safely removed. Baber and Spickard, "Crafting Culture," p. 227.

39. *Ever after Blog.*

40. I will be forever grateful to Georgia Essig for pointing out the newlywed mouse ear phenomenon.

41. Chalmers, "Great American Passport Myth."

42. Kincaid, *Erotic Innocence,* p. 52.

43. Blank, *Virgin,* pp. 193–96.

44. Bernstein, *Racial Innocence,* pp. 41–42.

45. Urbina, "Perils of Climate Change Could Swamp Coastal Real Estate."

46. Wallace-Wells, "Uninhabitable Earth."

47. Barr and Malik, "Revealed."

48. Goodnough, "Disney Is Selling a Town It Built to Reflect the Past."

CONCLUSION

1. Sachs, "Restoring American Happiness," pp. 181–82.

2. Ibid., p. 183.

3. Kimmel, "Community in History," pp. 37–38. For more on the role that television played in the creation of the suburbs, see Spigel, *Welcome to the Dreamhouse.*

4. See Howard, "Building a 'Family-Friendly' Metropolis," for how state policies facilitated a concentration of straight, white, nuclear families in the suburbs while simultaneously making the cities more queer and less white.

5. "The Return of the Multi-Generational Family Household."

6. Vespa, Lewis, and Kreider, "America's Families and Living Arrangements: 2012," p. 1. See also DePaulo, "America Is no Longer a Nation of Nuclear Families."

7. For instance, Brigitte Berger argues that the nuclear family has been a primary site of child rearing for several hundred years and is likely to continue to be so because of the advantages it brings to children, but also for the stability it provides societies predicated on opportunity and happiness for all. *Family in the Modern Age.*

8. Hanchett, "Financing Suburbia," p. 312.

9. Wolfinger, "The American Dream—For All Americans," p. 432.

10. For instance, see Roediger, *Working toward Whiteness.*

11. Howard, "Building a 'Family-Friendly' Metropolis," p. 938.

12. Spigel, *Welcome to the Dreamhouse,* pp. 31–32.

13. Mintz and Kellogg, *Domestic Revolutions,* p. 178.

14. Toossi, "A Century of Change," p. 22.

15. Desilver, "U.S. Income Inequality, on Rise for Decades, Is Now Highest since 1928."

16. Vesselinov and Le Goix, "From Picket Fences to Iron Gates," p. 207.

17. Low, "Maintaining Whiteness," p. 87.

18. Benjamin, *Searching for Whitopia,* loc. 101.

19. Ibid, loc. 4661.

20. For instance, see Vanassche, Swicegood, and Matthijs, "Marriage and Children as Key to Happiness?"

21. Sachs, "Restoring American Happiness."

22. "What Disney's City of the Future, Built to Look like the Past, Says about the Present."

23. Byrnes, "How Michael Bierut Branded Celebration, Florida."

24. Goodnough, "Disney Is Selling a Town It Built to Reflect the Past."

25. Pilkington, "How the Disney Dream Died in Celebration."

26. "Celebration CDP, Florida."

27. Louis C. K.'s bit can be seen on YouTube at, www.youtube.com/watch?v = 87LGmm1M5Is.

28. Bezdecny, "Imagineering Uneven Geographical Development in Central Florida," p. 336.

29. Seaver, "This Mass Lesbian Wedding and Vow Renewal Is the Most Joyful Thing We've Seen."

30. Filipovic, *The H-Spot*, p. 144.

31. Email, from Bride Pride organizers Baldwin and Mitnick, December 2017.

32. Solnit, *Hope in the Dark*, p. 4.

BIBLIOGRAPHY

"21 Epic Same-Sex Wedding Proposals That Will Make You Cry." 2014. www
.youtube.com/watch?v=rkSQaCooWXI.

"The 365 Day Proposal." n.d. www.youtube.com/watch?v=ECRqF4BHkGk.

"2017 Newlywed Report." Wedding Wire, 2017. http://publications.weddingwire
.com/i/795912-weddingwire-2017-newlywed-report/2.

Abrams, Rachel. "Sex Toy Shops Prepare for Tie-Ins to 'Fifty Shades of Grey.'"
New York Times, February 1, 2015. Media sec. www.nytimes.com/2015/02
/02/business/media/50-shades-of-green-shops-prepare-for-tie-ins-to-fifty-
shades-of-grey-film.html.

Adams-Campbell, Melissa M. *New World Courtships: Transatlantic Alternatives to
Companionate Marriage.* Hanover, NH: Dartmouth College Press, 2015.

Ahlm, Jody. "Respectable Promiscuity: Digital Cruising in an Era of Queer
Liberalism." *Sexualities* 20, no. 3 (March 1, 2017): 364–79. https://doi.org/10.1177
/1363460716665783.

Ahmed, Sara. "A Phenomenology of Whiteness." *Feminist Theory* 8, no. 2
(August 1, 2007): 149–68. https://doi.org/10.1177/1464700107078139.

"AMAZING!!!—A Pitch Perfect Proposal." September 6, 2014. www.youtube.
com/watch?v=ojk8hnZTDhU.

Anderson, L.V. "J.K. Rowling Is Wrong: Harry Potter Should Not Have
Ended Up with Hermione." *Slate,* February 3, 2014. www.slate.com/blogs
/browbeat/2014/02/03/j_k_rowling_says_harry_should_have_ended_up_
with_hermione_j_k_rowling_is.html.

"Annual Earnings of Young Adults." National Center for Education Statistics, April 2017. https://nces.ed.gov/programs/coe/indicator_cba.asp.

Aughinbaugh, Alison, Omar Robles, and Hugette Sun. "Marriage and Divorce: Patterns by Gender, Race, and Educational Attainment." Monthly Labor Review, US Bureau of Labor Statistics. October 2013. www.bls.gov/opub /mlr/2013/article/marriage-and-divorce-patterns-by-gender-race-and-educational-attainment-1.htm.

"Aussie Guy Proposes to Girlfriend in Packed Cinema: Best Wedding Proposal EVER!" January 18, 2015. www.youtube.com/watch?v=zcQZzYecaJg.

Baber, Katherine, and James Spickard. "Crafting Culture: 'Tradition,' Art, and Music in Disney's 'It's a Small World.'" *Journal of Popular Culture* 48, no. 2 (April 1, 2015): 225–39. https://doi.org/10.1111/jpcu.12253.

Bagehot. "Set the Royal Family Free." *Economist,* April 20, 2011. www.economist.com/blogs/bagehot/2011/04/british_monarchy.

Bagg, Allison. "Go Home, Everyone, This Is The Most Elaborate Marriage Proposal Ever." BuzzFeed. Accessed November 2, 2017. www.buzzfeed.com /abagg/this-insane-marriage-proposal-is-basically-an-episode-of-gle.

Baldwin, James. *James Baldwin: Collected Essays.* Edited by Toni Morrison. New York: Library of America, 1998.

Baker, Aryn. "The Fight against Blood Diamonds Continues." *Time,* August 27, 2015. http://time.com/blood-diamonds/.

Balk, Gene. "As Seattle Incomes Soar, Gap Grows between Rich and Poor." *Seattle Times,* October 6, 2014. http://blogs.seattletimes.com/fyi-guy/2014 /10/06/as-seattle-incomes-soar-gap-grows-between-rich-and-poor/.

———. "Census: Seattle Saw Steepest Rent Hike among Major U.S. Cities." *Seattle Times,* September 18, 2014. http://blogs.seattletimes.com/fyi-guy/2014 /09/18/census-seattle-saw-steepest-rent-hike-among-major-u-s-cities/.

Barr, Caelainn, and Shiv Malik. "Revealed: The 30-Year Economic Betrayal Dragging down Generation Y's Income." *Guardian,* March 7, 2016. News sec. www.theguardian.com/world/2016/mar/07/revealed-30-year-economic-betrayal-dragging-down-generation-y-income.

Baudrillard, Jean. *Jean Baudrillard: Selected Writings,* edited by Mark Poster. Stanford, CA: Stanford University Press, 1988.

Baumgardner, Jennifer, and Amy Richards. *Manifesta: Young Women, Feminism, and the Future.* New York: Macmillan, 2000.

Bazelon, Emily. "Marriage of Convenience." *New York Times Magazine,* February 1, 2015.

"Becky G Plans the Perfect Cheer #Promposal—Ep. 2." April 26, 2014. www .youtube.com/watch?v=2cFwfCy4w9Y.

Benjamin, Melanie. "America's Royal Wedding: General and Mrs. Tom Thumb." *Huffington Post*, April 19, 2011. www. Huffingtonpost.com/melani-benjamin/royal-wedding_b_850540.html.

Benjamin, Rich. *Searching for Whitopia: An Improbable Journey to the Heart of White America*. New York: Hyperion, 2009. Kindle.

Berger, Brigitte. *The Family in the Modern Age: More Than a Lifestyle Choice*. New New York: Routledge, 2002.

Berlant, Lauren. *Cruel Optimism*. Durham, NC: Duke University Press, 2011.

Bernard, Tara Siegel. "With Engagement Rings Love Meets Budget." *New York Times*, January 31, 2014. www.nytimes.com/2014/02/01/your-money /with-engagement-rings-love-meets-budget.html.

Bernstein, Robin. *Racial Innocence: Performing American Childhood from Slavery to Civil Rights*. New York: New York University Press, 2011.

Best, Amy L. *Prom Night: Youth, Schools and Popular Culture*. New York: Routledge, 2000.

"Best Marriage Proposal of 2015 (Warning Will Make You Cry!)—365 Day Proposal." January 18, 2015. www.youtube.com/watch?v=ECRqF4BHkGk.

Bezdecny, Kris. "Imagineering Uneven Geographical Development in Central Florida." *Geographical Review* 105, no. 3 (July 2015): 324–43.

Bhabha, Homi. "Of Mimicry and Man: The Ambivalence of Colonial Discourse." *October* 28 (1984): 125–33. https://doi.org/10.2307/778467.

Blank, Hanne. *Virgin: The Untouched History*. New York: Bloomsbury USA, 2007.

Borgia, Danielle N. "Twilight: The Glamorization of Abuse, Codependency, and White Privilege." *Journal of Popular Culture* 47, no. 1 (February 1, 2014): 153–73. https://doi.org/10.1111/j.1540-5931.2011.00872.x.

"Boston Marriage Proposal Ideas." The Heart Bandits. Accessed November 2, 2017. www.theheartbandits.com/boston-proposal-ideas.html.

Bourdieu, Pierre. *Distinction: A Social Critique of the Judgement of Taste*. London: Routledge, 1986.

Bourque, Andre. "Technology Profit and Pivots in the $300 Billion Wedding Space." *Huffington Post* (blog), May 2, 2015. www.huffingtonpost.com/andre-bourque/technology-profit-and-piv_b_7193112.html.

"Box Office History for Twilight Movies." The Numbers. Accessed November 1, 2017. www.the-numbers.com/movies/franchise/Twilight#tab=summary.

Boym, Svetlana. "'Banality of Evil,' Mimicry, and the Soviet Subject: Varlam Shalamov and Hannah Arendt." *Slavic Review* 67, no. 2 (2008): 342–63.

"Bridal Magazine Girl." Flash Games Spot. Accessed November 3, 2017. http://flashgamesspot.com/play/bridal-magazine-girl-every-little-girl-dreams-abo/flash-game/.

"Bridezilla Britain: Six in Ten SINGLE Women Have Already Planned Their Wedding—Including Dress, Flowers, Bridesmaids." *Daily Mail*, Feburary 25, 2014. www.dailymail.co.uk/femail/article-2567408/Bridezilla-Britain-Six-ten-SINGLE-women-planned-wedding-including-dress-flowers-bridesmaids.html.

Bridezillas. WE Tv (blog). Accessed November 4, 2017. www.wetv.com/shows/bridezillas.

"Brothers Grimm: Fairy Tales, History, Facts, and More." *National Geographic*, 1999.www.nationalgeographic.com/grimm/index2.html.

Brubaker, Jed R., Mike Ananny, and Kate Crawford. "Departing Glances: A Sociotechnical Account of 'Leaving' Grindr." *New Media and Society* 18, no. 3 (July 7, 2014): 373–90. https://doi.org/10.1177/1461444814542311.

Buchheit, Paul. "The One Percent Just Keeps Getting Richer." *Mother Jones* (blog). November 3, 2014. www.motherjones.com/politics/2014/11/2014-global-wealth-report/.

Bulcroff, Kris, Richard Bulcroff, Linda Smeins, and Helen Cranage. "The Social Construction of the North American Honeymoon, 1880–1995." *Journal of Family History* 22, no. 4 (October 1, 1997): 462–90. https://doi.org/10.1177/036319909702200404.

Byrnes, Mark. "How Michael Bierut Branded Celebration, Florida." *CityLab*, November 4, 2015. www.citylab.com/design/2015/11/how-michael-bierut-branded-celebration-florida/413752/.

Callahan, David. "How the GI Bill Left Out African Americans." Demos, November 11, 2013. www.demos.org/blog/11/11/13/how-gi-bill-left-out-african-americans.

Candiday, Margot. *The Straight State: Sexuality and Citizenship in Twentieth-Century America*. Princeton, NJ: Princeton University Press, 2011.

Casserly, Meghan. "When Wedding Planning Becomes a Full-Time Job." *Forbes*, July 22, 2010. www.forbes.com/2010/07/22/wedding-planning-the-knot-wedding-channel-websites-forbes-woman-time-working-brides.html.

Cawley, Laurence. "DeBeers Myth: Do People Spend a Month's Salary on an Engagement Ring?" *BBC News*, May 16, 2014. www.bbc.com/news/magazine-27371208.

"Celebration CDP, Florida." US Census Bureau. www.census.gov/quickfacts /fact/table/celebrationcdpflorida,FL/RHI105210#viewtop.

Chalmers, William D. "The Great American Passport Myth: Why Just 3.5% of Us Travel Overseas!" *Huffington Post* (blog), September 29, 2012. www .huffingtonpost.com/william-d-chalmers/the-great-american-passpo_b_ 1920287.html.

Chandler, Daniel, and Rod Munday. *A Dictionary of Social Media.* Oxford: Oxford University Press, 2016.

Chang, Juju, Marjorie McAfee, and Lauren Effron. "Teens Stage Elaborate 'Promposals' to Score Dates, Social Media 'Likes.'" ABC News, May 3, 2016. http://abcnews.go.com/Lifestyle/teens-stage-elaborate-promposals- score-dates-social-media/story?id=38840417.

"Chart History." Hannah Montana Billboard. www.billboard.com/art- ist/276390/hannah+montana/chart?f=395.

"Chicago Bulls Luvabull Cheerleader Surprised with Marriage Proposal during Bulls/Heat Game." December 7, 2013. www.youtube.com/watch?v= d3qLrEipXeI.

"Children's Wedding Dream Comes True." CBS News, March 3, 2009. www .cbsnews.com/news/childrens-wedding-dream-comes-true/.

Clark, Tom. "Queen Enjoys Record Support in Guardian/ICM Poll." *Guardian,* May 24, 2012. www.theguardian.com/uk/2012/may/24/queen-diamond- jubilee-record-support.

Cohn, D'Vera. "Love and Marriage." *Pew Research Center's Social and Demographic Trends Project* (blog), February 13, 2013. www.pewsocialtrends.org /2013/02/13/love-and-marriage/.

Cokely, Carrie L. "'Someday My Prince Will Come,' Disney, the Heterosexual Imaginary and Animated Film." In *Thinking Straight: The Promise and Paradox of Heterosexuality,* edited by Chrys Ingraham. New York: Routledge, 2004.

"Common Data Set." Institutional Research, Washington State University. Accessed November 1, 2017. https://ir.wsu.edu/common-data-set/.

Constable, Catherine. *Adapting Philosophy: Jean Baudrillard and "The Matrix Trilogy."* Manchester, UK: Manchester University Press, 2009.

Cook, Daniel Thomas, and Susan B. Kaiser. "Betwixt and Be Tween: Age Ambiguity and the Sexualization of the Female Consuming Subject." *Journal of Consumer Culture* 4, no. 2 (July 1, 2004): 203–27. https://doi .org/10.1177/1469540504043682.

Coontz, Stephanie. *Marriage, a History: How Love Conquered Marriage.* New York: Penguin, 2006.

Cott, Nancy F. *Public Vows: A History of Marriage and the Nation.* Rev. ed. Cambridge, MA: Harvard University Press, 2002.

Covert, Bryce. "Nearly a Billion Dollars Spent on Marriage Promotion Programs Have Achieved Next to Nothing." Think Progress, February 11, 2014.https://thinkprogress.org/nearly-a-billion-dollars-spent-on-marriage-promotion-programs-have-achieved-next-to-nothing-e675f0d9b67/.

"The Cullen Cars." *Stephenie Meyer* (blog). Accessed November 1, 2017. https://stepheniemeyer.com/the-books/twilight/twilight-cullen-cars/.

"Cutest Lesbian Proposal EVER!" August 11, 2012. www.youtube.com/watch?v=l4HpWQmEXrM.

"Cutest Promposal!" May 27, 2012. www.youtube.com/watch?v=7kHxP-hW3JQ.

"Daniels PromPosal." April 16, 2015. www.youtube.com/watch?v=6BtI4EoiIzU.

"Daniels PromPosal Parody." April 20, 2015. www.youtube.com/watch?v=g6Sp6N6VurU.

Debord, Guy. *Society of the Spectacle.* Detroit: Black and Red, 2000.

Deitz, Bibi. "This Is the Average Cost of an Engagement Ring." Bustle, February 29, 2016. www.bustle.com/articles/144926-this-is-the-average-cost-of-an-engagement-ring.

DePaulo, Bella. "America Is no Longer a Nation of Nuclear Families." *Quartz,* June 20, 2015.https://qz.com/440167/america-is-no-longer-a-nation-of-nuclear-families/.

Desilver, Drew. "U.S. Income Inequality, on Rise for Decades, Is Now Highest since 1928." Pew Research Center. December 5, 2013. www.pewresearch.org/fact-tank/2013/12/05/u-s-income-inequality-on-rise-for-decades-is-now-highest-since-1928/.

Dhar, Rohin. "Diamonds Are Bullshit." *Priceonomics* (blog). Accessed November 2, 2017. http://blog.priceonomics.com/post/45768546804/diamonds-are-bullshit.

Dirks, Tim. "All Time Top Box Office Major Film Franchises." AMC Film Site. www.filmsite.org/series-boxoffice.html.

"Disney Posts Record Profits." *New York Times,* July 27, 1990. www.nytimes.com/1990/11/09/business/disney-profits-increase-9.html.

"Disney's Honeymoons." Disneyweddings. http://disneyweddings.disney.go.com/honeymoons/magical-places/overview.

Doll, Jen. "When the Proposal Costs More Than a Wedding." *Atlantic,* March 19, 2013. www.theatlantic.com/national/archive/2013/03/when-proposal-costs-more-wedding/317155/.

Dredge, Stuart. "42% of People Using Dating App Tinder Already Have a Partner, Claims Report." *Guardian,* May 7, 2015. Technology sec. www .theguardian.com/technology/2015/may/07/dating-app-tinder-married-relationship.

Dubinsky, Karen. *The Second Greatest Disappointment: Honeymooners, Heterosexuality, and the Tourist Industry at Niagara Falls.* New Brunswick, NJ: Rutgers University Press, 1999.

Dunning, Jenni. "1 in 4 Women Disliked Their Marriage Proposals: Survey." *Toronto Star,* March 18, 2011. Life sec. www.thestar.com/life/2011/03/18/1_in_4_women_disliked_their_marriage_proposals_survey.html.

Durkheim, Émile. *The Elementary Forms of Religious Life.* Oxford: Oxford University Press, 2001.

———. *Émile Durkheim on the Division of Labor in Society.* Translated by George Simpson. New York: Macmillan, 1933.

Dymock, Alex. "Flogging Sexual Transgression: Interrogating the Costs of the 'Fifty Shades Effect.'" *Sexualities* 16, no. 8 (December 1, 2013): 880–95. https://doi.org/10.1177/1363460713508884.

Edelman, Lee. *No Future: Queer Theory and the Death Drive.* Durham, NC: Duke University Press, 2004.

Edward-Jones, Imogen. "Bride and Gloom: The Rise of Post-Nuptial Depression," July 9, 2009, *Sunday Times.* http://women.timesonline.co.uk/tol/life_and_style/women/relationships/article6668905.ece.

Edwards, Jim. "Yes, You Can Make Six Figures as a YouTube Star … And Still End Up Poor." *Business Insider,* February 10, 2014. www.businessinsider .com/how-much-money-youtube-stars-actually-make-2014-2.

Edwards, Katie M., Kateryna M. Sylaska, Johanna E. Barry, Mary M. Moynihan, Victoria L. Banyard, Ellen S. Cohn, Wendy A. Walsh, and Sally K. Ward. "Physical Dating Violence, Sexual Violence, and Unwanted Pursuit Victimization: A Comparison of Incidence Rates among Sexual-Minority and Heterosexual College Students." *Journal of Interpersonal Violence* 30, no. 4 (February 1, 2015): 580–600. https://doi.org/10.1177/0886260514535260.

Eisenhart, Maddie. "Fair Trade Wedding Dresses." *A Practical Wedding,* June 8, 2015. https://apracticalwedding.com/fair-trade-wedding-dresses/.

Elliott, Larry, and Ed Pilkington. "New Oxfam Report Says Half of Global Wealth Held by the 1%." *Guardian,* January 19, 2015. Business sec. www .theguardian.com/business/2015/jan/19/global-wealth-oxfam-inequality-davos-economic-summit-switzerland.

England, Dawn Elizabeth, Lara Descartes, and Melissa A. Collier-Meek. "Gender Role Portrayal and the Disney Princesses." *Sex Roles* 64, no. 7–8 (April 1, 2011): 555–67. https://doi.org/10.1007/s11199–011–9930–7.

Essig, Laurie. "In the US, Fairy-Tale Royal Weddings Clash with Reality." The Conversation, May 17, 2018. https://theconversation.com/in-the-us-fairy-tale-royal-weddings-clash-with-reality-94719.

———. "The Mermaid and the Heterosexual Imagination." In *Thinking Straight: The Power and Paradox of Heterosexuality,* edited by Chrys Ingraham. New York: Routledge, 2005.

Ever after Blog. Disney Weddings. www.disneyweddings.com/ever-after-blog/.

"Families and Living Arrangements." US Census Bureau. Accessed November 3, 2017. www.census.gov/topics/families.html.

"Fast Facts: Disney's Fairy Tale Weddings and Honeymoons." Walt Disney World News. Accessed November 3, 2017. http://wdwnews.com/fact-sheets /2016/05/04/fast-facts-disneys-fairy-tale-weddings-and-honeymoons/.

Ferguson, Michaele L. "Choice Feminism and the Fear of Politics." *Perspectives on Politics* 8, no. 1 (2010): 247–53.

"Fifty Shades of Grey Bear." Vermont Teddy Bear Factory, n.d. www .vermontteddybear.com/sellgroup/fifty-shades-of-grey-bear.aspx?bhcp=1.

"'Fifty Shades of Grey' Movie Mansion Part of Vancouver Heritage House Tour." HuffPost Canada, May 26, 2014. www.huffingtonpost.ca/2014/05/26 /fifty-shades-of-grey-movie-house_n_5393978.html.

"Fifty Shades of Grey Sex Toys" Lovehoney. Accessed November 1, 2017. www.lovehoney.com/brands/fifty-shades-of-grey/.

Filipovic, Jill. *The H-Spot: The Feminist Pursuit of Happiness.* New York: Nation Books, 2017.

Fink, Megan P. "Tween Romances You'll Love." Flashlight Worthy Books. Accessed November 1, 2017. www.flashlightworthybooks.com/Best-Tween-Romance-Books/662?fwsource=fb.

Finkel, Eli J., Paul W. Eastwick, Benjamin R. Karney, Harry T. Reis, and Susan Sprecher. "Online Dating: A Critical Analysis from the Perspective of Psychological Science." *Psychological Science in the Public Interest* 13, no. 1 (January 1, 2012): 3–66. https://doi.org/10.1177/1529100612436522.

Fish, Stanley. *Inside the Mouse: Work and Play at Disney World.* Edited by Jane Kuenz, Susan Willis, and Shelton Waldrep. Durham, NC: Duke University Press, 1995.

Fisher, Helen. "Biology: Your Brain In Love." *Time,* January 19, 2004. http:// content.time.com/time/magazine/article/0,9171,993160,00.html.

———. "The Forgotten Sex: Men." *Official Match.com Blog,* February 4, 2011. https://matchuptodate.wordpress.com/2011/02/04/the-forgotten-sex-men/.

"Forget Kate's Dress: It's Diana's Bridal Gown That's Still Drawing Millions across the World." *Daily Mail,* May 9, 2011. www.dailymail.co.uk/femail /article-1384783/Forget-Kate-Middletons-dress-Princess-Dianas-bridal-gown-thats-drawing-millions-world.html.

Foster, Jill. "Deflated after the Big Day? You've Got PND! (That's Post Nuptial Depression)." *Daily Mail,* May 4, 2011.

Frankel, Todd C. "Whitney Wolfe, Founder of Dating App Bumble, Has Had Quite the Year. She Just Can't Discuss Parts of It." *Washington Post,* December 2, 2015. www.washingtonpost.com/news/the-switch/wp/2015/12/02 /whitney-wolfe-founder-of-dating-app-bumble-has-had-quite-the-year-she-just-cant-discuss-parts-of-it/.

Fraser, Nancy. "Transnationalizing the Public Sphere: On the Legitimacy and Efficacy of Public Opinion in a Post-Westphalian World." *Theory, Culture and Society* 24, no. 4 (2007): 21.

Fried, Carla. "The Royal Wedding: What Will It Cost?" CBS News. April 28, 2011. www.cbsnews.com/news/the-royal-wedding-what-will-it-cost/.

Friedman, Uri. "How an Ad Campaign Invented the Diamond Engagement Ring." *Atlantic,* February 13, 2015. www.theatlantic.com/international /archive/2015/02/how-an-ad-campaign-invented-the-diamond-engagement-ring/385376/.

Fry, Richard. "Four Takeaways from Tuesday's Census Income and Poverty Release." *Pew Research Center* (blog), September 18, 2013. www.pewresearch. org/fact-tank/2013/09/18/four-takeaways-from-tuesdays-census-income-and-poverty-release/.

Gaffney, Adam. "The Devastating Effects of Dental Inequality in America." *New Republic,* May 25, 2017. https://newrepublic.com/article/142368 /devastating-effects-dental-inequality-america.

Garland, Poppy. "Americans Are Spending Less Time, More Money on Vacation." *Conde Nast Traveler,* July 4, 2016.

"Genepartner.com: DNA Matching—Love Is No Coincidence." Accessed November 1, 2017. http://www.genepartner.com/.

Giddens, Anthony. *The Transformation of Intimacy: Sexuality, Love, and Eroticism in Modern Societies.* Stanford, CA: Stanford University Press, 1993.

Giroux, Henry A. "Are Disney Movies Good for Your Kids?" In *Kinderculture: The Corporate Construction of Childhood,* edited by S.R. Steinberg and J.L. Kincheloe. Boulder, CO: Westview Press, 1997.

———. *The Mouse That Roared: Disney and the End of Innocence.* Lanham, MD: Rowman and Littlefield, 1999.

"Global Travel and Tourism Industry—Statistics and Facts." Statista. Accessed November 3, 2017. www.statista.com/topics/962/global-tourism/.

"Global Wealth Data Bank 2013." Credit Suisse, October 2013. www.international-adviser.com/ia/media/Media/Credit-Suisse-Global-Wealth-Databook-2013.pdf.

Goodnough, Abby. "Disney Is Selling a Town It Built to Reflect the Past." *New York Times,* January 16, 2004. www.nytimes.com/2004/01/16/us/disney-is-selling-a-town-it-built-to-reflect-the-past.html.

"Greatest Marriage Proposal EVER!!!" 2011. www.youtube.com/watch?v=pnVAE91E7kM.

Greenwood, Shannon, Andrew Perrin, and Maeve Duggan. "Social Media Update 2016." *Pew Research Center: Internet, Science and Tech* (blog), November 11, 2016. www.pewinternet.org/2016/11/11/social-media-update-2016/.

Grice, Andrew. "Polls Reveal Big Rise in Support for Monarchy." *Independent,* April 9, 2002. www.independent.co.uk/news/uk/home-news/poll-reveals-big-rise-in-support-for-monarchy-656892.html.

Hanchett, Thomas W. "Financing Suburbia: Prudential Insurance and the Post–World War II Transformation of the American City." *Journal of Urban History* 26, no. 3 (March 1, 2000): 312–28. https://doi.org/10.1177/009614420002600302.

"He Loved Her since They Were 10: This Is How He Proposed (Matty Mac—The Proposal)." May 22, 2015. www.youtube.com/watch?v=OuXKkROBkiI.

"Her Fantasy Proposal That Exceeded Her Expectations." January 8, 2014. www.youtube.com/watch?v=GBbxM6k-leU.

Hess, Amanda. "The Awkward Charm of the Promposal." *New York Times,* April 8, 2016.

Himmelstein, Kathryn E. W., and Hannah Brückner. "Criminal-Justice and School Sanctions against Nonheterosexual Youth: A National Longitudinal Study." *Pediatrics* 127, no. 1 (January 1, 2011): 49–57. https://doi.org/10.1542/peds.2009–2306.

Holland, Kelley. "The High Economic and Social Costs of Student Loan Debt." *CNBC,* June 15, 2015. www.cnbc.com/2015/06/15/the-high-economic-and-social-costs-of-student-loan-debt.html.

Houston, H. Rika, and Laurie A. Meamber. "Consuming the 'World': Reflexivity, Aesthetics, and Authenticity at Disney World's EPCOT Center." *Consumption Markets and Culture* 14, no. 2 (June 1, 2011): 177–91. https://doi.org/10.1080/10253866.2011.562019.

Howard, Clayton. "Building a 'Family-Friendly' Metropolis: Sexuality, the State, and Postwar Housing Policy." *Journal of Urban History* 39, no. 5 (2013): 933–55.

How Heroes of Fiction Propose and How Heroines Reply: Together with Familiar Quotations in Poetry and Prose; with Parallel Passages from the Most Famous Writers of the World. New York: P. F. Collier, 1890. http://hdl.handle.net/2027/nyp.33433082179643.

Illouz, Eva. *Cold Intimacies: The Making of Emotional Capitalism.* Malden, MA: Polity, 2007.

———. *Why Love Hurts: A Sociological Explanation.* Malden, MA: Polity, 2013.

Ingraham, Chrys. *White Weddings: Romancing Heterosexuality in Popular Culture.* New York: Taylor and Francis, 2008.

Inside Bella's Closet (blog). Accessed November 1, 2017. https://insidebellascloset.wordpress.com/.

"Introducing Tinder Online—Swipe Anywhere." Tinder, March 28, 2017. http://blog.gotinder.com/introducing-tinder-online/.

"Isaac's Live Lip-Dub Proposal." May 25, 2012. www.youtube.com/watch?v=5_v7QrIWozY.

James, E. L. *Fifty Shades Freed.* New York: Vintage, 2012.

———. *Fifty Shades of Grey.* New York: Vintage, 2011. Kindle.

"Jamin's Downtown Disney Flashmob Proposal." September 26, 2011. www.youtube.com/watch?v=Su1YLAjty-U.

Jessee, Catherine. "Your Inner Disney Princess? Take the Quiz." *The Knot.* www.theknot.com/content/disney-princess-honeymoon-quiz."Justin and Emily: The Proposal." October 8, 2013. www.youtube.com/watch?v=hVTr5MNa_8Y.

"A Just Incredible Proposal." May 27, 2012. www.youtube.com/watch?v=2bY4GuZXjSo.

Kaminetsky, Heather. "The 5 Biggest International Holidays for E-Commerce." *Business Insider,* September 24, 2012. www.businessinsider.com/5-international-holidays-for-ecommerce-2012-9.

Katz, Jonathan M., and Erik Eckholm. "Anti-Gay Laws Bring Backlash in Mississippi and North Carolina." *New York Times,* April 5, 2016. www.nytimes.com/2016/04/06/us/gay-rights-mississippi-north-carolina.html.

Kelly, Helen. "Royal Wedding 2018 Viewing Figures: How Many People Watched Meghan Markle Marry Harry." *Express,* May 20, 2018. www.express.co.uk/showbiz/tv-radio/962610/Royal-Wedding-viewing-figures-Meghan-Markle-Prince-Harry-kiss-David-Beckham.

Khoo. "Tinder Issues Lifetime Ban to Man Who Hurled Racist Slurs at Asian Woman." *HuffPost Canada,* March 2, 2017. www.huffingtonpost.ca/2017/03/02/tinder-lifetime-ban_n_15108620.html.

Kim, Eugene. "Here's How the Dating Service Company That Owns Tinder Makes Money." *Business Insider.* Accessed November 1, 2017. www .businessinsider.com/how-match-group-and-tinder-make-money-2015-10.

Kimmel, Chad M. "Community in History: Exploring the Infancy of America's 'Most Perfectly Planned Community,' Levittown, Pennsylvania." *Sociological Viewpoints* 26, no. 2 (Fall 2010): 37–51.

Kincaid, James. *Erotic Innocence: The Culture of Child Molesting.* Durham, NC: Duke University Press, 2000.

Kipnis, Laura. *Against Love: A Polemic.* New York: Vintage, 2004.

Kuenz, Jane, Susan Willis, and Shelton Waldrep, eds. *Inside the Mouse: Work and Play at Disney World.* Durham, NC: Duke University Press, 1995.

Kuperberg, Arielle, and Joseph E. Padgett. "The Date's Not Dead." The Society Pages, August 10, 2016. https://thesocietypages.org/ccf/2016/08/10 /the-dates-not-dead/.

Lapidot-Lefler, Noam, and Azy Barak. "Effects of Anonymity, Invisibility, and Lack of Eye-Contact on Toxic Online Disinhibition." *Computers in Human Behavior* 28, no. 2 (March 1, 2012): 434–43. https://doi.org/10.1016/j.chb.2011.10.014.

Lingan, John. "Bristling Dixie: Uncle Walt Thought *Song of the South* Would Be His Masterpiece: Now It's Invisible." *Slate,* January 4, 2013. www.slate.com /articles/arts/books/2013/01/song_of_the_south_disney_s_most_notorious_ film_by_jason_sperb_reviewed.html.

Lippe-McGraw, Jordi. "Yes Couples Are Now Taking 'Earlymoons' before Their Weddings." *Brides,* July 7, 2017. //www.brides.com/story/earlymoons-before-their-weddings.

"Living Wage Calculator." Poverty in America. Accessed November 1, 2017. http://livingwage.mit.edu/.

Long, Heather. "The Feel-Good Hallmark Channel Is Booming in the Age of Trump." *Washington Post,* August 21, 2017. www.washingtonpost.com/news /wonk/wp/2017/08/21/the-feel-good-hallmark-channel-is-booming-in-the-age-of-trump/?utm_term=.17d93b595b41.

Low, Setha. "Maintaining Whiteness: The Fear of Others and Niceness." *Transforming Anthropology* 17, no. 2 (October 2009): 79–92.

Luckerson, Victor. "The 13 Most Controversial Super Bowl Ads Ever." *Time,* January 27, 2014. http://business.time.com/2014/01/27/the-13-most-controversial-super-bowl-ads/slide/ashley-madison-wants-to-help-you-have-an-affair/.

Lugo-Lugo, Carmen R., and Mary K. Bloodsworth-Lugo. "'Look Out New World, Here We Come'?: Race, Racialization, and Sexuality in Four Children's Animated Films by Disney, Pixar, and DreamWorks" In *Cinematic Sociology: Social Life in Film,* edited by Jean-Anne Sutherland and Kathryn Feltey. 2nd ed. Thousand Oaks, CA: Sage.

"The Magic of the Monarchy: The Royal Moment Has Come." *Guardian,* April 1, 2011. Opinion sec. www.theguardian.com/commentisfree/2011/apr/01 /magic-monarchy-royal-moment.

"Making the Movies Jealous—Matt & Ginny's Wedding—by Ray Roman." n.d. www.youtube.com/watch?v=DJ4DNqIuCcQ.

Mapes, Diane. "Anonymity Opens Up Split Personality Zone." NBC News, September 24, 2008. www.nbcnews.com/id/26837911/ns/health-behavior/t /anonymity-opens-split-personality-zone/.

Marin, Louis. *Utopics: Spatial Play.* Translated by Robert A. Vollrath. London: Palgrave Macmillan, 1984.

"Marriage Proposal Packages." The Yes Girls. Accessed November 2, 2017. https://theyesgirls.com/marriage-proposal-packages.

Mason, Corinne Lysandra. "Tinder and Humanitarian Hook-Ups: The Erotics of Social Media Racism." *Feminist Media Studies* 16, no. 5 (September 2, 2016): 822–37. https://doi.org/10.1080/14680777.2015.1137339.

"Matt and Ginny on Ellen." November 29, 2012. www.youtube.com/watch?v= q1uUIjqAKvo.

McClintock, Anne. *Imperial Leather: Race, Gender, and Sexuality in the Colonial Contest.* New York: Routledge, 1995.

McGee, Micki. *Self-Help, Inc.: Makeover Culture in American Life.* Oxford: Oxford University Press, 2007.

Melander-Dayton, Adele. "'Bridalplasty': The Reality TV Apocalypse No One Watched." *Salon,* January 31, 2011. www.salon.com/2011/02/01/bridalplasty_ finale/.

Meyer, Stephenie. *Breaking Dawn.* New York: Little, Brown, 2008.

———. *Twilight.* New York: Little, Brown, 2005.

Miller, Kevin. "The Simple Truth about the Gender Pay Gap." *AAUW: Empowering Women since 1881* (blog). Accessed November 1, 2017. www.aauw.org /research/the-simple-truth-about-the-gender-pay-gap/.

Mintz, Steven, and Susan Kellogg. *Domestic Revolutions: A Social History of American Family Life.* New York: Free Press, 1989.

"Monarchy/Royal Family Trends: Monarchy v Republic, 1993–2013." Ipsos MORI, July 19, 2013. www.ipsos-mori.com/researchpublications/research archive/122 /MonarchyRoyal-Family-Trends-Maonarchy-v-Republic-19932013.aspx?view= wide.

Moraski, Lauren. "Miley Cyrus' Booty-Shaking VMA Performance Gets Quite the Reaction." September 21, 2013. www.cbsnews.com/news/miley-cyrus-booty-shaking-vma-performance-gets-quite-the-reaction/.

"Most Epic Prom Proposal." December 7, 2013. www.youtube.com/watch?v=Ti-VwlT-NTE.

Mutch, Deborah. "Coming out of the Coffin: The Vampire and Transnationalism in the Twilight and Sookie Stackhouse Series." *Critical Survey* 23, no. 2 (2011): 75–90.

"myRWA: The Romance Genre; Romance Industry Statistics." Accessed October 21, 2017. www.rwa.org/page/romance-industry-statistics.

Nazayran, Alexander. "'Fifty Shades of Grey' Tops Ten Million Sales: Reading Public Craves Christian Grey, Anastasia Steele—and Nothing Else." *New York Daily News.* Accessed November 1, 2017. www.nydailynews.com/blogs/pageviews/fifty-shades-grey-tops-ten-million-sales-reading-public-craves-christian-grey-anastasia-steele-blog-entry-1.1638369.

Negra, Diane, and Yvonne Tasker. "Neoliberal Frames and Genres of Inequality: Recession-Era Chick Flicks and Male-Centred Corporate Melodrama." *European Journal of Cultural Studies* 16, no. 3 (June 1, 2013): 344–61. https://doi.org/10.1177/1367549413481880.

"New Ferrari Cars." *Motortrend Magazine.* www.motortrend.com/new_cars/01/ferrari/#__federated=1.

"Niagara Falls—Facts and Summary." History. Accessed November 4, 2017. www.history.com/topics/niagara-falls.

"Noel Biderman, CEO Of AshleyMadison.com—Changing the Face of Matrimony—Zing Talk." February 14, 2011. www.youtube.com/watch?v=umkghboC7Rw.O'Brien, Sara Ashley. "81-Year-Old eHarmony Founder on Gay Marriage and Tinder." CNNMoney, February 12, 2016. http://money.cnn.com/2016/02/12/technology/eharmony-neil-clark-warren/index.html.

"On this Day, 29 July 1981: Charles and Diana Marry," July 29, 1981. BBC News. http://news.bbc.co.uk/onthisday/hi/dates/stories/july/29/newsid_2494000/2494949.stm.

Otnes, Cele C., and Elizabeth Pleck. *Cinderella Dreams: The Allure of the Lavish Wedding.* Berkeley: University of California Press, 2003.

"Our Lady of Perpetual Exemption." *Last Week Tonight with John Oliver,* August 16, 2015. HBO.

Patten, Eileen, and Kim Parker. "A Gender Reversal on Career Aspirations." *Pew Research Center's Social and Demographic Trends Project* (blog), April 19, 2012. www.pewsocialtrends.org/2012/04/19/a-gender-reversal-on-career-aspirations/.

Pavlo, Walter. "Fraud Thriving in U.S. Churches, but You Wouldn't Know It." *Forbes,* November 18, 2013. www.forbes.com/sites/walterpavlo/2013/11/18 /fraud-thriving-in-u-s-churches-but-you-wouldnt-know-it/#4b35692fd9d4.

Peiss, Kathy. *Cheap Amusements: Working Women and Leisure in Turn-of-the-Century New York.* Philadelphia: Temple University Press, 1986.

Pepitone, Julianne. "Buy Edward Cullen's Twilight House." CNNMoney, February 23, 2010. http://money.cnn.com/galleries/2009/real_estate/0911 /gallery.twilight_cullen_house/.

Peppers, Margot. "How Much Would You Spend on Your Bridal Dress? Probably the Same as your GREAT GRANDMOTHER: The Surprising History of Wedding Costs since the 1930s." *Daily Mail,* July 3, 2014. www.dailymail .co.uk/femail/article-2679539/How-did-spend-bridal-dress-Probably-GREAT-GRANDMOTHER-The-surprising-history-wedding-costs-1930s.html.

Perez, Sarah. "U.S. Consumers Now Spend 5 Hours per Day on Mobile Devices." *TechCrunch* (blog). Accessed November 2, 2017. http://social .techcrunch.com/2017/03/03/u-s-consumers-now-spend-5-hours-per-day-on-mobile-devices/.

Phillips, Mark. "Royal Wedding Could Cost UK Economy $50 Billion." CBS News, April 22, 2011. www.cbsnews.com/news/royal-wedding-could-cost-uk-economy-50-billion/.

Pilkington, Ed. "How the Disney Dream Died in Celebration." *Guardian,* December 13, 2010. www.theguardian.com/world/2010/dec/13/celebration-death-of-a-dream.

Polikoff, Nancy D. *Beyond (Straight and Gay) Marriage: Valuing All Families under the Law.* Boston: Beacon Press, 2009.

"Popular Tween Romance Books." Goodreads. Accessed November 1, 2017. www.goodreads.com/shelf/show/tween-romance.

Porter, Rick. "Monday Final Ratings: 'Jane the Virgin' Adjusts down but Still Hits Season High, 'Scorpion' Adjusts Up." *TV by the Numbers,* November 17, 2015. http://tvbythenumbers.zap2it.com/2015/11/17/monday-final-ratings-nov-16-2015/.

Pous, Terri. "Top 10 Short-Lived Celebrity Marriages." *Time,* November 1, 2011. http://content.time.com/time/specials/packages/article/0,28804,2098279_ 2098285_2098286,00.html.

"Practical Money Skills for Life: 2015 Prom Spending Survey." VISA. www .practicalmoneyskills.com/resources/pdfs/Prom_Survey_2015.pdf.

Pressly, Linda. "The Cost of Weddings Spirals in China." BBC News, July 22, 2011. Business sec. www.bbc.com/news/business-14208448.

"Prom Flashmob with Becky G! #Promposals Ep. 1." April 19, 2014. www
.youtube.com/watch?v=ZCUYXOzCwQ8.

"Queen Victoria Wedding." *Victoriana Magazine.* Accessed November 3,
2017. www.queenvictoria.victoriana.com/RoyalWeddings/Queen-Victoria-
Wedding.html.

Radford, Benjamin. "Sweet Science of Seduction or Scam? Evaluating eHarmony." Committee for Skeptical Inquiry, December 2014. www.csicop.org
/si/show/sweet_science_of_seduction_or_scam_evaluating_eharmony.

Radway, Janice A. *Reading the Romance: Women, Patriarchy, and Popular Literature.*
2nd ed. Chapel Hill: University of North Carolina Press, 1991.

Rainie, Lee, and Andrew Perrin. "Slightly Fewer Americans Are Reading
Print Books, New Survey Finds." *Pew Research Center* (blog), October 19,
2015. www.pewresearch.org/fact-tank/2015/10/19/slightly-fewer-americans-
are-reading-print-books-new-survey-finds/.

"The Return of the Multi-Generational Family Household." *Pew Research
Center's Social and Demographic Trends Project* (blog), March 18, 2010. www
.pewsocialtrends.org/2010/03/18/the-return-of-the-multi-generational-family-
household/.

Reuters. "2011 Engagement & Jewelry Statistics Released by TheKnot.com
& WeddingChannel.com." August 30, 2011. www.reuters.com/article
/idUS198935+30-Aug-2011+BW20110830.

———. "Match Group Revenue Up as Tinder Attracts More Paid Users."
Fortune, May 3, 2016. http://fortune.com/2016/05/03/match-group-revenue-
tinder-paid-users/.

———. "Washington: More Tent Cities Sought for Homeless in Seattle." *New
York Times,* January 15, 2015. www.nytimes.com/2015/01/16/us/more-tent-
cities-sought-for-homeless-in-seattle.html.

"The Revenue of the Walt Disney Company in the Fiscal Years 2006 to 2017 in
Billion U.S. Dollars). statista.com, 2018. www.statista.com/statistics/273555
/global-revenue-of-the-walt-disney-company/#0.

Rich, Motoko. "Recession Fuels Readers' Escapist Urges." *New York Times,* April
7, 2009. Books sec. www.nytimes.com/2009/04/08/books/08roma.html.

Richardson, John M. "The Promposal: Youth Expressions of Identity and
'Love' in the Digital Age." *Learning, Media and Technology* 42, no. 1 (January
2, 2017): 74–86. https://doi.org/10.1080/17439884.2016.1130055.

Rochotte, Emily. "Engagementmoon: What It Is and Why You Should Take
One." *Equally Wed,* December 7, 2016. http://equallywed.com/engagementmoon-
take-one.

Roediger, David. *Working toward Whiteness: How America's Immigrants Became White.* New York: Basic Books, 2006.

Roiphe, Katie. "Spanking Goes Mainstream." *Daily Beast,* April 16, 2012. www .thedailybeast.com/newsweek/2012/04/15/working-women-s-fantasies.html.

Romeyn, Kathryn. "The Top 100 Honeymoon Destinations for 2017." *Brides,* November 15, 2016. www.brides.com/gallery/100-best-honeymoon-destinations.

Rosenberg, Yuval. "Economics of Happiness: Where the US Ranks." MSN Money, April 6, 2012. http://money.msn.com/politics/post.aspx?post= 79d88065-08a9-434d-9f3a-56d662608ea0.

Roser, Max, and Esteban Ortiz-Ospina. "Literacy." *Our World in Data* (blog). Accessed November 2, 2017. https://ourworldindata.org/literacy/.

"Royal Wedding Watch." *InStyle.* April 29, 2011. news.instyle.com/photo-gallery /?postgallery=52730#12.

Rubin, Gayle. "Thinking Sex: Notes toward a Radical Theory of the Politics of Sexuality." In *Pleasure and Danger: Exploring Female Sexuality,* edited by Carole Vance. New York: Routledge and Kegan Paul, 1984.

Russell, Dora. *Hypatia; or Woman and Knowledge.* London: Kegan Paul, Trench, Trubner, 1925.

Sachs, Michael D. "Restoring American Happiness." In *The World Happiness Report, 2017.* http://worldhappiness.report/ed/2017/.

Sales, Nancy Jo. "Tinder and the Dawn of the 'Dating Apocalypse.'" *Vanity Fair,* September 2015. www.vanityfair.com/culture/2015/08/tinder-hook-up-culture-end-of-dating.

Sardone, Susan Breslow. "Wedding Statistics and Honeymoon Facts and Figures." TripSavvy. Accessed November 3, 2017. www.tripsavvy.com/wedding-statistics-and-honeymoon-facts-1860546.

Schabner, Dean. "Americans Work More Than Anyone." ABC News, January 7, 2006. http://abcnews.go.com/US/story?id=93364&page=1.

Schwartz, Barry. *The Paradox of Choice: Why More Is Less.* New York: HarperCollins, 2005.

Schweingruber, David, Alicia D. Cast, and Sine Anahita. "'A Story and a Ring': Audience Judgments about Engagement Proposals." *Sex Roles* 58, no. 3–4 (February 1, 2008): 165–78. https://doi.org/10.1007/s11199-007-9330-1.

Seaver, Maggie. "The National Average Cost of a Wedding is $33,391." *The Knot.* www.theknot.com/content/average-wedding-cost-2017.

———. "This Mass Lesbian Wedding and Vow Renewal Is the Most Joyful Thing We've Seen." *The Knot,* n.d. www.theknot.com/content/bride-pride-same-sex-mass-wedding.

Shaw, Frances. "'Bitch I Said Hi': The Bye Felipe Campaign and Discursive Activism in Mobile Dating Apps." *Social Media and Society* 2, no. 4 (November 1, 2016): 2056305116672889. https://doi.org/10.1177/2056305116672889.

Sheftell, Jason. "Breathless 'Grey' Apartment Is No Work of Fiction." *New York Daily News.* Accessed November 1, 2017. www.nydailynews.com/life-style/real-estate/breathless-fifty-shades-grey-apartment-no-work-fiction-article-1.1105633.

Simmons-Duffin, Selena. "'School for Good and Evil' Is a Kids' Fantasy Series for the Fake News Era." *All Things Considered,* NPR, September 18, 2017.

"Single by Choice: Why Fewer American Women Are Married Than Ever Before." NPR. March 1, 2016. www.npr.org/2016/03/01/468688887/single-by-choice-why-fewer-american-women-are-married-than-ever-before.

"Singles in America 2017." Accessed November 2, 2017. Match.com. www.singlesinamerica.com/.

Smith, Aaron, and Monica Anderson. "5 Facts about Online Dating." *Pew Research Center* (blog), February 29, 2016. www.pewresearch.org/fact-tank/2016/02/29/5-facts-about-online-dating/.

"Socioeconomics and Obesity." State of Obesity. Accessed November 1, 2017. https://stateofobesity.org/socioeconomics-obesity/.

Solnit, Rebecca. *Hope in the Dark: Untold Histories, Wild Possibilities.* Chicago: Haymarket, 2016.

Somerville, Siobhan B. *Queering the Color Line: Race and the Invention of Homosexuality in American Culture.* Durham, NC: Duke University Press, 2000.

Sorren, Martha. "14 Times during Kim Kardashian & Kris Humphries' Wedding You Could Tell They Were Doomed." *Bustle,* August 20, 2014. www.bustle.com/articles/35470-14-times-during-kim-kardashian-kris-humphries-wedding-you-could-tell-they-were-doomed.

"Spencer's Home Depot Marriage Proposal." September 11, 2013. www.youtube.com/watch?v=l4HpWQmEXrM.

Sperb, Jason. "'Take a Frown, Turn It Upside Down': Splash Mountain, Walt Disney World, and the Cultural De-Rac(e)-Ination of Disney's Song of the South (1946)." *Journal of Popular Culture,* no. 5 (2005). https://doi.org/http://dx.doi.org/10.1111/j.0022-3840.2005.00148.x.

Spigel, Lynn. *Welcome to the Dreamhouse: Popular Media and Postwar Suburbs.* Durham, NC: Duke University Press, 2001.

Stampler, Laura. "Americans Could Spend $703 Million on Their Pets This Valentine's Day." *Time,* January 27, 2015. http://time.com/3684556/valentines-day-pets/.

Steverman, Ben. "Americans Work 25% More Than Europeans, Study Finds." *Bloomberg,* October 18, 2016. www.bloomberg.com/news/articles/2016–10–18/americans-work-25-more-than-europeans-study-finds.

Stiglitz, Joseph E. "Of the 1%, by the 1%, for the 1%." *Vanity Fair,* May 2011. www.vanityfair.com/news/2011/05/top-one-percent-201105.

Stopes, Marie. *Married Love.* London: Fifield, 1918.

Sumter, Sindy R., Laura Vandenbosch, and Loes Ligtenberg. "Love Me Tinder: Untangling Emerging Adults' Motivations for Using the Dating Application Tinder." *Telematics and Informatics* 34, no. 1 (February 1, 2017): 67–78. https://doi.org/10.1016/j.tele.2016.04.009.

"Surprise Ending—Flash Mob Marriage Proposal." June 15, 2012. www.youtube.com/watch?v=5uCP1bkpe90.

"The Sweetest Peter Pan Marriage Proposal." January 16, 2013. www.youtube.com/watch?v=HRlMURMTYPw.

Sykes, Tom. "William and Kate Honeymoon Photos Published." *Daily Beast,* July 10, 2012. www.thedailybeast.com/william-and-kate-honeymoon-photos-published.

Taylor, Anthea. "'The Urge towards Love Is an Urge towards (Un)Death': Romance, Masochistic Desire and Postfeminism in the Twilight Novels." *International Journal of Cultural Studies* 15, no. 1 (January 1, 2012): 31–46. https://doi.org/10.1177/1367877911399204.

"Televangelists." *Last Week Tonight with John Oliver.* HBO. 2015. www.youtube.com/watch?v=7y1xJAVZxXg.

Tempesta, Erica. "Proof That Promposals Are TOTALLY out of Control: Arizona Teen Books His Girlfriend a Trip to HAWAII as Part of His Prom Invitation to Celebrate Their Ninth Dance Together." *Daily Mail,* April 27, 2016. www.dailymail.co.uk/femail/article-3562020/How-allowance-Arizona-teen-books-girlfriend-trip-HAWAII-extravagant-promposal-celebrate-ninth-high-school-dance-together.html.

"Tents, Tiaras and a Few Tears as a Million Turn Out for Wills and Kate." *Daily Mail,* April 30, 2011. www.dailymail.co.uk/news/article-1381820/Royal-Wedding-route-A-MILLION-turn-celebrate-Kate-Middleton-Prince-William.html.

Tepper, Fitz. "Bumble Is Finally Monetizing with Paid Features to Better Help You Find a Match." *TechCrunch* (blog). Accessed November 1, 2017.

http://social.techcrunch.com/2016/08/15/bumble-is-finally-monetizing-with-paid-features-to-better-help-you-find-a-match/.

Toossi, Mitra. "A Century of Change: The U.S. Labor Force, 1950–2050." *Monthly Labor Review*, U.S. Bureau of Labor Statistics. May 2002. www.bls.gov/opub/mlr/2002/05/art2full.pdf.

"Top 5 Marriage Proposal Fails." December 24, 2011. www.youtube.com/watch?v=22ec807p2bI.

Traister, Rebecca. *All the Single Ladies: Unmarried Women and the Rise of an Independent Nation.* New York: Simon and Schuster, 2016.

Urbina, Ian. "Perils of Climate Change Could Swamp Coastal Real Estate." *New York Times,* November 24, 2016. Science sec. www.nytimes.com/2016/11/24/science/global-warming-coastal-real-estate.html?_r=0.

Vanassche, Sofie, Gray Swicegood, and Koen Matthijs. "Marriage and Children as Key to Happiness? Cross-National Differences in the Effects of Marital Status and Children on Well-Being." *Journal of Happiness Studies,* 14, no. 2 (April 2012): 501–24. doi: 10.1007/s10902–012–9340–8.

VanDerWerf, Todd. "How Hallmark Took Over Your TV Every Christmas," *Vox,* December 14, 2017. www.vox.com/culture/2017/12/14/16752012/hallmark-christmas-movies-explained.

Vannini, Phillip. "Will You Marry Me?: Spectacle and Consumption in the Ritual of Marriage Proposals." *Journal of Popular Culture* 38, no. 1 (August 2004): 169–85.

Vasel, Kathryn. "Couples Are Spending a Record Amount of Cash to Get Married." CNNMoney, February 2, 2017. http://money.cnn.com/2017/02/02/pf/cost-of-wedding-budget-2016-the-knot/index.html.

Velasco, Schuyler, and Jacob Turcotte. "Are Americans Working Too Much?" *Christian Science Monitor,* August 18, 2016. www.csmonitor.com/Business/2016/0818/Are-Americans-working-too-much.

Vella, Matt. "Apple's Latest Ad Is Probably Going to Give You Chills." *Time.* Accessed October 21, 2017. http://business.time.com/2014/01/13/apples-latest-ad-is-probably-going-to-give-you-chills/.

"A Very Sweet Proposal (When He Cries, You'll Cry) from HowHeAsked.com." April 4, 2014. www.youtube.com/watch?v=Su_l8r3CqTM.

Vespa, Jonathan, Jamie M. Lewis, and Rose M. Kreider. "America's Families and Living Arrangements: 2012." US Census Bureau. August 2013. www.census.gov/prod/2013pubs/p20–570.pdf.

Vesselinov, Elena, and Renaud Le Goix. "From Picket Fences to Iron Gates: Suburbanization and Gated Communities in Phoenix, Las Vegas and Seattle." *GeoJournal* 77, no. 2 (2012): 203–22.

Vilhauer, Jennice. "This Is Why Ghosting Hurts So Much." *Psychology Today.* November 27, 2015. www.psychologytoday.com/blog/living-forward/201511 /is-why-ghosting-hurts-so-much.

Wade, Lisa. *American Hookup: The New Culture of Sex on Campus.* New York: W. W. Norton, 2017.

Walker, Rebecca A. "Fill/Flash/Memory: A History of Flash Mobs." *Text and Performance Quarterly* 33, no. 2 (April 1, 2013): 115–32. https://doi.org/10.1080 /10462937.2013.764002.

Wallace-Wells, David. "The Uninhabitable Earth: Famine, Economic Collapse, a Sun That Cooks Us; What Climate Change Could Wreak— Sooner Than You Think." *New York Magazine,* July 9, 2017. http://nymag .com/daily/intelligencer/2017/07/climate-change-earth-too-hot-for-humans .html.

Walters, Suzanna Danuta. *The Tolerance Trap: How God, Genes, and Good Intentions Are Sabotaging Gay Equality.* New York: New York University Press, 2014.

Weber, Max. *The Protestant Ethic and the Spirit of Capitalism.* 2nd ed. London: Allen and Unwin, 1976.

"Wedding Proposal That Will Leave You Breathless." January 8, 2014. www .youtube.com/watch?v=IU-aHsjv5eA.

Wesley, Daniel. "How Much Will You Spend for Valentine's Day?" *Credit Loan* (blog), n.d. http://visualeconomics.creditloan.com/how-much-will-you-spend-for-valentines-day/.

"What Disney's City of the Future, Built to Look like the Past, Says about the Present." *Economist,* December 24, 2016. www.economist.com/news /united-states/21712156-utopia-i-4-what-disneys-city-future-built-look-past-says-about.

Whitty, Monica T. "Anatomy of the Online Dating Romance Scam." *Security Journal* 28, no. 4 (October 2015): 443–55. doi.org/10.1057/sj.2012.57.

"Why Don't Women Propose to Men?" CBS News. Accessed November 2, 2017. www.cbsnews.com/news/why-dont-women-propose-to-men/.

Wolfinger, James. "'The American Dream—For All Americans': Race, Politics, and the Campaign to Desegregate Levittown." *Journal of Urban History* 38, no. 3 (2012): 430–51.

"The World Factbook." Central Intelligence Agency. Accessed November 3, 2017. www.cia.gov/library/publications/the-world-factbook/docs/notesanddefs .html.

Yuknavitch, Lidia. *The Book of Joan: A Novel*. New York: Harper, 2017.

Zane, Zachary. "Tough Love: Why You May Never Find the One." INTO. Accessed November 1, 2017. https://intomore.com/into/tough-love-why-you-may-never-find-the-one/1cdf717a646b4148.

Zelizer, Viviana A. *The Purchase of Intimacy*. Princeton, NJ: Princeton University Press, 2005.

INDEX

abortion, 38

addiction, love as, 22

adulthood: Disney as placing romance as cornerstone of, 32, 148; marriage as determination of, 11, 148

advertising: deceptive, online dating sites and, 64–65; for Disney World honeymoons, 145–46; "happily ever after" used to sell products via, 7–8; and ritual of bended knee and diamond ring, 87–90, 89, 190nn10,15; "tweens" as invented by, 34; for wedding products, 7. *See also* capitalism

African Americans: dating sites for, 63; discrimination against, and honeymoons, 144; at Disney World, 151; Disney World honeymoons of, 152, 154, 156–58; erasure of Jim Crow and white violence, 149; and fairy-tale romance of Kate and William, 126; and income inequality, 14; and minstrelsy, Disney as washing blackface from, 149; racial composition of interviewees, 72; royal wedding of Harry and Meghan, 114; and

spectacular proposals, 94, 111; voting rights loss of, 8. *See also* race hierarchies

age differences: and desire to find a relationship, 77; and expectation of men proposing and women answering, 85; and importance of sex, 76–77; and remembrance of pre-internet dating practices, 73, 81; and sex on first date, 76. *See also* college students

ageism: and Disney fantasy of the future, 150; fairy-tale romance as requiring youthful body, 116; gay male dating apps and, 69; popular spectacular proposals and, 99, 111; proposal fails and, 103

Ahmed, Sara, 123

Aladdin (film), 156–57

Albert, Prince, 117–19

alienation of labor, 11, 13

amour passion, 29

Andersen, Hans Christian, "The Little Mermaid," 25

anxiety: about gay marriage, 16–17; about single-mother families, 16–17; about virgin brides and need for